The New Era of Home-Based Work

The New Era of Home-Based Work

DIRECTIONS AND POLICIES

EDITED BY

Kathleen E. Christensen

Routledge
Taylor & Francis Group
LONDON AND NEW YORK

First published 1988 by Westview Press

Published 2019 by Routledge
52 Vanderbilt Avenue, New York, NY 10017
2 Park Square, Milton Park, Abingdon, Oxon OX14 4RN

Routledge is an imprint of the Taylor & Francis Group, an informa business

Library of Congress Cataloging-in-Publication Data
The New era of home-based work.
Includes index.
1. Home-based businesses. 2. Telecommuting.
I. Christensen, K. (Kathleen)
HD2333.N48 1988 331.25 88-14148

ISBN 13: 978-0-367-29435-9 (hbk)
ISBN 13: 978-0-367-30981-7 (pbk)

Contents

Tables and Figures

Tables

Figures

Foreword

This important book conveys some of the profound changes occurring in the assumptions, meanings, and practice of workplace and workforce. The simple view of the Industrial Revolution is that work shifted from farm and home to mill. Yet that view profoundly neglects the continuing importance of women's household labor in making men and women available for work outside the home—what has come to be called "the reproduction of labor"; in addition, the separation of work and home has never been complete. Homework defined as paid industrial labor performed at home has persisted in the United States despite legislative attempts to limit it. Many office workers and professionals are expected to continue their salaried duties after employer-based "working hours": Witness the "briefcase brigade" of commuters and others.

This book analyzes a significant emerging chapter in the continuous and sometimes tumultuous renegotiations involving employers, employees, technology, workplace, and workhours. The work relationship is not a fixed set of formulas, agreements, procedures, or rules. For example, the Wagner Act of the 1930s moved labor relations toward greater participation of unions in bargaining for employees. Today, the theme of improving U.S. participation and competitiveness in global markets has weakened workers' and unions' influence in workplace relations. Employers are asking their unionized factory workers to be more flexible about job titles, pay schedules, seniority, and work task regulations (sometimes providing incentives such as year-end bonuses tied to profits).

Home-based white-collar work can be seen as part of the expansion of contingent work: part-time, temporary, or off-the-premises employment. An alternative interpretation might be that it is the human resource equivalent of the Japanese practice of "just-in-time" inventory process, since it avoids the stockpiling of staff. Many expect that both contingent work and its home-based white-collar component will grow rapidly as they fit into the business desire for employer flexibility and lower wage and fringe benefits' costs. If they do grow as expected, safeguards may be necessary to regulate these work patterns, for the many who work in these ways are particularly vulnerable to exploitation.

Today's home-based white-collar work is not an add-on to the working day as is the briefcase brigade, but rather, it is the major form of paid work for a growing number of women and for a smaller number of men. As the authors in *The New Era of Home-Based Work* dispassionately point out, home-based workers sometimes pay a price for the flexibility of place and time that such work offers.

Although white-collar home-based work can be viewed as continuing past traditions of home-as-workplace, it should also be seen as moving onto new tracks made possible by the high technology of computer processing. For example, U.S. employers' insistence on physical and social control of the work process, thus requiring a large supervisory force, is overcome in home-based work. Performance or output measures, eased by the computer's capacity for data processing, are deemed sufficient. White-collar home-based work assumes that employees will provide the physical infrastructure usually supplied and controlled by employers. The split between formal and informal work sectors has never been sharp; home-based work may foretell a formal informal sector in which on-the-books, regular employers operate through the premises of those who are presumably employees.[1]

Home-based white-collar work should be seen as transactional, for both employees and employers are involved in structuring this arrangement. The former may desire the arrangement as much as many employers who seek reduced labor and space costs. Home-based work should be viewed in broader terms than an economic arrangement.

Among its negative components is that home-based work impinges more obviously and perhaps directly on family relations and child development than do centralized work settings. A mother working at home may be more physically present than if she worked in a faraway office, but she may also be preoccupied with her work demands because she has no fixed, limited work schedule. The home may not be a haven for any of its members.

The new arrangements raise questions of the legal and economic relationship of employers and those who are paid by them. This issue is evident in the debate about who is an independent contractor and to what extent that designation is a dodge to reduce burdens on and responsibilities of employers.

Michael Piore informs us that the profound separation in manufacturing between home and work led to the invention of the concept of "unemployment."[2] In our new, unfolding work world, these lines are again blurred. It is a real contribution to have a book that moves beyond anecdote and occasional journalism to sustained analysis and research.

The contributors' diversity of vantage points (academic, government, unions) aids us in interpreting the swiftly moving phenomenon of home-based white-collar work. Their chapters help us consider what is changeable and inexorable in the future of home-based white-collar work and which options and choices to pursue or set aside. Areas of ignorance are pointed out rather than covered by rhetoric.

As workplace and workforce change, our received wisdoms about desirable directions need reappraisal. Research that is both historical and contemporary aids our understanding of the continuous process of renegotiation in the relationships of market and society. *The New Era of Home-Based Work* initiates a new stage in the study of one important component of the significant changes that are occurring and that will likely speed up. It is an excellent beginning.

S. M. Miller
Boston University

Notes

1. The September 1987 issue of *The Annals* is devoted to the informal economy.

2. Michael J. Piore, "Historical Perspectives and the Interpretation of Unemployment," *Journal of Economic Literature* 25 (December 1987):1834–1850.

Acknowledgments

I am grateful to the Administration for Children, Youth and Family (ACYF) of the U.S. Department of Health and Human Services (HHS) for sponsoring and funding the February 1987 conference at Airlie House, which formed the basis for this book. In particular, Paget Wilson Hinch and Joan Gaffney of ACYF deserve special thanks. They recognized the significance of home-based work to broader social and economic trends in contemporary American society and backed the conference from the outset. Others were also instrumental to the success of that two-day conference: Alan Gartner offered insightful and challenging direction as the moderator of our meetings; S. M. Miller delivered a thoughtful wrap-up to the conference; and Judith Kubran provided valuable administrative support in the planning of the conference. Clearly, there could have been no conference at all without the generosity of the 37 people who gathered for those two snowy days of discussion and debate in Airlie, Virginia. I extend my thanks to all of the participants, and especially those who prepared papers.

No book is ever the product of only one person, and this book is no exception. Audrey Gartner was an invaluable editor whose insights and talents contributed markedly to the book. Halina Maslanka assumed overall responsibility for the coding of the manuscript and skillfully brought it to completion. And Adrianne Royals typed and retyped what I am sure at times seemed like countless versions of chapters. Special thanks to Jack Murray for his comments on various stages of the manuscript and to Beverly LeSuer of Westview Press for her insights and sustained efforts as project editor. Finally, I want to thank Miriam Gilbert of Westview Press for her wisdom and humor throughout this project. It has been a pleasure to work with her.

Kathleen E. Christensen
New York City

Introduction: White-Collar Home-Based Work— The Changing U.S. Economy and Family

Kathleen E. Christensen

Home-based work constitutes one of the most controversial labor issues in the 1980s. Advocates argue that working at home increases autonomy on the job, enhances flexibility in balancing the demands of work and family, and protects the basic right of U.S. citizens to work where they want. Critics maintain that working at home creates an invisible workforce that is easily exploited, forces women back into the home, and precludes the development of a national policy of child care and elder care supports.

The public debates on homework, both industrial as well as white-collar, have been intense and vociferous. Yet, according to May 1985 data collected by the U.S. Bureau of Labor Statistics (BLS), only 1.9 million Americans work exclusively in their homes—representing only a small fraction of the entire American workforce. Why has such a minority of workers been able to claim so much U.S. political, economic, and social attention?

One of the most likely reasons is that the move toward white-collar homework is indicative of larger trends that are propelling American firms and families to rethink the traditional division between the home and workplace.

Although home-based work is certainly not new to American society, the emergence of white-collar office homework is. Until the Industrial Revolution, agricultural and cottage industries dominated the economy, and, throughout history, certain groups such as scholars, writers, craftspeople, and artists have worked at home, seeking a measure of solitude. However, since the advent of the industrial era, other needs such as supervision, communication, and the cooperative use of resources and equipment have predominated, leading to the centralization of the workplace, first in factories, then in offices. The notion of work and family as separate and relatively autonomous behavioral spheres grew out of this physical separation of the centralized workplace and the home.

Current changes in the economy and the family are precipitating changes in attitudes toward the separation of the home from the workplace. The move toward a "lean and mean" corporate labor force and the shifting boundaries between work and family are resulting in new work arrangements for men and women.

This book focuses on the causes and consequences of paid white-collar work in the home, including work that is professional, managerial, clerical, technical, and sales. It is directed to audiences concerned with both the policy issues and the research challenges raised by working at home.

There are a number of terms currently in vogue to cover gainful employment in the home; here, the most inclusive—"home-based work" and "homework"—are used. These terms can be used interchangeably to characterize any paid work done in the home regardless of the employment status of the worker. In addition, they can cover work that is either done exclusively in the home or based out of the home. For example, authors usually work in their homes, whereas sales representatives spend much of their time on the road, working out of their homes.

More restrictive terms than home-based work and homework also exist to cover computer-mediated homework. Futurist Jack Nilles of the University of Southern California coined "telecommuting" to describe computer work done by a company employee at home that substitutes the computer for the commute. In effect, both technology and employment status are embedded in the label.

The notion of the electronic cottage, originally forged by futurist Alvin Toffler in *The Third Wave,* focuses on the technological, rather than employment, aspect of the homework. Wired for electronic work, the home often sits in an electronic network made possible by advanced telecommunication technology. Although the electronic cottage houses both the employed and self-employed, it refers most often to the self-employed, including sole proprietorships, partnerships, and corporations.

Much of the media's attention to homework has been limited to telecommuting and to the electronic cottage, implying that the technology causes work to be done at home. Yet, contrary to the conventional wisdom, which holds that computers will enable millions of people to work in their homes, we will argue that the causes for any large-scale movement to white-collar homework, whether it is computer-mediated, will have more to do with prevailing conditions in the economy and the family than in the availability of computer technology.

Structural Changes in the U.S. Economy

In the United States, as elsewhere in the developed world, several forces are converging to affect the structure, design, and distribution of jobs. First, the internationalization of the economy has forced Americans to recognize that competition from abroad is exerting as much of an influence on jobs as is competition from within the U.S. economy. Foreign competition has been especially strong from Japan and the Far East in the electronics, automotive, and garment industries as well as others. U.S. firms are trying to find ways to cut labor costs, maintain quality, and remain competitive in a world economy in which other countries frequently can compete more favorably than ours.

Technology constitutes a second driving force affecting both the design and distribution of jobs. Office work increasingly is being automated, and estimates are that by 1995, 15 million computer terminals will be used in the United States. Although Wassily Leontief and Faye Duchin (in *The Future Impact of Automation on Workers,* Oxford University Press, 1986) found that technological change would result in absolute gains in jobs in most occupations, they projected an absolute decline in the number of clerical jobs and slow growth for those in management. Technology cannot be divorced from the first force, the internationalization of the economy, either. Advanced telecommunication equipment is making it possible to transport data-entry work offshore.

The third factor affecting the design and distribution of jobs is perhaps the most profound: the transformation of the U.S. economy from an industrial to a service economy. Service-related jobs in retail and business have grown at a much faster rate than industrial jobs over the last decade. These new service jobs vary in their skill requirements; some necessitate higher educational and skill levels, others call for minimal training. Moreover, service-sector jobs have a time and space independence that industrial jobs do not. Not only can the jobs be moved to different regions of the country to save on labor costs or to provide amenable work environments, they can also be done off-site from a centralized office, contributing to the rise of white-collar home employment.

The effects of foreign competition, technological change, and the growth of the service sector on the design, structure, and nature of jobs in the United States can be seen in many areas of the economy. Some of the most notable evidence of change is revealed in the recent massive layoffs of American workers.

According to BLS figures, 5.1 million Americans were dislocated from their jobs between 1981 and 1985 due to plant closings, slack work, or abolishment of shifts or jobs. Of these 5.1 million, nearly 800,000 managers or professionals and over 500,000 workers in technical, sales, and administrative support (including clerical) were laid off. These layoffs were often precipitated by an overall drive to cut costs in order to stay competitive. One way many firms have dealt with the layoffs is to move to a flexible, variable cost, two-tiered workforce of core and peripheral workers. While the core consists of full-time salaried employees, the peripheral rings consist of workers hired on part-time, temporary, and/or an independent-contract basis; the workforce can be reduced, expanded, or redeployed according to demand.

These peripheral workers have been referred to as contingent workers, marginal workers, or a just-in-time workforce. According to Thomas Plewes, associate commissioner of the Bureau of Labor Statistics, as "companies have changed to just-in-time inventories," which refers to the maintenance of inventories just sufficient to meet current demand, "they have also turned to a just-in-time workforce." For companies, the major impetus behind a just-in-time workforce is to remain flexible; a secondary goal is to cut costs. For example, by hiring workers as self-employed independent contractors rather than employees, an employer can save from 30 to 40 percent on each worker due to several factors. Because the worker is self-employed, the employer pays only for the work done, not for any lag times between projects. Furthermore the firm is not responsible for contributing to the worker's social security account or providing him or her with health or pension coverage.

The home becomes an important worksite for many contingent workers who are hired on a contract basis. Many of these self-employed workers are euphemistically described at times as entrepreneurs, free-lancers, or consultants. Because of their inability to find jobs, as well as the financial advantages of using a home as an office, many of these newly self-employed start their businesses at home. Sometimes the home-based contractor may be a laid-off middle manager who is hired back as a management consultant; other times she may be a woman who wants the opportunity to earn some money while she stays home with her young children.

Structural Changes in the American Family

The traditional family in which the father goes out to work and the mother stays home has undergone rapid change. Less than one-tenth of U.S. families (7 percent) fit that model. In fact, the norm is much more likely to be the dual-earner family in which both spouses have paying jobs or the female-headed family where the woman is the sole breadwinner. By March 1985, nearly 17 percent of all families, approximately 10.5 million, were headed by women who were divorced, separated, widowed, or never married.

One result of these changes in the family is that the traditional boundaries between women's work and men's work have changed. Significantly, no longer is women's work solely unpaid labor in the home and men's work solely paid labor outside the home. Women's entrance into the workforce in large numbers over the last several years has profoundly reconfigured the boundaries between work and family.

Yet, the burden of these changes has fallen primarily on women who now work the double day: paid labor one shift, unpaid domestic work another. The vaunted ideal remains flexibility—an ability to set hours or stretch days in such a fashion that both shifts can be accomplished.

There are a variety of ways that women seek flexible work; the most prevalent is through part-time employment. Over a quarter (28 percent) of all women workers in nonagricultural industries hold part-time jobs (less than 35 hours a week). But there is a penalty paid for part-time work. On average, the hourly wage for part-time work is $4.50 contrasted to an hourly average wage of $7.80 for full-time work. Furthermore, part-time work typically pays no health benefits, offers little opportunity for advancement, and provides no pension coverage.

For many women, self-employment offers more opportunity and flexibility than does the current part-time labor market. According to the U.S. Small Business Administration, women-owned businesses are the fastest growing segment of the small business population. Between 1977 and 1982, the number of female nonfarm sole proprietorships grew at an annual rate of 6.9 percent, nearly double the overall annual rate of 3.7 percent. For those women with family responsibilities, a small business appears to offer more autonomy in setting a work schedule that suits their needs. For those women who have been out of the labor market, self-employment may provide more opportunities for reentry than does the conventional job market.

Indications are that the home provides the workplace for many women who are in business for themselves. According to the May 1985 Current Population Survey, the BLS found that 9 million Americans worked at least eight hours or more a week at home as part of their primary job and were predominantly wage and salary workers, implying that most of them were doing overtime work at home. Of those, however, who worked 35 hours or more at home, nearly 70 percent were self-employed in home-based unincorporated businesses. Furthermore, for the 1.9 million persons who worked exclusively in their homes in nonfarm-related occupations, two-thirds were women who averaged 27.7 hours and were likely to be self-employed. The reality appears to be that the home becomes the workplace for part-time self-employment for women.

Much of the public debate indicates that mothers with children under 18 are the prime candidates for home-based work. Yet the BLS 1985 figures indicate that of the women who work 35 or more hours a week at home, approximately 259,000 have children under 18, but almost an equal number are women without children. Circumstances propelling these women to work at home are varied. Some are trying to reenter the labor force after years out raising their children, others are approaching retirement and need supplemental income, and others find that they have increasing responsibility for elderly family members.

The issue of elder care is likely to assume major proportions over the next several decades as more of the U.S. population ages. By the year 2000, the Census Bureau estimates that the "oldest old," those Americans aged 85 or older, will number five million and are likely to be women who have little or no retirement benefits. According to Dana Friedman of the Conference Board, a private nonprofit business research institute in New York City, nearly 80 percent of the oldest old live outside nursing homes and thereby require some type of assistance. For example, in 1986, The Travelers Corporation of Hartford, Connecticut, surveyed their employees and found that almost one out of every five of the employees over the age of 30 provided some type of care to an elderly parent. Most of those who needed care were widowed mothers or mothers-in-law, while most of those who provided care were women.

Although U.S. corporations are beginning to recognize the significance of the pressures of elder care on their employees, most jobs are not designed in such a way to accommodate the needs of employees who have competing family responsibilities. As a result, women turn to self-employment and part-time work, often at home, as a way to create a balance between their work and family responsibilities. Although men are increasingly taking on more of the emotional and practical responsibilities of family life, the burdens remain largely borne by women.

Work-at-Home Alternatives

Home-based work, when it is more than a simple cost-cutting strategy, can meet the needs of both the employer and many employees. For example, Mountain Bell, Pacific Bell, and J.C. Penney have developed home-based programs that permit valued employees already on their payrolls to work at home for part of each week. Although these companies are in the minority of firms who hire home-based workers, their programs warrant attention as work-at-home alternatives.

Since 1985, Mountain Bell has had an at-home program for its managers. Although the company sees working at home as providing advantages for their employees, they don't view it as a special arrangement, but rather as one of many flexible work alternatives. In 1986, Pacific Bell of California instituted a year-long pilot telecommuting program for 200 managerial level workers. The firm's philosophy was simple and direct: In order for an employee to work at home, it must be demonstrated that "it will suit the needs of the company and the needs of the employee."

Both Mountain Bell and Pacific Bell have found that what counts in home-based work has more to do with the person than the task. To be successful, a person working at home must be a self-starter, who can work without social interaction with colleagues or management, and who has the capacity to complete specific tasks.

Both Mountain and Pacific Bell view the arrangement as a way to attract and retain valuable employees, to reduce absenteeism, and to cut the costs of office space. What is important about the programs is that employees maintain their employee status, are paid exactly what they would be paid if they worked in the office, and receive all of the health and pension benefits they would get as on-site employees. In addition, they are considered for promotion. The company pays for all equipment and telephone costs. To ensure that the home-based employee maintains a high profile in the company, Pacific Bell requires the employees to come into the office at least one day a week.

Pacific Bell does not think that working at home should be treated as a regular solution to child care, but it does believe that telecommuting can solve some short-term child care problems such as when a child is too sick to go to school but not so sick as to need constant attention.

Perhaps because of this attitude that discourages using homework for child care, the majority of women at Pacific Bell who telecommute are unmarried professional women who do not have young children and whose primary motivation for working at home runs parallel to that of the men in the program—to avoid the time, expense, and effort of commuting.

These telephone companies are not alone in approaching home-based work as a way to attract and retain valuable employees. In 1981, J.C. Penney decided that hiring telephone sales associates to work in their homes would suit the needs of the company and the desires of some workers. According to the program manager, Carl Kirkpatrick, "We wanted to find a way to have more flexibility. If, for example, during a half-hour, we had planned for only 500 calls and we got 1,000, we needed to find a way to respond quickly to this unexpected surge in demand." Penney saw home-based work as one of many alternatives and now hires about 126 associates to work at home in five cities: Atlanta, Milwaukee, Columbus, Grand Rapids, and Pittsburgh.

"There are absolutely no differences between our in-home associates and our phone-center associates," Kirkpatrick says. "They are paid exactly the same. They receive the same benefits. They don't pay for any equipment or telephone costs. And their ability to apply and be considered for any jobs in the company is the same."

After nearly five years with the in-home associates program, Kirkpatrick says, "We have been tremendously pleased with all aspects of the program . . . and not one in-home worker has come back to work at the phone center. The associates love it because they have more time with their families."

The company feels that it has benefited in a number of ways. The in-home program has opened up a market of associates who would not have been able to leave their homes to come to work; it allows the company to handle a sudden surge in demand; and the productivity for individual workers has remained the same or increased, although the company has made no added demands on in-home associates.

These three programs at Mountain Bell, Pacific Bell, and J.C. Penney embody some of the best principles for home-based work programs, providing excellent models for companies embarking on the same path. They maintain the employee status of those who work at home; they provide the same pay and benefits to home-based workers as they do to those in the office; and they consider all workers equally when it comes to promotion and training. These model companies may lose the short-term savings on salaries and benefits that they would gain if they contracted out the work, but they are likely to gain long-term benefits in loyalty and quality.

In addition, firms such as these may augur well for the type of enlightened and strategic planning that U.S. business increasingly will need as the United States moves toward the turn of the century. According to a recent study commissioned by the Department of Labor, the pool of young workers entering the labor market will shrink, and those who will constitute an increasing share of the future workforce "are more likely to be functionally illiterate, to drop out of school, to become pregnant as teenagers, or to abuse drugs and alcohol." The composition of the projected workforce is forcing some large U.S. firms to think seriously about ways to retain their own valued employees. For these firms a move toward a work-at-home alternative may be just one of many ways to cultivate good workers who need or want flexibility.

About This Book

Home-based work not only raises issues specific to wage-earning work in the home, it also serves as a lens through which larger structural changes in the contemporary American workplace and family can be seen.

It was within this climate that a national conference was convened in February 1987 to examine the "New Era of Home-based Work: Directions and Responsibilities." Thirty-seven experts gathered for two days at Airlie House, outside Washington, D.C., to explore and discuss issues related to white-collar home employment. The participants came from government, the private sector, organized labor, advocacy groups, and academia. Thirteen papers were commissioned prior to the conference and one was added subsequent to it. These papers make up this book, which is organized, as was the conference, around three themes: Part I, the trends and patterns in white-collar home-based work; Part II, the forces driving as well as impeding its growth; and Part III, the consequences of the arrangement on the health and welfare of homeworkers and the communities in which they live and work.

In Part I, Eileen Boris, of Howard University, adopts a historical approach and looks to past experiences in the United States with industrial homework in order to explore what lessons we can learn in dealing with current white-collar homework. Robert Kraut, of Bell Communication, describes the contemporary scene by drawing on national data to develop an analytic framework that distinguishes between and profiles primary homeworkers from supplementary homeworkers. In an important comparative analysis Judith Gerson, of Rutgers University, and Robert Kraut compare home-based clerical workers with office-based clericals with regard to their compensation and satisfaction. The empirical evidence of these researchers reveals that homework will be neither the extreme form of exploitation feared nor the utopian fantasy sought.

From a management perspective, Gil Gordon, of Gil Gordon Associates, addresses the factors that encourage U.S. business to pursue telecommuting and those factors that promote organizational lethargy around the issue. He also shows that telecommunication technology serves both as a catalyst and obstacle to a firm's decision to allow work-at-home arrangements. While Gordon's chapter focuses exclusively on company employees who work at home, Kathleen Christensen turns to self-employed home-based workers, specifically those hired as independent contractors. Because they are at the center of much of the public debate regarding homeworker abuses, she identifies and defines the issues and provides an analytic framework for distinguishing who benefits and who loses from the arrangement.

In Part II, the focus turns to the forces driving the trend toward homework. Roberta McKay, of the Women's Bureau, argues that the international economy has created an intensely competitive climate for U.S. businesses that in turn has affected both their overall levels of employment as well as their particular staffing arrangements, including the move to a two-tiered workforce. She argues that homeworkers have become a part of the second tier of contingent workers. Vary Coates, of the U.S. Congress Office of Technology Assessment, takes the argument a step further, maintaining that home-based clerical work and off-shore data entry are alternative and competitive techniques by which U.S. business can reduce its labor costs. New advances in telecommunication and computing may enhance some of these trends, while other advances could actually abort wide-scale use of home-based clerical work or off-shore data entry.

The focus then shifts to the countervailing factors that may impede any full-scale growth in home-based white-collar work. Margrethe Olson, of New York University, argues that the contemporary American corporate culture will not encourage nor enable large numbers of employees to work at home—largely because of the difficulty in managing employees who cannot be seen. Cynthia Costello, of the Villers Foundation, examines the day-to-day realities that a working mother faces when she tries to balance simultaneously the demands of a paid job and the demands of children in the home. Although better than not working, the arrangement is by no means ideal for women with young children.

Part III explores both the consequences of working at home for white-collar workers and the responsibility of the federal government regarding these workers. Kristine Iverson, of the U.S. Senate Committee on Labor and Human Resources, situates the issue of home employment within the broader context of political philosophy. She sees the current debate over homework as a result of friction between two philosophies of government: the first focused on "responsible choice," the second on "protectionism." She argues the case for the former. Joy Simonson, of the U.S. House of Representatives Subcommittee on Employment and Housing, takes the counter position arguing that because of abuses in independent contracting among home-based workers, government has the responsibility to protect these workers through strict enforcement of federal laws regarding employee status. Dennis Chamot, of the Department of Professional Employees (DPE) of the AFL-CIO, furthers that stance and calls for a clear distinction between blue-collar and white-collar homeworkers and self-employed versus employed. He clearly presents the history and rationale of the AFL-CIO's proposed ban on computer homework; in light of that ban he proposes a series of approaches to protect the welfare of homeworkers.

In assessing the advantages and disadvantages of home-based work, of sustained concern are those women who fall outside of the safety net regarding social security, pension, and health coverages. Charlotte Muller, of the Graduate School and University Center of the City University of New York, examines precisely what those long-term effects have been and provides recommendations for further monitoring and analysis of the impacts of homework on the health and welfare of home-based working women. Although most of the attention of the book has been on homeworkers directly, JoAnn Butler, of Sachnoff, Weaver, and Rubenstein Ltd., focuses on protecting the neighborhood from home-workers by examining current trends in municipal zoning ordinances.

Home-based work is situated within powerful economic and social trends that are affecting the American family and workplace. Any discussion of home-based work rapidly becomes a discussion of work and family issues, women's participation in the labor market, corporate trends toward a two-tiered workforce of a core of salaried employees and rings of contingent workers, and a growing class of underprotected workers in terms of health and pension coverage. The chapters in this book address both the specific issues regarding home-based work as well as the larger issues they illuminate.

PART I

Trends and Patterns in Home-Based Work

1
Homework in the Past, Its Meaning for the Future

Eileen Boris

A historical perspective provides a framework for understanding home-based work—the complexity of the homework issue, why homework regulation has been difficult, how homework has met the needs of working class families, and how it incorporated workers into the labor force on terms that reinforced occupational segmentation by sex. In particular, analysis of the historical record reveals the conditions under which current regulations have emerged. A study of the past will help us understand how the present situation came into being and suggest actions that we can take to shape future developments.

Home-based work, defined as gainful employment within the confines of the home, developed in the United States as an integral part of the industrialization process. Even though the putting-out of work marked only an intermediary stage in the growth of textile factories, outwork grew along with the shift from a family-labor system to a wage-labor system in shoemaking, clothing, and a host of other industries that both met the trade with the South and expanded urban consumer needs in the 1830s and 1840s. In New England, while some daughters headed to the mill towns of Lawrence and Lowell, others remained at home in their agricultural villages, supplementing the family income and earning money for their dowries well into the 1880s by braiding straw and palm-leaf hats, sewing shoes and garments, and even weaving on handlooms.[1]

As early as the 1820s, however, in port cities like New York and Boston, merchant tailors were expanding production by sending out work to seamstresses in their homes. These women cared for children under crowded urban conditions and stretched the often inadequate wages that men earned; their other options for wage earning were limited both by family labor and the lack of other forms of "women's work."

The "core" of this labor force consisted of widows and deserted wives, though single women and those still married increasingly were drawn into the system as its demand for labor expanded. As historian Christine Stansell has concluded, "If employers in some settings utilized outwork only until they overcame the barriers to women working outside the home, New York employers capitalized upon and profited from those very obstacles. Through the outside system, the immobility and apparent marginality of women workers became institutionalized and formalized in urban industrial capitalism."[2]

Initially, sewing women made an entire shirt, but their meager average earnings of $1.20 a week barely covered the cost of rent. Many were forced to turn to charity, which, ironically, further lowered the price paid by the garment contractors who knew that such women had other sources of sustenance. Yet, the manufacturers, beset by competition, could not have paid more even if they wanted to.[3]

From its origins in the "slop" shops of the 1820s, producing rough clothes for seamen and slaves, the clothing industry suffered from the very entrepreneurial conditions that promised upward mobility to immigrants and other workingmen. Beset by competition, low start-up costs, undercapitalization, and a highly seasonal and variable product, garment manufacturers resorted to a system of central shops and contractors, run on credit. This organization collapsed prices and led to underpayment, withheld payment, and long hours, all of which were exacerbated by an oversupply of contractors and workers.

The sewing machine, introduced in the 1850s, allowed better capitalized manufacturers to increase efficiency through standardization of production with the consequence that the sewing woman made buttonholes or collars rather than an entire shirt. This division into those who had machines and those who lacked them further encouraged contracting and its resultant cutthroat competition.[4]

By the last quarter of the century, reformers and commentators named this organization of production, the sweating system. As defined by the Illinois Bureau of Labor Statistics in 1892, "Sweating consists of the farming out by competing manufacturers as to competing contractors of the material for garments, which in turn is distributed among competing men and women to be made up."[5] Either in small workshops crowded with machines and people, called sweatshops, or at home, the sweating system encouraged the exploitation of workers because the various middlemen, jobbers, or contractors had to get their take even as they underbid each other in costs and time to receive jobs from larger manufacturers. Thus, they tended to reduce piece-rates paid to the actual producers and passed along to them the overhead costs of production—lighting, rental of machines, needles, and thread. Workers also absorbed the costs of mistakes, with contractors refusing to pay for spoiled goods; workers further suffered from the instability of their employers who often closed shop and disappeared before payday. Not limited to clothing, homework flourished in other labor-intensive or handicraft industries in the secondary market of the economy, especially consumer goods such as cigars, artificial flowers, hair brushes, coffee beans, nuts, and lamp-shades.[6]

Although manufacturing processes dominated homework, some clerical work also took place at home. Prior to the invention of the typewriter, "deserving" widows received work to copy at home, especially from government agencies. Although the transformation of clerical work, with the growth of the modern corporation and the mechanization of copying, centralized such labor into offices, some clerical home labor persisted on an ad hoc basis. In the 1920s, for example, an Ohio publishing company gave out envelope addressing to 100 married women who were former employees. But not until the 1940s, when war demands for female labor led to a shortage of typists, did clerical homework grow in the direct mail industry.[7]

In an uncertain market, homework employers gained flexibility. With their workforce scattered in homes, they also lessened the chance of strikes or union organization. (Refusing to take any more work or spoiling work became chief forms of resistance to the system.) Home-workers also faced uncertainty as to amount of work, when it would be available, when it had to be returned, and even the kind of work they would be given to do. Rush jobs forced homeworkers to recruit children, husbands, relatives, and neighbors to aid them; low piece-rates also compelled them to find more hands, so to increase production and wages.[8]

The underemployment and intermittent work of homeworkers was not unique in the early twentieth century. In an era before unionization or government regulation, the U.S. economy experienced irrationalities and production bottlenecks similar to, if not identical with, the homework system. Much of U.S. manufacturing suffered from seasonality, unpaid layoffs for factory maintenance or stylistic changeover, or irregular rhythms of production. Labor turnover was high due to protests by dissatisfied workers and to structural defects. Factory or office work, 40 hours a week with two weeks' vacation, is a product of New Deal reforms, the reorganization of capital during that period, and union demands—relatively recent developments.[9]

The homework system, however, maintained characteristics forged in the mid- and late-nineteenth century, one of the foremost of which was relying on a largely female, often immigrant, sometimes rural, workforce that had few other wage-earning options. Even though early labor standards for legislation targeted women and children, mothers benefited least from the initial systematizing of industry because their workplace remained the home.[10]

A Social Portrait of Homeworkers

The first homeworkers, as we have seen, were sewing women, both urban and rural, native born and Irish immigrant, who stitched shirts or bound shoe uppers in the transitional economy of the pre–Civil War period. While mothers and daughters continued to take in outwork in farming and other rural regions during the last third of the nineteenth century, industrial homework in garments, cigarmaking, nut packing, and other hand processes was concentrated in urban tenements among immigrants from Southern and Eastern Europe.

Until the turn of the century, women were engaged in homework as part of family manufacturing; that is, male artisans (such as Bohemian cigar makers or Jewish tailors) enlisted the services of their wives and children. But as tailoring and other trades became more divided, some processes remained in workshops, some entered more mechanized and rationalized factories, while the most labor intensive stayed or went into the homes.

By 1912, Italian mothers and their school-age children (too young to get working papers) dominated hand-finishing of pants, assembling of artificial flowers, willowing of feathers, and the performing of at least 100 other different operations that required little machinery. In the Chinese and Japanese sections of Northern California, continuing into the 1920s and 1930s, women made garments and embroidered them. Though the majority of black women in Chicago went out to work, some stayed at home and assembled artificial flowers and lampshades at home during the 1920s.[11]

Women, whose cultural traditions and/or family responsibilities kept them home, took in homework. These women—most of whom were married—worked because their men held seasonal, casual jobs and made too little to sustain their families. For the most part, homeworking families shared with reformers the assumption that mothers should stay at home with children, but unable to live on the income of husbands, other family members, or "the relief dole," such women accepted the exploitative conditions of homework for family survival. Among Jewish and Italian immigrants, in particular, mothers sewed in the home while daughters worked at similar jobs in the factory (or in the 1920s and 1930s, entered clerical work). Husbands and sons cut and pressed garments inside the shops, a segmentation of the labor market that reflected not only ethnic, racial, and sexual divisions, but also an occupational segregation by kinship position that narrowed the options for mothers who chose or needed to work.

In the early twentieth century, the vast majority of homeworkers were between the ages of 25 and 45, the prime childbearing and caring years, and nearly half of the women had children under three. Reformers estimated at least a quarter of a million homeworkers in New York City, the center of the homework system. Although a small number of deserted, widowed, or divorced women were homeworkers, compared to a majority in the 1830s, in general such women could not support families on the meager income that homework brought: an average of $126 a year. Thus, in this period before welfare, homeworkers often were also on private charity, with both philanthropists and manufacturers counting on the other to supplement what each gave to homeworkers.[12]

These general patterns persisted into the 1930s. While Italian women predominated the home-based workforce during the entire 1900 to 1940 period, in the Southwest, Mexican and Chicana women were homeworkers. In New York City, Puerto Ricans also began to engage in homework in the interwar years. Like the Italians, their culture prescribed mothers staying at home; like other racial/ethnic women, they were relegated to the bottom of a segmented labor market. Among Chicanas, family members engaged in pecan shelling, but garment sewing or embroidery was women's work alone.[13]

Sometimes men would engage in homework, although they were reluctant to be seen by outsiders as doing women's work. This was as true in the New York tenements in 1912 as it would be for Italians in Rhode Island in the thirties, when depression conditions led some men in the mill towns to swallow their pride and pull lace.[14]

Most of the men doing homework were usually helping their wives and children. Whole families would assemble garters or flowers, or pick coffee beans or nuts. Some husbands of slip stitchers would fold and pin neckties, while other husbands aided their wives by picking up and delivering work by car to the factory or contractor. Some even went to demand money owed their wives. Still, domestic work remained women's work, with only a rare husband doing the housework so that the family could benefit from the skill of an embroiderer or sewer during the rush season. Some husbands saw homework as an affront to their self-esteem as an adequate breadwinner. As one women reported to an agent of the Women's Bureau in 1931, "Husband wouldn't let [her] do it if he could find a job." Children would help in both the most simple and less-skilled forms of labor and in child care and domestic maintenance.[15]

When questioned why they worked at home, the majority of homeworkers in most studies cited the care of their children. One Connecticut woman explained in 1931, "baby cried mornings when she had to get up . . . it broke my heart to see her . . . my baby was too small to make get up when she wanted to sleep." So she "asked the boss would he please give me work at home . . . I tell him my children need me." Significantly, at home she made about 26 cents an hour, about half of her shop rate, and, as she reported, "I work till 1:00 A.M. to make anything." She had three other children, and her husband was irregularly employed, so she needed to work. Such women placed their children's needs first, and turned to homework as the only viable option to earn wages.[16]

Respondents also listed housework, physical disability, or old age as reasons for turning to homework. Some preferred homework because they could set their own pace, determine their own hours, and still earn wages as they would in a factory. As one 55-year-old mother of seven put it, "If in factory have to work whether you feel like it or not—if at home, can do housework in A.M. [plus] work on neckties late." Other women combined homework with caring for sick relatives or taking in boarders. Still others felt that it was beneath them to work in a factory, or that it was impossible to find such work due to their lack of English skills or because of general economic conditions.

During the Depression, discrimination against married women certainly limited some women to homework. Mrs. L., though she had a young child, "prefers organized work in fact . . . also pays better," jotted down a Women's Bureau investigator. But she couldn't find such a job; neither could Mrs. B. who "looked the town over many times. Some places will not take married women . . . some places have no work for anybody," she complained.[17] Most women, however, actively chose homework, even if it was less than ideal, as the best they could get. For the most part, then, family labor kept these women at homework.[18]

Many claimed that homework provided the margin of survival for their families, but a few protested its exploitative wages and long hours. As one elderly embroiderer complained, "They take advantage of homeworkers. You must use all your skill to make the designs very accurate no matter how difficult the pattern. . . . All this takes time and you get nothing—practically nothing for it—¾ cents per dress! They say homeworkers never count their time."[19] Hidden from public view, homework appeared to fade into the domestic realm and seemed even in the eyes of some homeworkers not to be real work; at least, employers generally paid for it as if it were only pin money. Yet homeworking families in the Depression and earlier relied on such earnings; they lived so close to the margin.

Attempts at Regulation

Regulation of homework, with the goal of abolishing it, began in the nineteenth century as a crusade against "sweated labor" and its contaminated products. Reformers condemned homework for undermining labor standards such as minimum wage, maximum hour, and health and safety, yet they further attacked it for "commercializing" the home and for degrading motherhood, childhood, and family life. They also emphasized the demoralizing environment of the home factory in ways that suggested that the home should remain separate from the factory and women should stay within the home. As one local official proclaimed in the 1890s,

> The home is the hope of the Republic. A home means privacy. Within its walls, however humble, a sacred sanctity shuts out the intrusive gaze. Whatever tends to immodesty of thought or act, whatever tends to mix in unseemly confusion the innocence of childhood with the vulgar immodesty of men or women tends to sap the foundation of the State. A tenement house without all the modern improvements for seclusion and sanitary purposes is in its nature and by necessity a demoralizing power. When these houses are converted into tenement factories the evils are multiplied. They are a return to the barbarous system of long ago.[20]

Yet some industrial commissioners, especially in southern states like Mississippi and Louisiana, as late as the 1920s saw sewing homework as "relatively harmless," because it went "into homes of comparative refinement and cleanliness," maintaining the genteel status of "respectable, clean persons." By the mid-1930s, however, state labor law administrators condemned homework on economic grounds, particularly its undermining "decently run industry." But they did so in terms that linked labor standards to the dominant gender ideology. Thus, Mr. Toohney, of New Jersey, told the Twenty-Second Convention of the International Association of Governmental Labor Officials: "My primary interest is in preserving for women and children the home and its influence for good for future generations."[21]

Beginning with the 1884 New York State prohibition against cigar manufacturing in tenements, struck down by the courts as a violation of a man's right to privacy in his home, most of these regulations proposed to protect the consumer rather than monitor the working conditions of producers. New York's 1892 tenement house law legalized homework through a licensing system: first, for individual apartments; then, as amended, for entire buildings, according to sanitary and building codes and with specified items prohibited. Not until 1913, through the efforts of the National Consumers' League and the National Child Labor Committee, did the state prohibit child labor or the manufacturing of dolls' clothing or items worn by children and infants.

During the next decade, even advanced industrial states lacked adequate machinery to regulate homework. Connecticut had no law that permitted inspectors inside individual homes and, therefore, depended upon information given by manufacturers. Its homework law applied only to tenements or houses "used by others than the immediate members of the family living therein." Instead of requiring a license, it asked that those engaged in homework "notify the labor commissioner" and that "the work shall be done in clean, sanitary rooms properly lighted and ventilated." Illinois applied only its child labor law and garment manufacturing law to homework, neither of which had any teeth. Massachusetts, in contrast, had a licensing and recordkeeping system under the state department of labor and industries, but still allowed family members to engage in unprohibited homework in their own homes. Only California, which regulated homework as part of the state regulation of the hours and wages of women and minors, and Wisconsin, which required that the homework piece-rate equal the minimum wage, moved to protect the labor standards of the worker (though California lacked adequate funding for enforcement).[22]

In 1934, New York extended its licensing system statewide, including private dwellings; the next year it overhauled the law with the intent to control and gradually eliminate homework. Justifying Article 13 of the state labor law under the police powers of the state to protect women and minors from "wages unreasonably low and conditions injurious to their health and general welfare," proponents argued that homework presented such a situation. The law also allowed the industrial commissioner, after proper study, to restrict or prohibit homework in industries where it undermined labor standards of factory workers or harmed the "health and welfare" of homeworkers. Employers had to receive annual permits, and homeworkers, a certificate. Workers also had to be covered by workmen's compensation.[23]

Under the power of this law, the commissioner prohibited homework in 1936 for the men's and boys' outer-clothing industry, in 1937 for the men's and boys' neckwear industry, in 1938 for the artificial flower and feather industry, and in 1941 for the glove industry. Each order made room for exceptions, including the aged, ill, or their caretakers, who, unable to leave home, could continue homework. Employers who had engaged in the practice before a specified date could supply these special homeworkers; they had to be paid the same rate as factory workers, however. By 1939, 16 states had joined New York with laws regulating homework, though none had the enforcement machinery necessary to investigate the practice fully. Over the 1910 to 1930s period, union agreements in the garment trades simultaneously attempted to stamp out homework.[24]

Women reformers, particularly groups like the National Consumers' League and the Women's Trade Union League, played a key role in shaping social welfare and labor policy. The New Deal first attempted to prohibit homework in 1933 through the National Recovery Administration (NRA) codes of fair competition. In the ensuing debate, a common conception of womanhood equated women with mothers and mothers with the home. The reason that business proponents gave for permitting homework—that mothers could earn wages and still watch children—suggested the very circumstances under which union, New Deal, and social reform opponents rejected homework: A mother could not properly care for children while engaged in the low-wage piecework of sewing dresses, knitting sweaters, or soldering jewelry.[25]

Women reformers and organized labor opposed homework for its effect on labor standards and union organizing, but protection of the working-class family and the family wage lay at the center of these concerns. As Mary Anderson, head of the Woman's Bureau, argued, "The only thing to do about homework is to abolish it and to arrange for higher wages for the breadwinner in a family so that his wife and children do not have to supplement the family income by doing homework, or, if there is no regular breadwinner, to provide pensions or relief."[26]

During the brief period that homework was banned in 1933 to 1935, mothers took factory jobs and discovered the advantages of "shorter and more regular hours of work, no night work, the opportunity of working without the interruptions of household duties, and well-equipped quarters in which to work," as well as "increased earnings and the relief of a home freed from the 'everlasting clutter' of work." One woman explained, "My house is better. I have more time to do my housework when I go to the factory. . . . I take better care of the children, and I am not so nervous and tired and cranky."[27]

Prohibiting homework, however, cut off an avenue for women's supplemental wage earning without truly alleviating the inadequate income and responsibility for child care that brought mothers to homework in the first place. Public policy in these years never linked the homework problem with child care or the other reasons why women took work into their homes.[28]

The NRA was declared unconstitutional in 1935 (the act improperly delegated legislative powers to the executive, and its codes regulated intrastate, rather than interstate commerce). The women of the Labor Department then turned to state laws and joint administrative efforts before they won passage of the Fair Labor Standards Act (FLSA) in

1938. The framers of the FLSA viewed an administrative ban on homework as crucial for carrying out the act; the initial Black-Connery bill specified homework as one of a number of activities that the administrator, through industry wage boards, could regulate in order to enforce the act. The Senate committee eliminated this specific provision in the belief that their expanded definition of "employ"—to suffer or permit to work—sufficiently covered homeworkers. Amendments introduced in 1939 to authorize the administrator to allow the employment of rural homeworkers at lower rates than the statutory minimum were not only defeated but confirmed the intent of the act to treat "homeworkers just as any other type of employee."[29]

Meanwhile, administrative hearings led to special and extra recordkeeping on the part of employers of homeworkers in an attempt to enforce the act. This recordkeeping program proved inadequate, as employers and employees not only failed to fill out the handbooks correctly but also deliberately falsified them.[30] Thus, the administrator in the early 1940s, because of widespread violations, banned homework in seven garment-related industries (women's apparel, jewelry, knitted outerwear, handkerchiefs, gloves and mittens, embroidery, and buckles and belts), an action upheld by the Supreme Court in *Gemsco v. Walling* (1945).[31]

The labor needs of World War II further encouraged these bans on homework. Responding to rising illegal as well as legal homework, New York State issued a general homework order in 1945 that banned new employers from distributing such work and limited existing homeworkers to a strict quota system in all industries not covered by special orders.[32]

In the late 1940s, under pressure from the organized sector of the direct mail industry, New York considered a special order regulating the growth of home typing. Though the State Department of Labor decided that the industrial homework law applied to clerical homework, in 1953 the state legislature exempted typing, bookkeeping, and related processes from the 1935 law. Thus, the law defined clerical homeworkers as independent contractors even if their actual relation to production differed little from industrial homeworkers.[33]

In 1949 Congress incorporated the existing prohibitions into the FLSA as Section 11(d). Simultaneously, it reaffirmed the national scope of the act by rejecting a House amendment that would have permitted homework on the part of a rural person who was "not subject to any supervision or control by any person whomsoever, and who buys raw material and makes and completes any articles and sells the same to any person, even though it is made according to specifications and the requirements of some single purchaser." This description fits some today

who label themselves "independent contractors" but are defined as employees under the FLSA. Although couched in gender-neutral terms, as most federal legislation, actually "person" here referred to several hundred women, mainly farmers' wives, who crocheted and knitted baby articles for another woman in the district of Tennessee Representative John Sherman Cooper, the amendment's sponsor.[34] Still, federal law and administrative rulings provided no consistent definition of who was an independent contractor and who was an employee.[35] With the exception of exempting jewelry made on Indian reservations, federal action shifted to enforcement until the 1980s.

Lessons for the Future

The advent of the microcomputer and possibility of telecommuting presents a complex situation: intensified deskilling of office work along with the development of new skills.[36] Not all white-collar home-based labor is, or will be, the same. From home programmers and other professionals to insurance keypunchers and other routine clericals, we can expect a range of conditions, of control over the labor process, of payment and employment status. Much clerical homework, however, exhibits similarities with industrial homework of the past or opens itself up to these features: the employee-employer relation, possibility of abuse through piece-rate payment systems, lack of benefits or job ladders, hidden costs for employee (no payment for waiting, supplies, or employee overhead), use of home-bound workers to undercut unionization and/or labor standards of inside workers.[37]

Homework will persist in unregulated, highly competitive, and relatively low-capital economic markets. New technologies may permit expansion into other markets. The labor standards of homeworkers will affect inside workers, while the struggles for unionization or organization among such workers can control homework—either through contracts with employers or by forcing government to act. Employers who reject the use of homeworkers—either because their employees force them or because they can operate more rationally and efficiently without homework—can be counted on to further press against homework. Usually these are big firms, which means that homework persists as a strategy among smaller, newer, often immigrant-owned competitors.

But state and federal governments can only control homework if there is a consensus about its role within the economy. New technologies may make it possible to monitor homework in such a way as to calculate a more accurate minimum wage so homeworkers will have a true record of output per hour, bringing them up to the minimum even if their piece-rate drops them below, much as the real wages of inside workers are adjusted in garments and other piece-rate employments. This monitoring can only occur if job security exists, as homeworkers in the past have falsified their own hours in fear that employers will stop giving them work.

The conditions and terms of homework are not tied to their past manifestations. If homework is a good production choice, there is no reason it should not be paid the same as inside work or that its workers not receive benefits and promotion opportunities. Perhaps we should think of a continuum of work experiences and work sites, but such possibilities will be a product of future struggle between workers, employers, and the state.

But is homework good for women? The merger of home and workplace provides an alternative to the dominant organization of labor but does not challenge the place of the home in the economy, nor of women within the home. Neither will it provide a living wage for women and their children. Instead, it encourages the view that women are only secondary earners who need not have jobs that pay better, and who only want to work a few hours a day. Letting women take in homework in itself hardly solves the underlying problems of why women choose homework: women's nearly exclusive responsibility for care of dependents, a sex-segmented labor market where women's work earns about 60 percent of men's, and the undervaluing of women's labor in both the family and market.

Women's place within the family, a factor that encouraged homework in the origins of industrialization, persists as a reason for its continued attractiveness, but also reinforces the very sex-segmentation behind the system. Moreover, the undermining of labor standards persists as a possibility with homework. Only with a new home and a new workplace could homework be a good deal for some women. People rather than technologies will determine whether the new white-collar homework will break with the historical legacy of industrial homework.

Notes

1. Sandra Albrecht, "Industrial Home Work in the United States: Historical Dimensions and Contemporary Perspective," *Economic and Industrial Democracy* 3 (1982):413–430; Thomas Dublin, "Women and Outwork in a Nineteenth-Century New England Town: Fitzwilliam, New Hampshire, 1830–1850," in Steven Hahn and Jonathan Prude, eds., *The Countryside in the Age of Capitalist Transformation: Essays in the Social History of Rural America* (Chapel Hill: University of North Carolina Press, 1985), pp. 51–69; Mary Blewett, "The Social Relations of Production in an Early Nineteenth Century Rural New England Outwork System" (unpublished paper, 1986).

2. Christine Stansell, "The Origins of the Sweatshop: Women and Early Industrialization in New York City," in Michael Frisch and Daniel Walkowitz, eds., *Working-Class America: Essays on Labor, Community, and American Society* (Urbana: University of Illinois Press, 1983), pp. 78–103.

3. Carol Lasser, "Mistress, Maid and Market: The Transformation of Domestic Service in New England, 1790–1870" (Ph.D. diss., Harvard University, 1981), p. 93; Stansell, "The Origins of the Sweatshop," pp. 88–89.

4. Stansell, op. cit.

5. Illinois Bureau of Labor Statistics, quoted in Albrecht, "Industrial Home Work," p. 421.

6. Eileen Boris, "Tenement Homework and the Reorganization of Immigrant Life" (unpublished paper, American Studies Association, November 1985); "The Commercialization of the Home Through Industrial Home Work," *Bulletin of the Women's Bureau,* no. 135 (1935):1–2.

7. Joan Wallach Scott, "The Mechanization of Women's Work," *Scientific American* (September 1982):166–187; Margery Davies, *Women's Place Is at the Typewriter* (Philadelphia: Temple University Press, 1982).

8. For a dramatic example of the impact of uncertainty on homework, see the survey interviews of Connecticut garment sewers in 1931, "Home Visit Schedules" (Papers of the Women's Bureau, National Archives, Washington, D.C.). I have analyzed these in "Homeworkers on Homework: Self-Perceptions from Depression America" (unpublished paper, Social Science History Conference, October 1986).

9. Daniel Nelson, *Managers and Workers: Origins of the New Factory System in the United States, 1880–1920* (Madison: University of Wisconsin Press, 1975); Ronald Schatz, *Electrical Workers: A History of Labor at General Electric and Westinghouse, 1923–60* (Urbana: University of Illinois Press, 1983).

10. On the history of protective legislation, see Judith Baer, *The Chains of Protection: The Judicial Response to Women's Labor Legislation* (Westport, Conn.: Greenwood Press, 1978); for its impact on homework, see Eileen Boris, "The Quest for Labor Standards in the Era of Eleanor Roosevelt: The Case of Industrial Homework," *Wisconsin Women's Law Journal* 2 (1986):53–74.

11. "Report of Committee on Industrial Home Work," in United States Department of Labor, Bureau of Labor Statistics, *Proceedings of the Fourteenth Annual Convention of the Association of Governmental Labor Officials of the United States and Canada,"* bulletin no. 455 (Washington, D.C.: U.S. Government Printing Office, 1927), pp. 77–78; Myra Hill Colson, "Home Work Among Negro Women in Chicago" (Master's thesis, University of Chicago, 1928); and Colson, "Negro Home Workers in Chicago," *The Social Service Review* 11 (September 1928):385–413.

12. *Report of the U.S. Industrial Commission on the Relations and Conditions of Capital and Labor,* vol. 7 (Washington, D.C.: U.S. Government Printing Office, 1901), pp. 181–190, 243–256; Mary Van Kleeck, "Women and Children Who Make Men's Clothes," *Survey* 26 (April 1, 1911):68–69; Elizabeth C. Watson, "Report on Manufacturing in Tenements in New York State," *Second Report of the Factory Investigating Commission, 1913,* vol. 1 (Albany, 1913), Appendix IV.

See also Cynthia R. Daniels, "Between Home and Factory: Homeworkers of New York, 1900–1914," in *Working Mothers and the State* (Ph.D. diss., University of Massachusetts, 1984), pp. 42–81.

13. Mary Loretta Sullivan and Bertha Blair, "Women in Texas Industries: Hours, Wages, Working Conditions, and Home Work," *Bulletin of the Women's Bureau,* no. 126 (1936):71–79; Virginia Sanchez Korrol, "On the Other Side of the Ocean: The Work Experiences of Early Puerto Rican Migrant Women," *Caribbean Review* 8 (January–March 1979):22–29.

14. Harriet A. Byrne and Bertha Blair, "Industrial Home Work in Rhode Island, with Special Reference to the Lace Industry," *Bulletin of the Women's Bureau,* no. 131 (1935):8.

15. Lewis Hine, *Tenement House Scrapbook* (Washington, D.C.: Prints and Photographs Division, Library of Congress, 1911); "Home Visit Schedules."

16. For example, Nellie Swartz, "Social and Economic Aspects of Homework," *Special Bulletin,* no. 158 (New York: Department of Labor, 1929), pp. 10–21; "Home Visit Schedules."

17. "Home Visit Schedules."

18. Lois Scharf, *To Work and to Wed: Female Employment, Feminism, and the Great Depression* (Westport: Greenwood Press, 1980), pp. 43–65.

19. "Home Visit Schedules."

20. New York State, Bureau of Labor Statistics, "Tenement Cigarmaking in New York City," *Thirteenth Annual Report, 1895* (Albany: Wynkeop Hallenbeck Crawford Co., 1896), p. 551; *Proceedings of the Fourteenth Annual Convention,* pp. 82–85.

21. United States Department of Labor, Bureau of Labor Statistics, "Home Work," *Labor Laws and Their Administration, 1936: Proceedings of the Twenty-Second Convention of the International Association of Governmental Labor Officials,* bulletin no. 629 (Washington, D.C.: U.S. Government Printing Office, 1936), pp. 176–177.

22. Ruth Shallcross, *Industrial Homework: An Analysis of Homework Regulation Here and Abroad* (New York: Industrial Affairs Publishing Company, 1939); *Proceedings of the Fourteenth Annual Convention,* pp. 78–81, 83–84, 95–96.

23. Article 13, Section 351 Labor Law, State of New York.

24. Mary Skinner, "Industrial Home Work Under the National Recovery Administration," *Children's Bureau Publication,* no. 234 (Washington, D.C.: U.S. Government Printing Office, 1936), pp. 2–6.

25. Eileen Boris, "Regulating Industrial Homework: The Triumph of Sacred Motherhood," *Journal of American History* 71 (March 1985):745–763.

26. Mary Anderson, *Women at Work: The Autobiography of Mary Anderson as Told to Mary N. Winslow* (Minneapolis: University of Minnesota Press, 1951), p. 244.

27. Mary Skinner, "Prohibition of Industrial Home Work in Selected Industries Under the National Recovery Administration," *Children's Bureau Publication,* no. 244 (Washington, D.C.: U.S. Government Printing Office, pp. 21–25; "Regulation and Control of Home Work by State Labor Departments," in

United States Department of Labor, Bureau of Labor Statistics, *Labor Laws and Their Administration: Proceedings of the Twenty-First Convention of the International Association of Government Labor Officials*, bulletin no. 619 (Washington, D.C.: U.S. Government Printing Office, 1936), pp. 123–124.

28. Susan Ware, *Beyond Suffrage: Women in the New Deal* (Cambridge: Harvard University Press, 1981).

29. For the legislative history of the FLSA, *Mitchell v. Nutter*, 161 F. Supp. 799 (April 28, 1958); Brief for the Petitioner, *Mitchell v. Whitaker House Cooperative* in the Supreme Court of the United States, October term, 1960 (no. 274), pp. 20–45.

30. "In the Matter of: Hearing on Proposed Amendments to Part 516 of Regulations with Respect to the Keeping of Special or Additional Records by Employers of Industrial Home Workers, in the United States and Puerto Rico," *Report of Proceedings Before the Division of Wages and Hours of the Department of Labor* (Washington D.C.: U.S. Government Printing Office, January 6, 1939).

31. *Gemsco v. Walling*, 324 U.S. 244.

32. State of New York, Department of Labor, Division of Women, Child Labor, and Minimum Wage, "Trends in Homework Industries in New York State" (typescript, August 1944).

33. I have traced this history in the files of the Division of Labor Standards, New York Department of Labor, 1 Main Street, Brooklyn, New York. See, especially, the following unpublished papers: "Minutes of Public Hearing on Industrial Homework in the Direct Mail Industry" (October 5, 1949); "Order No. 5 Governing Homework on Typing, Addressing, Mailing, and Related Processes and Operations" (July 1950); and Inter Office Memorandum, "To: Supervisions; From: George Ostrow, Assistant Director; Re: Direct Mail Order" (August 17, 1953).

34. Brief for the Petitioner, *Mitchell v. Whitaker House Cooperative*, pp. 40–43.

35. For the persistence of this question, see House Committee on Government Operations, *Report: Home-Based Clerical Workers: Are They Victims of Exploitation?* 99th Cong., 2d sess., July 16, 1986, pp. 3–6.

36. Paul Adler, "Technology and Us," *Socialist Review* 85 (January-February 1985):67–96.

37. National Academy of Sciences, *Office Workstations in the Home* (Washington, D.C.: National Academy Press, 1985); House Committee on Government Operations, *Hearing: Pros and Cons of Home-Based Clerical Work*, 99th Cong., 2d sess., February 26, 1986.

2
Homework: What Is It and Who Does It?

Robert E. Kraut

Today, changes in the nature of white-collar work and in the composition of the labor force have refocused attention on home-based employment in the public policy, business, and research literatures. The increasing proportions of the American workforce doing information work and the decreasing costs of computer and telecommunications services equipment are two trends that may allow large numbers of white-collar workers to work from their homes. In addition, the increase in employment among women with young children and increases in self-employment may make home-based work an attractive work arrangement (U.S. Congress 1985). Finally, changes in Labor Department policies are resulting in the elimination of restrictions on commercial home-based employment at the same time entrepreneurs are proselytizing for this work style (for example, Schiff 1983; Kelley and Gordon 1986).

Yet recent policy debate and business planning about home-based employment have been underinformed by current, representative data and confused by conflicting definitions. Estimates of the numbers of people currently working at home, projections of future trends, and the characteristics of homeworkers vary widely. In terms of numbers, analyses based on the 1980 Census of the Population estimate that 1.3 million people or 1.6 percent of the nonfarm labor force work at home as their primary place of employment on their primary job, a percentage that has fallen by half since 1960 (Kraut and Grambsch 1988). At the other extreme, an American Telephone and Telegraph (AT&T) marketing study conducted in 1982 estimated that 23 million people performed job-related, income-producing work at home, representing 26 percent of the U.S. labor force (AT&T 1982). Somewhere in between is a recent estimate based on a May 1985 Current Population Survey (CPS) that 17.3 million people do some work at home for their primary employer and that 8.4

million people or over 11 percent of the nonfarm labor force work at home at least eight hours per week (Horvath 1986). Finally, a taxpayer usage study of Internal Revenue Service (IRS) income tax returns (Grayson 1983, reported in Pratt and Davis 1985) estimated that 5.1 million businesses were conducted from home.

This chapter will investigate these estimates to determine why they vary so greatly and to assess their usefulness. Some of the characteristics of selected classes of home-based workers will also be described.

Problems in Measuring Home-Based Employment: Definitions

Variability in home-based employment estimates and difficulties in describing both the characteristics of home-based workers and the consequences of working at home result from diverse definitions of homeworking and from methodological problems in identifying people who fit any particular definition. Let us consider definitional issues first.

The definitions on which these estimates are based vary on their inclusiveness. The AT&T estimate, which counted anyone who performed any work for any job at home as a homeworker, is an order of magnitude higher than the Census Bureau estimate, which counted only those who worked at home a majority of their time for their primary employer. The CPS estimate, which asked about regularly scheduled work done for the principal employer at home, imposed an arbitrary cut-off of eight hours per week before a respondent was considered for further analysis (Horvath 1986). The IRS estimate was based on business units rather than individuals, with individuals potentially having multiple businesses (Grayson 1983).

Which of these estimates is correct? Although this is the question often asked, unfortunately, it is the wrong question. A more appropriate one is, Which of these estimates is the most useful? The answer, in turn, depends on the purposes for which the estimate is used.

When investigating the economic or social-psychological consequences of working at home for workers and their families, a census-like definition that distinguishes people working at home a substantial amount from those doing little or no work at home is appropriate. A similar definition is appropriate for determining the need for protective labor legislation, although counts may be limited to those who are neither self-employed nor employees of their own corporations (but see Christensen 1985, for the difficulties in distinguishing bona fide employees from the bona fide self-employed). For other purposes, a more inclusive definition is appropriate. To determine the need for telecommunications infrastructure, to assess the demand for goods and services that appeal to homeworkers, or to assess the impact of homework on managerial productivity, a comparison of individuals performing any work at home with those performing none would be useful. Finally, for tax enforcement purposes and for purposes of fostering small businesses, the number of businesses conducted from home is of interest. More generally, although legislation requires discrete classification of homeworkers and nonhomeworkers, most research on the topic is better served by collecting continuous variables that index the extent to which people work from home and then letting individual researchers and policy analysts impose classifications for their own purposes.

In classifying a person as a homeworker, these and other definitions differ on several dimensions. The primary classification variable is the extent (in number of hours) to which a person works at home. This variable can be treated continuously, with each hour making a person a little more of a homeworker, or dichotomously, as is done in the Census Bureau and CPS estimates, so that only persons working at home over a certain threshold are classified as homeworkers. For the census, the threshold varies per person, so that he or she is classified as a homeworker if he or she "usually" works at home rather than at some other location; presumably respondents answer this question affirmatively if they spend more than 50 percent of their time in their primary occupation working at home. Distinguishing the degree to which people work at home is important because, as we shall see below, people who work only a few hours per week at home differ substantially from those who work most of their time at home.

Researchers also use a number of secondary dimensions to distinguish homeworkers from others. One is whether the work is for a primary employer or another employer. Thus, both the Census Bureau and CPS estimates explicitly exclude moonlighters and other multiple jobholders (who work at home on their secondary jobs) by asking only about work location for the primary employer. On the other hand, the AT&T survey explicitly asked about work location for any work, whether a main or additional job. Presumably the Census Bureau and the CPS concentrate on the primary occupation for methodological convenience. This concentration reduces the number of questions a respondent must answer to a reasonable number and generates useful data from many respondents. For many purposes—from assessing the needs for protective legislation to assessing the growth in small businesses to developing a marketing database—the wider data collection, which asks about all jobs from home, is preferred.

The third variable affecting classification is whether the work is done *at* home or *from* home. Daycare providers who supervise children in their homes meet the classification for all studies, but plumbers who keep their books at home and travel from there to bathrooms and kitchens in other locations are excluded by some definitions.

A fourth variable is whether the work is paid or unpaid. The unpaid bookkeeper in a family business conducted from home could be classified as a homeworker; this type of worker was excluded in the AT&T estimate, however.

Methodological Problems in Identifying Homeworkers

Compounding these definitional differences are some methodological difficulties that lead to undercounts of the total numbers of home-based workers and that obscure distinctions among them. Because even generous estimates find that a relatively small proportion of the labor force works at home for a minimum of eight hours per day, research on homeworkers' characteristics require large samples, often beyond the means of standard small-scale surveys used by academic researchers.

The need for large samples is especially important to the extent that a specific research project focuses on the characteristics of subgroups of homeworkers, such as undocumented immigrants or female heads of household with young children. For example, consider the sample size needed to examine the welfare of homeworkers in female-headed households with young children. In 1983 less than 2 percent of the labor force consisted of single, widowed, separated, or divorced women with children less than six years old. As only 11 percent of the workforce worked at home even eight hours per week (according to the CPS estimate), one would need a nonstratified random sample of over 20,000 workers to examine the characteristics of just 50 female heads of household with young children working from home at least one day a week. The study would assume that work location and family characteristics are independent. These sample requirements would be substantially higher if one were interested in women whose primary workplace was the home or who were clerical workers or if, as we shall see below, unmarried women with young children are less likely than others to work at home. The AT&T survey with its sample of under 300 respondents and even the CPS survey with its sample of over 60,000 respondents may be too small to answer some questions of public policy interest.

A second methodological problem is that many people who actually work at home are unlikely to reveal this fact to researchers. As much homework is part of the underground economy, homeworkers may fear negative consequences of revealing the existence of work that was not reported to the IRS, that violates zoning ordinances, or that they believe compromises their loyalty to their primary employer. On the other hand, some respondents may fabricate an at-home business or at-home work to acquire tax advantages or company perquisites.

A third methodological problem is that many research questions draw on information that is recorded less reliably for homeworkers than for conventional workers. Even such fundamental information as the number of hours worked, necessary to determine the extent to which people work at home and to compute hourly wage rates for purposes of both research and minimum wage enforcement, is less reliably recorded for homeworkers than for conventional workers. The boundary between employment and personal activity is more blurred for homeworkers. In addition, they are more likely to be part-time workers who, as a result, are likely to forget a short burst of paid employment. Similarly, the distinction between self-employed and employee status is less clear for homeworkers than for conventional workers, both because of company employment practices and conflicting definitions adopted by the IRS and the U.S. Department of Labor.

Despite these caveats, it is possible from current research to sketch portraits of at least two types of home-based workers. The first we might label *primary homeworkers;* these individuals work at home for a substantial part of their work week instead of working at a more conventional work location. To describe primary homeworkers, I use data on the nonfarm[1] labor force obtained from the 1980 U.S. Decennial Census (U.S. Bureau of the Census 1980, Public-Use Microdata Sample A; Kraut and Grambsch 1988). Homeworkers were identified as such if the respondents indicated on a means-of-transportation-to-work question that they worked at home as their principal place of work in the reference week.

The second type of home-based worker might be labeled a *supplementary homeworker,* who supplements his or her primary work at a conventional work site with a relatively small amount of overflow work done at home. The data that describe these workers are more impressionistic and come primarily from both quantitative and qualitative case studies in specific industries or companies.

Characteristics of Primary Homeworkers

According to data derived from the journey-to-work question in the decennial census, the percentage of the labor force working at home in 1980 was small and had been decreasing over the preceding two decades. In 1960, only 3.6 percent of the nonfarm labor force worked at home as their primary place of employment. In 1970 the figure was 2.0 percent, and in 1980 it was 1.6 percent. Although these figures are old and do not encompass the 1980s with the rapid changes in technology and labor force arrangements, they do encompass the last major wave of office automation in banking and insurance in the 1970s. If home-based work has been increasing in the 1980s, it must counter a general decline since 1960.

As Table 2.1 and Table 2.4 show, the distribution of homeworkers varied widely across occupations. Primary homeworkers in the nonfarm labor force were disproportionately in private household service occupations and in farming, forestry, and fishing. A small amount of homework occurs among white-collar workers (executives, professionals, technicians, salespeople, and administrative support personnel), and an even smaller amount among traditional blue-collar workers. Horvath (1986) found similar results. Other analyses from the 1980 census not presented in Table 2.1 show that among white-collar workers, homeworkers were disproportionately managers and executives, writers, editors, entertainers, salespeople, information clerks, and social workers. On the other hand, white-collar workers who worked disproportionately in conventional locations included communications equipment operators, college teachers, scientists and engineers, mathematics professionals, health professionals, and administrative support personnel.

Table 2.2 compares statistics on white-collar homeworkers with on-site workers. Compared to on-site workers, homeworkers were overwhelmingly self-employed or employees of their own corporation. Presumably, the self-employed reduce their overhead costs substantially by working from home, using their household budgets to subsidize rent, utilities, and their other costs of doing business. In addition, working from home enhances the freedom from supervision and schedules for which many people create their own businesses.

Compared to on-site workers, homeworkers were also far more likely to work part-time. From Table 2.2 one can see that 59 percent of homeworkers and only 40 percent of on-site workers work fewer than 35 hours per week or fewer than 50 weeks per year, with perhaps a quarter of this part-time employment being involuntary (U.S. Department of Labor 1985). As Horvath (1986) documented, homeworkers who worked only part-time were primarily women, suggesting that women were using both part-time work and work from home as a way to achieve time flexibility in employment.

Homeworkers were more likely to be older than on-site workers and to have a work or transportation limiting disability. Overall, however, they were not more likely to be women. Among women, those who were married and living in intact households with children, especially young children, were overrepresented among homeworkers, while among men the unmarried with no children were overrepresented. This association of homework with family structure is consistent with the hypothesis that women, but not men, use homework as a mechanism

Table 2.1
Percentage of Homework by Occupations, 1980

Occupational grouping	N in occupation (thousands)	% of occupation working at home
Total (all nonfarm workers)	82,235	1.6
Executive, administrative & managerial	10,079	2.1
Professional	12,409	1.9
Technicians & related support	3,002	.6
Sales Occupation	9,478	1.8
Administrative support, incl. clerical	16,441	1.1
Private household service	480	11.7
Protective service	1,276	.4
Service, except private and protective	10,089	2.3
Farming, forestry, & fishing	1,552	8.8
Precision production, craft and repair	12,396	1.1
Machine operators	6,156	.6
Fabricators, assemblers, and hand work	3,073	.6
Transportation & material moving	3,336	.5
Handlers, cleaners, helpers, laborers	5,385	.5

Source: U.S. Bureau of the Census. Census of Population and Housing 1980: Public-Use Microdata Sample A. Washington, D.C.: U.S. Bureau of the Census, 1980.

Table 2.2
Descriptive Statistics
for Conventional Workers versus Homeworkers
(white-collar, nonfarm workers only)

	Work-site last week			
	On-site		Home	
Variable	Male	Female	Male	Female
N (thousands)	23,648	26,936	371.2	456.0
White	91.1%	87.9	95.6	96.1
Age (years)	38.8	36.1	46.8	43.3
Education (years)	14.8	13.5	14.6	13.5
Married couple household	57.1%	31.9	44.9	54.0
Own children at home	44.7%	42.5	32.0	47.6
Preschool children at home	17.9%	13.2	10.8	19.7
Work limiting disability	4.9%	3.2	10.6	7.1
Part-year or part-time	25.8%	51.8%	40.6	74.0
Self-employed or employee of own corporation	14.0%	3.7	65.0	50.8
Wages & self employment income (all wc workers)	$18.0K	8.0	12.0	3.0
Wages & self employment income (fulltime wc workers)	$20.0K	10.8	17.0	8.1
Below poverty cutoff	2.6%	4.1	8.3	6.7

Source: U.S. Bureau of the Census. Census of Population and Housing 1980: Public-Use Microdata Sample A. Washington, D.C.: U.S. Bureau of the Census, 1980.

to combine family responsibilities with paid employment. This is a hypothesis that will be explored in more detail below.

Finally, homeworkers earned less money per year than conventional workers, even if they worked full time, and were more likely to live in families below the poverty line. These findings of lower income for homeworkers must be tempered, however, with the reminder that homeworkers worked in different occupations than did on-site workers and had other characteristics (for example, increasing age, disability, or rural status) that could negatively affect their income. Analyses below examine the effects of homework on income, controlling for occupation and other confounding variables.

To examine more precisely who works at home and to test hypotheses about the manner in which people use work location to mediate the demands of employment and family responsibilities, my colleagues and I used multivariate, logistic regression (Anderson 1972) to construct a model explaining who worked at home. After preliminary analyses, we concluded that a logistic regression model should include the following

Table 2.3
Influences on the Odds of Working at Home, Logistic Regression Analysis

	Female beta	Male beta	Female S.E.	Male S.E.	t for Sex Difference
Intercept	-7.303*	-6.197*	0.232	0.220	-3.459*
Age	0.045*	0.041*	0.002	0.002	1.142
Education	0.063*	0.021*	0.011	0.009	2.805*
Quadratic education	0.010*	0.008*	0.002	0.002	1.483
Urban	-0.100*	-0.112*	0.021	0.023	0.378
Race (black)	-0.630*	-0.377*	0.082	0.091	-2.077*
Race x Marriage	-0.295*	-0.060	0.081	0.090	-1.939
Marriage	-0.071	-0.387*	0.086	0.107	2.299*
Children	0.202*	-0.012	0.046	0.070	2.561*
Preschool children	0.348*	-0.010	0.080	0.133	2.311*
Marriage x children	0.184*	0.017	0.045	0.070	2.023*
Marriage x preschool	0.064	0.089	0.080	0.002	-0.160
Other household income	0.014*	0.014*	0.002	0.002	0.193
Disability	0.331*	0.202*	0.066	0.058	1.476

* $p <= .05$

Source: Computed from previous tables.

terms: *age* (in years), *education* (years of schooling), *quadratic education* (years of schooling minus mean years of schooling squared), *urbanization* (1 = lives outside a standard metropolitan statistical area (SMSA), . . . , 5 = central city of SMSA), *race* (1 = black, −1 = nonblack), *marital status* (1 = married and living in a married couple household, −1 = unmarried), *children* (1 = own children live in household, −1 = no children present), *preschool children* (1 = own child less than six in household, 0 = no children in household, −1 = own children in household six or older), *disability* (1 = physical disability that limits employment or use of public transportation, −1 = no disability), and *other household income* (respondent's total household income minus his or her wage, salary, and self-employment income in thousands of dollars). We also included three interaction terms, race × married, married × children, and married × preschool, formed in the standard way by multiplying the relevant factor.

Table 2.3 presents the results of the regression analysis, listing the influence of each independent variable separately for women and men (beta), the standard error of the beta coefficient, and whether the influence of any dependent variable is larger for women than for men (t-value). The table shows that increasing age, a more rural environment, a disability, and a greater other household income all increased the odds of working at home. The impact of these variables is about the same for men and

Figure 2.1
Age and Probability of Homework for Nonblacks

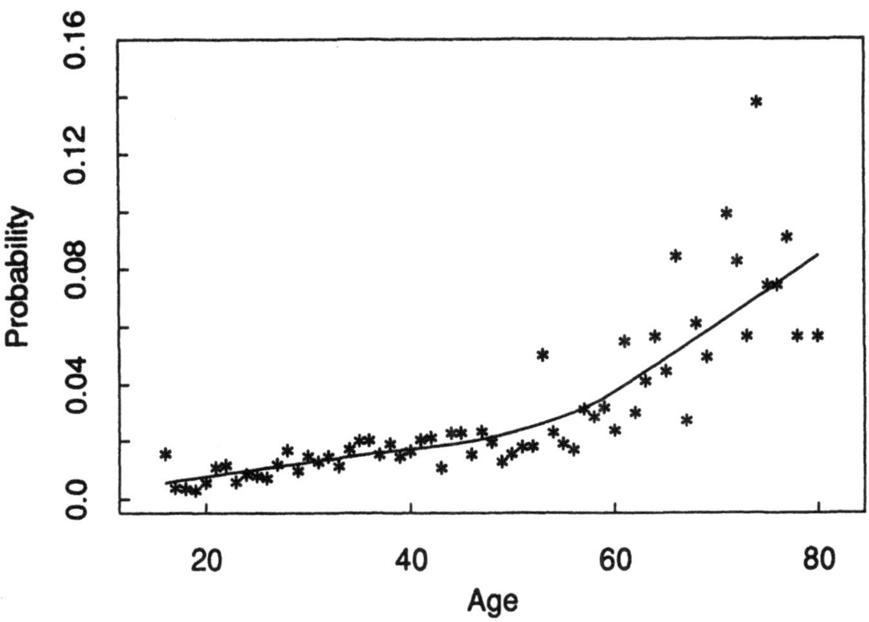

women. More concretely, adding ten years to one's age, living in a rural rather than an urban environment, being disabled, and having $30,000 more in other household income all increased the odds of working at home about one-and-a-half times.

The age effect deserves additional explanation, as it reflects more than mere retirement. Figure 2.1 shows a plot of the probabilities of working at home for each age from 16 to 80. A smooth curve passed through these points using the LOWESS smoothing procedure (Cleveland 1979) shows that the probability of working at home increased at all ages, but the rate of increase steepens appreciably around retirement age.

In part, the age effect is the result of limited employment options for older people with conventional employers because of mandatory or voluntary retirement, because older workers are less physically vigorous, or because they prefer shorter commutes. In addition, older people are more established and may have amassed sufficient experience, clients, or capital for home-based work. Finally, the association of age and homework may be partially a cohort effect. Older people who started their work experience earlier in the century did so at a time when the climate for working at home was more favorable, with higher rates of both home-based work and self-employment (Employment and Training

Figure 2.2
Probability of Working at Home for Women

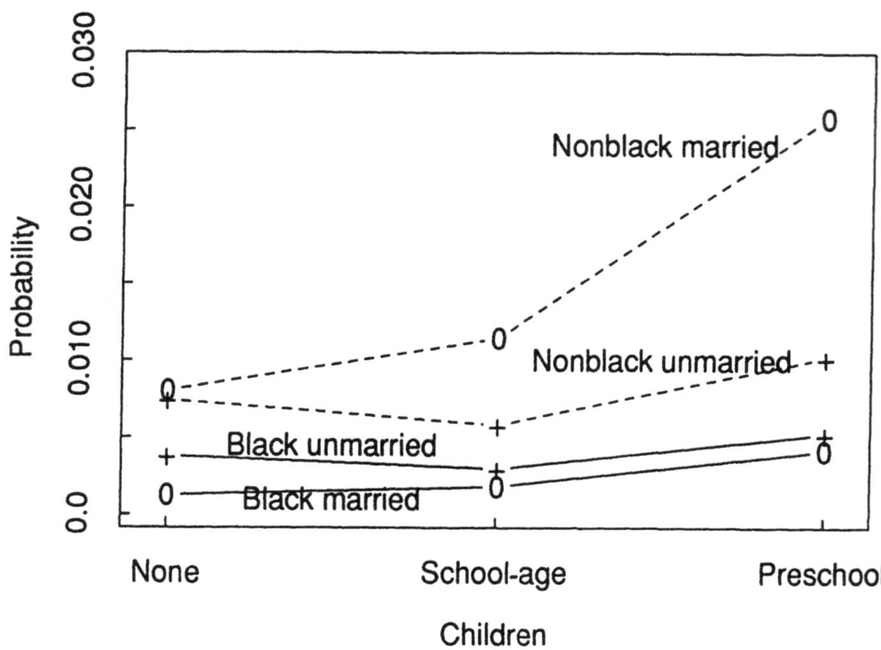

Report of the President 1981); their current work arrangements may be an outgrowth of these earlier decisions.

Race and the family structure variables had different effects on men and women. The picture is simple for men: Being black rather than nonblack or being married rather than unmarried halved the odds of a man working at home. The presence of children had little effect.

For women, the picture is much more complex. The relationships are most easily shown by plots of the probability of working at home for women of different family structures and races. Figure 2.2 shows the probability from the fitted logistic model of working at home as a function of the presence of children, for black married women, for black unmarried women, for nonblack married women, and for nonblack unmarried women, controlling for age, education, urbanization, disability, and other household income. The plot shows first that marriage decreased the probability of working at home for black women, but increased the probability for nonblack women. Second, living with children, especially with young children, increased the probability of working at home for women, both black and nonblack, but this effect occurred only for married women. Finally, for women as for men, nonblacks were more likely to work at home than blacks, but this effect was much larger for married women.

Effects of Primary Homework on Income

Earlier we had seen that homeworkers earn less on average than do on-site workers. Do these results remain when one controls for demographic and job-related variables known to influence income or the probability of working at home? The simple answer is yes.

To answer this question we used multiple regression, examining the effect of work location on the sum of 1979 wage and salary income and self-employment income. Only individuals reporting full-time employment (50 or more weeks of work and 35 or more hours of work per week in 1979) were included in the analysis to control for time worked. In this way we reduced the bias of homeworkers (because of their part-time employment) to forget small intervals of work (U.S. Bureau of the Census 1983). This correction, however, is likely to lead to a conservative estimate of the negative impact of home-based employment on earnings. The regression looked at the effect of homework on log annual earnings for full-time workers, controlling for age, degree of urbanization, race, years of schooling, self-employment, family structure variables, the presence or absence of disability, and some of their interactions.

The top two lines of Table 2.4 present the results. There was a negative effect of working at home on log income for both men and women that is both statistically significant and large in real world terms. Overall, homeworkers working full-time received 70 percent of the income of conventional workers.

To control for the influence of occupation, we added two analyses. We first controlled for occupation by subtracting the mean income of a respondent's occupational group from his or her own income in the log scale. The adjustment resulted in only minor changes. In particular, the large and significantly negative main effect for homework remained; in this analysis, homeworkers earned only 76 percent of nonhomeworkers.

The second analysis controlled for occupation by looking at the impact of homework on income for each of several occupations separately. We chose occupations with sufficient homeworkers and nonhomeworkers in the data set for the results to be believable and reliable. We found 17 such occupations, spanning the spectrum of white-collar work, including managerial, clerical, sales, technical, and professional positions. The small numbers in the individual occupations forced us to combine the men and women into one data set, to include only nonblacks who were not disabled, and to include only main effects as independent

Table 2.4
Effects of Homework on Income, 1980

	Census Code	Sample N	Beta	S.E.	Income of Non-homeworkers (thousands of dollars)	Homeworkers' Proportion of Income(a)	Percent in Occupation Working at Home
All white-collar workers (males)	3-389	3642	-.200*	0.024	19.5	0.67	1.6
All white-collar workers (females)	3-389	2393	-.178*	0.031	10.6	0.70	1.7
Bookkeepers	337	775	0.044	-0.072	10.0	0.87	3.2
General Office Clerks	379	442	0.197	-0.113*	10.0	0.80	1.0
Secretaries	313	1294	0.102	-0.147*	10.0	0.75	1.1
Purchasing Agents	29	251	0.134	-0.410*	14.4	0.44	1.1
Sales Supervisors and Proprietors	249	912	0.129	-0.248*	15.0	0.61	2.5
Business Service Sales	257	211	0.094	-0.093	16.5	0.83	1.9
Accountants	23	493	0.143	-0.299*	17.0	0.63	1.7
Computer Programmers	229	122	0.396	0.014	17.2	1.03	0.7
Technicians	213-218	405	0.123	-0.022	17.3	0.96	0.7
Designers	185	246	0.124	0.261	17.5	1.68	4.6
Insurance Sales	253	370	0.224	-0.110*	19.0	0.80	2.3
Mathematicians and Computer Scientists	64-67	137	0.161	0.039	20.4	1.08	0.6
Engineers	44-59	631	0.119	-0.068	24.0	0.87	0.7
Management Analysts	26	156	0.088	-0.099	24.5	0.82	9.8
Advertising, Marketing, and Public Relations Managers	13	428	0.171	-0.133*	25.0	0.77	1.4
Lawyers	178	265	0.253	-0.335*	29.5	0.51	1.5
Physicians	84	242	0.267	-0.105*	50.0	0.81	1.2

* $p \leq .05$

[a] The proportion of the income of a conventional worker received by a homeworker.

variables: age, quadratic age (age minus mean age squared), urbanization, education, self-employment, gender, marriage, children, preschool children, and homework.

The results in the lower section of Table 2.4 show a clear negative impact of working at home on income. In 9 of the 17 occupations, homeworkers earned significantly less than on-site workers, and in none did they earn significantly more. The weighted average of the homework effect indicates that, on average, homeworkers made only 78.3 percent of the income of nonhomeworkers.

Although these analyses show that homework was associated with lower income, we have by no means demonstrated a causal link between the two. Our controls may have been too gross; it is possible still that lower paid specialties, like real estate law, are done from home, while higher paid specialities, like corporate law, are done from conventional office locations. Historical comparisons, however, suggest that homeworking is one mechanism by which employers pay those with few labor market alternatives less than they do other workers (for example, see Daniels 1985).

The estimates we provided on the income of homeworkers and conventional workers underrepresent the total compensation gap between them because they do not include differentials in part-time work or in fringe benefits. Homeworkers earn substantially lower income than our analyses have shown because they are less likely to be working full-time, year-round. In addition, homeworkers receive fewer fringe benefits than on-site workers. For example, Gerson and Kraut (1986) found that compared to similar conventional workers, secretaries working from home were half as likely to receive company-sponsored health benefits or social security contributions and only an eighth as likely to have paid vacations. In summary, there is no doubt that, given their social position as part-time, part-year, self-employed workers, homeworkers have a much smaller total compensation than do conventional workers, which explains why they are almost twice as likely than others to live in households below the poverty line. Home-based employment by itself can account for some of the compensation gap.

Characteristics of Supplemental Homeworkers

Most writing and discussion about home-based employment has focused on primary homeworkers, even though many more supplemental homeworkers exist. Large numbers of people perform at least some of their income-producing work from home on a casual basis, often in the evening or on weekends. The crucial observation about supplemental homeworkers is that they differ dramatically from primary homeworkers in terms of occupation, demographics, benefits gained from working at home, and motivations for doing so. As a broad generalization, primary homeworkers work at home for personal and financial reasons—to gain independence, to subsidize a fledgling business, or to mesh personal constraints with employment—whereas supplemental homeworkers work at home for task-related reasons—to gain extra and uninterrupted time for work.

Much of what they do at home is work that overflows the conventional workday and insinuates itself into the home. At the extreme of those with overflow work are college presidents, doctors, and other holders of "two-person careers," whose work is so demanding that it consumes not only their own time, but also requires substantial sacrifices from all members of their families.

The CPS survey found that 18 percent of the nonfarm labor force did some work at home in a typical work week, but about 50 percent of these nominal homeworkers worked at home less than eight hours per week. The AT&T survey described earlier reported that 30 percent of those who were employed outside the home brought work home with them. Those who brought work home were primarily employed in white-collar, information-sector office jobs. For example, 88 percent of those who brought work home were in managerial, professional, technical, sales, or administrative support occupations, compared to only 52 percent of those who brought no work home. Similarly, 60 percent of those who brought work home had an office or school as the location of their outside employment versus only 36 percent of those who brought no work home.

As Horvath (1986) noted among workers in the service industries, 71 percent of those who worked at home between 8 and 34 hours a week were wage and salary workers, while almost 75 percent of those who worked at home 35 hours per week or more were self-employed or employees of their own firms. Teachers, who might grade papers or prepare class assignments at home, comprised about 15 percent of those with more than 8 hours of work at home, but virtually none worked 35 or more hours per week at home.

According to the AT&T study, those who bring work home from a conventional job differed in their motivations from those who ran a business from home or used their home as their primary work place. The primary homeworkers worked at home to mesh their desires for independence with their family and work responsibilities, whereas supplemental homeworkers worked at home because the tasks they performed required a concentration that was unobtainable in a conventional office. For example, those who brought work home saw being able to work without interruptions as the major advantage, although they were frustrated by the difficulties of arranging access to much of the information they needed. On the other hand, those with a business at home said being with their families and enjoying flexible hours were the important reasons for working from home. Those with a business at home were also more likely to believe homeworkers can enjoy their independence, earn money, and be with their children at the same time (AT&T 1982).

In a previous study of supplemental homeworkers in a research and development company (Kraut 1987), we found that almost 50 percent of our sample of managers and professionals worked at home on an informal basis, but they tended to augment work at their conventional offices, not substitute for it. Although they worked at home an average of 7.5 hours per week (that is, a full working day in their company),

Table 2.5
Tasks in Office and at Home

Category	Task	Office (extent)	Home (extent)	t (Home > Office)
Cognitive	Read	1.02	1.50	5.0
	Write	0.78	1.16	4.6
	Program	0.28	0.86	22.1
Social	Talk about work (face-to-face)	1.30	0.16	-1.5
	Talk about nonwork (face-to-face)	0.18	0.08	-7.3
	Attend meetings	0.28	0.0	-3.9
	Telephone	0.72	0.39	-3.9
	Electronic mail	0.34	0.67	4.3

Note: Entries have been standardized within location, so that a 0 indicates an activity was never performed at a given location and a 1 indicates that an activity was performed a standard deviation more frequently than other activities at that location.

they also worked 36.5 hours at a company location. Supplemental homeworkers tended to be higher status, better educated employees who put in almost a third more time on the job per week than did employees working exclusively on-site. These results are consistent with Olson's (1985) findings that telecommunications and computer professionals generally work at home primarily to supplement their more conventional work arrangements and for overflow work, although some also moonlighted on second jobs.

Our previous study (Kraut 1987) suggested the type of work that managers and professionals do from home. Homeworkers showed a division of labor across locations. A comparison of the work they did at home with the work they did in their conventional offices is presented in Table 2.5. Respondents estimated the frequency with which they engaged in each of a number of work tasks, separately for tasks performed at home and at an on-site location. One can summarize the findings by noting that employees used their conventional office for social tasks and their home for cognitive tasks. Thus, as the table shows, compared to their work in an office, when these employees worked at home they were more likely to read and write and computer program, and less likely to talk to colleagues face-to-face or on the phone. These results were confirmed in in-depth interviews, where respondents stressed the need to do work requiring sustained concentration as a major motivation for working at home.

The AT&T study, although providing no comparison with activities in a conventional work location, showed that the dominant activities done by employees at home were cognitive: reading papers, memos, magazines, articles, and books; preparing schedules; or writing letters, notes, and memos. In addition, many homeworkers made telephone calls, but for short periods of time; these were not substitutes for office meetings.

Conclusion

This chapter has reviewed some methodological and definitional difficulties in identifying homeworkers. Estimates of the numbers of homeworkers vary widely, primarily because estimates are based on inconsistent definitions. Failure to appreciate the differences among definitions is likely to lead to confusion about the extent of homework that exists, as well as about homeworkers' motivations for working there and the public policy, business, and personal consequences of their doing so.

Although much of the public policy debate in general and the discussion in this volume focuses on primary homeworkers—especially women clerical employees—this class represents a small fraction of the home-based labor force. Far more numerous are the supplemental homeworkers who augment conventional employment with overflow work done at home. Among primary homeworkers, owners of small businesses are the rule, not wage and hourly employees.

To generalize, primary homeworkers work at home to subsidize their businesses and to increase employment flexibility at the expense of lost income. Among the homeworkers are those who would have the most trouble being employed outside the home because of social or physical constraints. Thus, mothers of children at home, rural residents, the physically disabled, and the elderly are all more likely to work at home. One reason they need employment flexibility is to mediate the conflicting demands of employment with household responsibilities. This is especially true of married, white women with young children. By working at home they gain some flexibility in employment.

The data also suggest that homeworkers earn substantially less than do conventional workers, both because homeworkers work part time and are often self-employed, and simply because they work at home. As a result, homework is not a popular work style for those who have heavy demands for income. Thus, married white women with children whose pay supplements household income and who can rely on a spouse's fringe benefits are likely to work from home. On the other hand, some people literally cannot afford to work from home: married nonblack males, married black females, unmarried females with young children, and people who have no other source of household income but their own earnings.

We believe this equilibrium between income needs and flexibility needs partially explains the adoption of flexible work styles such as homework, as well as part-time employment and temporary employment. Various demographic groups differ in their familial obligations and resources and in their physical capabilities in ways that place constraints on the places and times they can work. They also differ in their expected return from engaging in full-time, office-based, conventional employment. As a result, they are differentially susceptible to homework and other modes of marginal labor force participation.

Many people are supplemental homeworkers, compared to the few who are primary homeworkers. Their workplace seems to be based on the demands of their jobs—they have too much work or they need to concentrate—rather than on economic and social constraints. Although in some sense, the family sphere encroaches on the work sphere for many primary homeworkers, the reverse is true for supplemental homeworkers. Many of them extend their employment into their family life. They bring overflow work home or work at home to escape the distractions and interruptions of the conventional workplace.

Even though this study was able to sketch some characteristics of primary and supplemental homeworkers, much remains to be known. Despite our knowledge of the demographics of people who work from home and our attempts to draw psychological inferences from them, we have little information about the texture of the lives of those who work from home and the ways working from home differs from working in a conventional location. For example, for both primary and supplemental homeworkers, we know little about the interaction between the family and work spheres and the manner in which accommodations between them are made. Nor do we know much about whether and how home-based employment influences more economic realms, such as worker productivity or the successful incubation of small businesses. Finally, we know little about how home-based employment as a work style innovation spreads, not only among workers but among employing firms as well.

Notes

1. In discussing census data in this chapter, the nonfarm labor force refers to people in the labor force who do not reside on farms, that is, places with $1,000 or more in sales of crops, livestock, or other farm products during the preceding year.

References

American Telephone and Telegraph. *The Structure of the Work-at-Home Market: Job/Volunteer/School.* Unpublished manuscript, 1982.

Anderson, J. A. "Separate Sample Logistic Discrimination." *Biometrika* 59 (1972):19–35.

Christensen, K. *Women Who Work at Home: An Invisible Labor Force Made Visible.* Center for Human Environments Working Paper 90-PD-01. New York: City University of New York Graduate Center, 1985.

Cleveland, W. S. "Robust Locally Weighted Regression and Smoothing Scatterplots," *Journal of the American Statistical Association* 74 (1979):829–836.

Daniels, C. R. "Between Home and Factory: Homeworkers of New York, 1900–1914." In *Working Mothers and the State.* Unpublished Ph.D. diss., Department of Political Science, University of Massachusetts, Amherst, 1985, pp. 42–81.

Employment and Training Report of the President. Washington, D.C.: U.S. Government Printing Office, 1981.

Gerson, J., and R. Kraut. "How Well Off Are Homeworkers? Psychological, Social, and Economic Outcomes for Secretarial Workers." Paper presented at the annual meeting of the American Sociological Association, New York, N.Y., 1986.

Grayson, P. "Male and Female Operated Nonfarm Proprietorships, Tax Year 1980." *Statistics of Income Bulletin* 2 (1983).

Horvath, F. W. "Work at Home: New Findings from the Current Population Survey." *Monthly Labor Review* (1986):31–35.

Kelley, M. M., and G. E. Gordon. *Telecommuting: How to Make It Work for You and Your Company.* Englewood Cliffs, N.J.: Prentice-Hall, 1986.

Kraut, R. "Telework as a Work-Style Innovation." In R. E. Kraut (ed.), *Technology and the Transformation of White-Collar Work.* Hillsdale, N.J.: Erlbaum, 1987.

Kraut, R. E., and P. Grambsch. "Home-Based, White-Collar Work: Lessons from the 1980 Census." *Social Forces* 66 (1988):410–426.

Olson, M. "Do You Telecommute?" *Datamation* (1985):129–132.

Pratt, J. H., and J. A. Davis. *Measurement and Evaluation of the Populations of Family-Owned and Home-Based Business.* Washington, D.C.: U.S. Small Business Administration, 1985.

Schiff, F. W. "Flexiplace: An Idea Whose Time Has Come." *IEEE Transactions on Engineering Management* (1983):26–30.

U.S. Bureau of the Census. *Census of Population and Housing, 1980: Public-Use Microdata Sample A. [MRDF].* Washington, D.C.: U.S. Bureau of the Census, 1980.

U.S. Bureau of the Census. *User's Guide to the Public-Use Microdata Sample for the 1980 Census.* Washington, D.C.: U.S. Government Printing Office, 1983.

U.S. Bureau of the Census. *Statistical Abstract of the United States: 1985,* 105th ed. Washington, D.C.: U.S. Government Printing Office, 1984.

U.S. Congress, Office of Technology Assessment. *Automation of America's Offices.* Washington, D.C.: U.S. Government Printing Office, 1985.

U.S. Department of Labor. *Employment and Earnings, Table A-31.* Washington, D.C.: U.S. Government Printing Office, 1985.

3
Clerical Work at Home or in the Office: The Difference It Makes

Judith M. Gerson
Robert E. Kraut

The current debate about the legal status of home-based work in the garment-related industries has extended public awareness and concern to other, nonindustrial forms of homework. Judging from the coverage in the mass media (for example, Herbers 1986; Keller 1984; Shabecoff 1981) as well as some of the testimony in legislative hearings (cf. Behr 1986; Elisburg 1986), the definition of the problem tends to focus on the larger, generalizable issues of home-based work, rather than on the particular dynamics of homework as they apply in specific occupational categories and industrial sectors. Although this emphasis on the generic issues of homework is not a deficit per se, the researcher is left wondering if the application is valid across all forms of homework.

Rather than continue to assume that all kinds of home-based work are essentially alike, this chapter compares home- and office-based work in one occupation—clerical work—within one industrial subsector—secretarial services. Clerical homework, like other nongarment forms of homework, has inherited the legacy of the debate over the moral, legal, social, and economic consequences of home-based work. This debate in its universal formulation has dichotomous versions, both positive and negative. This chapter begins with a review of these two work-at-home metatheories and then moves to a recapitulation of previous research findings on clerical homework. The major section, a comparison of home- and office-based clerical workers, is based on primary research data collected on a nationwide sample. The concluding section evaluates the validity of these general models for clerical homework and discusses the implications of the empirical findings.

The Metatheories of Homework

The first of these viewpoints portrays homeworkers as a relatively advantaged group of people who have consciously chosen to do their paid work within their homes (cf. Behr and Lazar 1983; Toffler 1980). Frequently, the desire for greater work autonomy and/or the wish to build a business enterprise precedes the decision to work at home. Homework seemingly is an ideal site to reduce both the effects of work supervision and the costs of starting a business. Or, perhaps homeworkers choose this work style because young children, sick, elderly, handicapped family members, or they themselves require assistance at home, making commuting to work either difficult or impossible. Thus, people work at home because they want to, even though that desire may occasionally and in part be based on necessity.

This viewpoint connotes the importance of individuals being able to choose where they work and argues that this choice ought to be a worker's right. Advocates of this position maintain that there are numerous advantages that accrue to homeworkers. They claim that homemakers have greater control over the scheduling and pacing of their work, working when they want. With both domestic and paid work concentrated in one domain, homeworkers are also able to integrate the normally inconsistent demands of domesticity and employment, thereby working more efficiently and having more leisure time. There are also savings available to the home-based worker, both in terms of time and monetary costs, including the expenses of commuting, eating out, and clothing. In addition, this view sees homeworkers as being financially successful, citing individual reports of earned incomes exceeding national averages.

Finally, this version of the metatheory depicts homeworkers as happy people because they seemingly have it all. They work when and where they want and can more easily deal with domestic responsibilities. Released from the time and costs of office jobs as well as the stresses of coping with the boss and coworkers, homeworkers tend to be more satisfied.

The contrasting metatheory, on the other hand, portrays homeworkers as an exceptionally exploited group of workers (cf. Berch 1985; Mattera 1983; Webb 1982). According to this perspective, homeworkers are forced to work for low wages, with few if any benefits, in substandard working conditions, often relying on the supplementary labor of young children. Frequently, people work at home simply because they do not have alternatives—employers or company policies may force them to or their personal circumstances may leave them no choice. The common reality of being paid piece-rate instead of a wage or salary means there is pressure to turn out enough work and do it quickly enough to earn sufficient money. If they are fortunate to earn an hourly wage, homeworkers still must toil long hours to compensate for the low-pay scale, often starting their workdays before dawn and not finishing until late into the night. In addition to low incomes, homeworkers cannot enjoy any of the supposed flexibility or freedom that ought to be theirs. Rather than gaining autonomy from the lack of direct supervision, they are the objects of indirect control from bosses, machines that regulate their work, and/or the low wages themselves.

The advantage of having everything at one's fingertips is also a myth according to this model. The integration of domestic responsibilities with paid work only means that women who work at home will assume even more of the housework and child care than is normally true. Homework reproduces their exploitation both as women and as workers because it reinforces the sexual division of labor (cf. Boris 1986). Working at home also contributes to the social isolation of workers, making it difficult for them to get needed support and assistance as well as derive any sociability from their work environments. Given the social and economic hardships depicted by this metatheory, homeworkers can be expected to experience more stress and lower job satisfaction than other on-site workers.

Previous Research on Home-Based Clerical Work

The research on clerical homework, though scant, has elaborated these metatheories, ultimately providing some support for both perspectives. Studies have addressed several closely related issues—what is clerical homework, who are clerical homeworkers, why do people work at home, and how many are there?

The definitional problem surrounding clerical homework is complicated by the concentration of some studies on the technological implications of widespread computer adoption, inadvertently assuming that all clerical homework is computerized. The term *telecommuter* means commuting from afar (U.S. Congress, Office of Technology Assessment 1985, p. 189) and usually applies to workers using some form of computing technology (Risman and Tomaskovic-Devey 1986). Yet, as Christensen (1986) has found, the electronic cottage image may be more mythical than real; only one-fourth of her sample used computers. Computer-based homework, therefore, is but one aspect of clerical homework, which more frequently is dependent on paper and pencil tasks, typewriters, calculators, and so forth.

The question of what is clerical homework is closely intertwined with who does it. A substantive emphasis on homework that is computer assisted and/or attributed to technology has meant that professionals working at home are occasionally lumped together with clerical workers if both groups use computers (cf. Pratt 1984; Ramsower 1985). Many researchers, however, have stressed the importance of distinguishing among types of clerical homeworkers (Christensen 1985; Leidner 1984; Olson and Primps 1984; Risman and Tomaskovic-Devey 1986). A recent report from the Office of Technology Assessment (1985) summarizes these distinctions, labeling three different phenomena often subsumed under the heading of office homework: (1) occasional homeworkers who work at home only when suitable, usually professional workers; (2) full-time entrepreneurs with several different clients; and (3) employees of a single company who are rarely if ever in the central office, usually women. There is some dissension with respect to the second category—entrepreneurs. Does ownership represent another dimension of labor force participation or can it appropriately be classified under office homework?

Judging from the design of recent studies, some researchers have decided to treat proprietorship as a separate entity and focus instead on comparisons between clerical and professional homeworkers (Leidner 1984; Olson and Primps 1984; Risman and Tomaskovic-Devey 1986). Nevertheless, the issue of entrepreneurship is an important one for clerical homeworkers. Frequently, companies and workers themselves believe that they are independent contractors, although they work for only one firm and there is essentially no independence in their work routine. The distinction assumes significance because fringe benefits, including social security, health insurance, and pensions, are generally not available to the independent contractor, and these workers are not protected under the Fair Labor Standards Act (cf. Christensen 1985).

These taxonomies, therefore, represent more than just descriptive categories. They are correlated with the metatheories discussed earlier. Professional workers and business owners provide empirical validation of the positive image of homework. Researchers have found that professional homeworkers voluntarily choose to work at home on some tasks rather than work at home all of the time. Thus, they often have the advantages of both work sites—the quiet and concentration afforded by the solitude of their homes and the sociability and support of their coworkers in the office. Moreover, they gain in autonomy and control over their jobs and report high levels of job satisfaction (Leidner 1984; Olson and Primps 1984; Risman and Tomaskovic-Devey 1986). Similarly, entrepreneurs are comparatively advantaged in terms of the pacing and scheduling of their work, pay, and job benefits in contrast to clerical employees (Christensen 1985).

Clerical employees, including those working as independent contractors for one employer, seem to work at home because of a set of constraints. Usually the needs of other family members requiring care or their own disabilities will cause women to seek home-based work. Workers receive lower wages, no fringe benefits, and have virtually no job mobility. For these women, homework is neither the solution to child care demands nor the path to keeping one's career on track (Christensen 1985, 1986; Costello 1986; Leidner 1984; Olson and Primps 1984; Risman and Tomaskovic-Devey 1986).

However, recent figures range from 15,000 telecommuters (U.S. Department of Labor 1985) to 1980 census-based estimates of 176,000 administrative support workers (which includes clerical workers), whose primary workplace is the home (Kraut and Grambsch 1988), to 406,000 secretaries, stenographers, and typists (Horvath 1986).

Although studies that estimate numbers of homeworkers are both necessary and useful, their utility does not extend beyond the broadest of descriptors in terms of occupational categories, industrial sectors, and number of hours worked. In addition to the information provided by such investigations, we would also want to know what effect if any do factors such as firm size, seniority in firm, and number of dependents have on the working conditions and outcomes for home- and office-based clerical workers. Such questions cannot be answered using presently available census data. And although other studies provide the in-depth analysis sought, the samples are non-random and very small, often with self-selected respondents. Thus, one cannot know how or to whom these findings might generalize.

This study fills part of the void remaining in our knowledge of the antecedents and consequences of clerical homework. Unlike previous studies of homeworkers, this investigation compares home-based workers with those in conventional offices, using random sampling techniques. The resulting sample size is sufficiently large to permit the use of appropriate statistical controls. Furthermore, limiting the analysis to one industrial sector and one occupational category allows us to control the variation due to occupation and industry. The research design is discussed first, followed by the analysis of our results.

Research Design

The present study of home- and office-based clerical workers is based on data collected jointly by both authors in 1985 using a four-part procedure. Cities with populations between 98,000 and 109,000 people, as recorded in the 1980 census, formed the potential study sites. Six cities were randomly selected within each of the four major geographic regions (Northeast, South, North Central, and West) as defined by the Census Bureau, for a total of 24 cities. In each of the cities selected, we used the local *Yellow Pages* to identify all the firms listed under "secretarial," "typing," and "word processing" services. We omitted national firms such as Kelly Services and Manpower from the sample because they did not have independent employment policies.

Following an introductory letter, we telephoned the president or manager of each firm to collect descriptive information about the firm and solicit their nominations of potential respondents. In a short telephone interview, managers of cooperating firms responded to questions about the number of employees, the number who were part- or full-time, the number who were office- or home-based, the firm's age, and types of services offered. Two hundred and forty-one out of the 453 firms contacted qualified for inclusion in the sample. Of these 241 establishments, 222 agreed to cooperate, giving a response rate of 92 percent for qualifying firms.

From each participating firm, we obtained the names and addresses of firm members who worked from their homes or in conventional offices. Preliminary analysis from census data had indicated that in secretarial businesses, homeworkers are underrepresented (Kraut and Grambsch 1988). Thus, we oversampled homeworkers by a factor of 2.552. There was an initial telephone call to potential respondents to secure their consent to participate in the study. This process identified 106 home-based workers and 260 office-based workers. People agreeing to participate received a written questionnaire to complete and return by mail. If necessary, as many as three follow-up reminders were sent. Eighty-seven percent returned their questionnaires, with no significant difference in response rates between the two groups. Our sampling suggests that in mid-sized cities, 35 percent of secretarial service firm members work from home. Because so few men work in secretarial firms, they are excluded from the present analysis. The results reported here are based on the 297 women out of the total final sample of 316 respondents.

The Processes and Consequences of Clerical Homework

Home- and office-based clerical workers were remarkably alike in terms of the actual work they did. In part, this similarity is an artifact; it results from the sampling design that required respondents to type in order to qualify for inclusion in the study. Nevertheless, both home and office workers performed a wide range of clerical tasks, including the preparation of address labels for bulk mailings to résumé advice and typing. Comparing task diversity, there seems to be no specialization associated with one work site or the other. In addition, data revealed that approximately 90 percent of both home and office workers used a computer in their work for word processing, form letters and bulk mailings, tape transcriptions, and so forth. Thus, the images of the computerized on-site office as well as the electronic cottage were validated.

Clerical homeworkers and office workers were markedly distinct, however, with respect to the degree and quality of their labor-force attachment. Homeworkers were much more likely than office workers to be the owners of their own businesses—70 percent of the homeworkers versus 33 percent of the office workers. Because of the sampling procedure, all managers also had to perform clerical work as well. In addition, homeworkers were more likely to be independent contractors with multiple clients than were their office counterparts, but less likely to be full-time employees of the firms. The relatively high proportion of owners and low proportion of full-time employees among the homeworkers reflected further differences in the structure of their work.

Table 3.1 indicates the type of monetary compensation workers received. Homeworkers were more apt to be paid in the profits of their firms, though this difference disappeared after controlling for firm ownership. Moreover, homeworkers were more likely to be paid piece-rate, by the project or by typed page, and less likely to be salaried workers. These differences remained after controlling for ownership, firm size, and firm age.

Income differences are interesting because they were not as large as expected. Homeworkers earned about $1,800 less per year than office workers, but this difference only approached statistical significance at the 0.10 level. Once we controlled for the number of hours worked, the earnings gap was only slightly diminished. Household income was significantly greater among homeworkers and reflects that a larger proportion of these families were dual earners.

One of the most important material differences between home and office clerical workers had to do with their fringe benefits. With the exception of contributions to pension plans in which neither group received appreciable benefits, office workers consistently had superior benefit packages.

Office workers had markedly better coverage for health insurance, social security contributions, unemployment compensation as well as pay for overtime work and vacations. For health insurance, however, married workers frequently were able to rely on the health plans provided by their husbands, thereby compensating for the lack of coverage provided in their own jobs and reducing the disparity in health coverage between the two groups. But other benefits were not as easily or as completely transferred among household members. Furthermore, after controlling

Table 3.1
Mean Differences Between Home and Office Clerical Workers: Labor Force Participation and Economic Outcomes

	Home Workers Mean	Office Workers Mean	T Value
LABOR FORCE ATTACHMENT			
% Owner	70	33	-5.94 ***
Total hours worked/week	33.8	41.1	2.92 **
Total weeks worked/year	42.9	42.9	- .02
Seniority in firm (years)	5.1	3.3	2.13 *
INCOME AND BENEFITS			
Income from firm ($1000s)	8.5	10.2	.13
% paid by profits	40	22	-3.32 ***
% paid piecerate	53	17	-4.67 ***
% paid salary	7	39	6.69 ***
Household income ($1000s)	37.6	31.4	-2.43 **
% with own health benefits	14	29	3.07 **
% with household health benefits	48	56	.44
% with social security	27	61	5.39 ***
% with pension contributions	11	9	.29
% with unemployment comp.	8	43	8.30 ***
% with overtime pay	10	30	4.25 ***
% with paid vacation	6	49	9.57 ***

N = 297
* $p \leq .05$
** $p \leq .01$
*** $p \leq .001$

for the number of hours and weeks per year worked, the inferior benefit package for homeworkers remained.

In sum, the economic picture for homeworkers is one in which they are relatively disadvantaged, though perhaps not to the extreme imagined by some. Despite the overall similarity in the actual work they do, home-based and office-based clerical workers have clearly different work experiences and rewards. The incomes of home-based clerical workers, though competitive in dollar amounts with conventional office workers, were based on a qualitatively distinct working relationship to the firms. Homeworkers were more likely to be either owners or independent contractors and were also more likely to be paid either with firm profits or piece-rate. Thus, their income was more susceptible to fluctuations. In addition to these qualitative differences, homeworkers appeared to be at a significant disadvantage in terms of their benefit packages. Even though married homeworkers compensated for this disadvantage in part by relying on husbands for health benefits, other benefits such as pensions could not be obtained from other family members.

Who Works at Home, and Why?

The answer to the query about the factors distinguishing home from office workers is multifaceted. Demographic data from the sample indicate that, in contrast to office workers, homeworkers were more likely to be married and have children under the age of six; yet they were also on the average more likely to be older (see Table 3.2). These differences are statistically significant. On the other hand, the two groups were not significantly different in their racial or ethnic identity, the amount of formal education attained, or the total number of children living with them. So, the first set of indicators seem to demonstrate that indeed clerical homeworkers are located where they are because of personal or familial circumstances. Marriage, the presence of young children, and advanced age are factors implying more need for flexibility in scheduling. But, do homeworkers perceive their personal or familial situation as forcing them to work at home?

To understand whether homeworkers felt coerced into working at home, we asked both groups to rate the relative advantages and disadvantages of the home and the conventional office as work sites. When describing their own behavior, homeworkers were most apt to remark that they worked at home because they wanted flexible hours and freedom from supervision. Married homeworkers were more likely than nonmarried homeworkers to cite flexibility as the reason for homework. At the same time, homeworkers generally stressed that neither their

Table 3.2
Mean Differences Between Home and Office Clerical Workers: Demographic Factors, Values, and Domestic Labor

	Home Workers Mean	Office Workers Mean	T Value
LABOR FORCE ATTACHMENT			
% Married	79	51	-4.97 ***
Age	42.4	36.6	-3.59 **
% with Children < 6	25	13	-1.79
Race (% Caucasian)	96	93	-1.29
Education (in years)	14.2	14.0	- .80
VALUES[a]			
Gender roles	- .40	.18	4.20 ***
Importance of family	- .02	.05	- .82
Importance of religion	.20	-.05	-1.95 *
Careerist orientation	- .34	.13	-2.08 *
DOMESTIC LABOR			
Housework hours/day	4.2	3.6	- .97
Childcare hours/day	2.0	1.6	.30
Money paid housework & childcare ($1000s)	5.2	2.9	-1.91 *

N = 297

* $p \leq .05$
** $p \leq .01$
*** $p \leq .001$

[a]Measures of values were transformed into Z scores ($\bar{X}$=0, s.d. =1).

inability to find other jobs or an employer's requirement that they work at home explained their motives. Other reasons fell in between these two strongest sets of factors and included the ability to accomplish more work, less distraction, as well as the reduction of expenses and elimination of commuting. Although most homeworkers did not cite the need to deal with personal or familial demands as reasons for working at home, there is one notable exception—women with young children who said that the need for child care motivated them to work at home.

Asked directly about their decision on work sites, homeworkers were more likely than office workers to state that their place of work was based on personal preference. Among homeworkers with young children, the feeling of freely choosing homework faded. Yet, after controlling for the presence of young children, homeworkers generally felt they had more choice in where they worked than did office workers. In other words, most homeworkers did not believe they were somehow forced to work at home, either because of an employer, the absence of other job opportunities, or because of family demands.

Homeworkers with young children, however, were an exception. They were considerably more likely to attribute working at home to the necessity of providing child care, and they were less likely to affirm that their work site was a matter of personal preference. Thus, it seems as if there is a disjuncture between the expressed needs for flexibility commensurate with homeworkers' demographic characteristics and how they understand their motivations. Whereas the outside observer construes the need for greater flexibility as resulting from added pressures, the homeworkers see themselves as making choices relatively unconcerned with structural conditions that might have predicted these outcomes. The distinction is one of emphasis: The researcher sees the competing demands of domesticity and employment resulting in homework as an accommodation; the homeworker envisions herself being able to choose homework given the realities of her life.

Therefore, the initial demographic indications revealed a pattern of homeworkers making their decision because of domestic needs. Yet, when asked more directly about these decisions, only the women with young children confirmed that their choice reflected familial responsibilities. This was not true of the older women and/or the married women who were either childless or had older offspring. Although married homeworkers regardless of age said they wanted the added flexibility of homework, they did not express those needs in terms of domesticity unless they had young children.

But do they actually make use of the possibility of integrating domestic demands with paid work? Even for the homeworkers with young children who made their choice to meet the competing requirements of domesticity and employment, working at home did not facilitate decreased dependence on child care (see Table 3.2). Homeworkers were almost as likely to use some type of child care as were office-based workers, after controlling for the effects of marital status, age of youngest child, and household income. In fact, homeworkers had higher child care expenses than did office workers and this difference was statistically significant. Nevertheless, homeworkers did more housework and child care, although the total amounts were not significant.

Another way of understanding why people work at home is to consider the personal values they hold. Generally speaking, when there were differences between home and office workers, homeworkers were more likely to express traditional values than were office workers. The strongest differences between the two groups occurred on attitudes regarding gender roles. Office-based workers were more likely to agree with statements advocating a shared household division of labor, equal employment opportunities for women and men, and other ideas expressing egalitarianism between women and men than were homeworkers. Not only were homeworkers more traditional than office workers with respect to gender relations, but they also placed greater emphasis on religion and less emphasis on career advancement. However, both home and office workers tended to value the family very highly. These value configurations suggest that homeworkers may be making decisions about work sites that are commensurate with personal belief systems. Homeworkers believed they ought to assume the major responsibility for housework and child care and not place too much importance on their careers. Presumably, work at home is congruent with this ideology.

Quality of the Work Environment and Job Satisfaction

Homeworkers were more apt to work in isolated settings such as a private office or study, working when no one was around to interrupt them. For homeworkers this need for solitude often meant that their workdays stretched beyond the standard nine-to-five. They were more likely, than office workers to be working before eight in the morning and again at night, after dinner. They also often used another individual—a babysitter, spouse—to ensure that people would not bother them while they were working. For the homeworker, most interruptions were not relevant to their work, but for office workers interruptions usually were considered job-related.

In terms of getting assistance with doing their work, as expected, home-based workers had less help than office workers. When they did get help it was from adult family members and not from the children as is commonly feared. In addition, homeworkers received *less* help from family members on housework and child care chores. However, homeworkers seemed to get more social and psychological support, even if that support did not translate directly into assistance with work. Thus, homeworkers were more likely to report that they could rely on others to discuss problems, to provide tangible support such as rides and help when sick, and for companionship at social gatherings.

Women working at home were also more satisfied with their jobs than were office workers. This difference remained, even after controlling for demographic variables, the hours worked, and household income. They also experienced less role conflict and overload, although previous research would have predicted otherwise. With potentially conflicting demands of domesticity and wage work concentrated in one domain, the expectations suggested from previous research seemingly point to heightened role strain or conflict.

Implications of Home-Based Work

Homework is neither the extreme form of exploitation feared, nor is it the utopian fantasy sought. There are, however, significant differences in material as well as social and psychological factors between home- and office-based clerical workers.

The homeworkers had a distinctly different working relationship with the target firm than the office workers. Homeworkers were much more likely to be either self-employed owners or independent contractors and much less likely to be full-time employees. The significance of this difference for a steady income cannot be minimized, although the actual earnings of home-based workers was not significantly lower.

The overall picture of material well-being of homeworkers is not particularly sanguine. Although they do not fare as poorly as one might have expected in terms of income, the relative absence of full benefit packages compromise the economic security of the worker. Even though husbands can, in some instances, provide health benefits for the entire family, this fact does not obviate the need to make full benefit packages available to all workers. When benefits duplicate those already available to the household, alternative packages could be offered.

The demographic composition of the home-based clerical workers suggests that they select their work location after recognizing their domestic constraints. Yet, when surveyed, the women did not generally conceptualize their familial responsibilities as demands or constraints on their labor force participation, with the notable exception of mothers of young children. For most homeworkers, the decision represents a choice rather than coercion. And after controlling for the presence of young children, homeworkers expressed more choice in where they worked than did office workers. The choices also were congruent with the personal values homeworkers had, which tended to be more traditional than the belief systems of office-based workers. On the whole, homeworkers report higher levels of job satisfaction and indicate that they have more support in their lives, even though this does not extend to support with their work. They also experience a lower level of role conflict than could be predicted from previous research.

The pacing of the average workday for the two groups is clearly distinguishable. Homeworkers' paid work is spread out more over the course of a day than is true of office workers, although on the average the homeworkers' work weeks are shorter. Homeworkers also are responsible for a higher proportion of both housework and child care in their households. Surprisingly, working at home does not eliminate the need to hire outside help for housework and child care. Homeworkers are as likely as their office counterparts to employ others to assist them with their domestic work.

Given the emphasis in many accounts of the importance of technology, it is important to note that homeworkers and office workers had nearly identical levels of computerized assistance. Only longitudinal studies will be able to tell us about the effects of more sophisticated forms of automation on the workers and the work environment. But technology does not operate as an isolated causal factor in shaping these outcomes. Nor is it technology per se that affects the work process, but the social relations that develop around a particular innovation.

What are the implications of this motley picture of homeworkers for the validity of the two metatheories? First, the accuracy of each model is determined in part by the level of analysis. At an individual level of analysis, homeworkers do relatively well, both in terms of material and subjective outcomes. And when we ask them, they report comparatively high levels of satisfaction. But at a structural level of understanding, the picture is not as optimistic. The lack of full-time employee status for many homeworkers, as well as the very weak provisions for fringe benefits, suggests that, for the aggregate, homework in its present state is neither the solution to domestic demands nor to the need for alternative forms of labor force participation. This does not imply, however, that homework does not have the potential of yielding advantages both at the structural level and for the individual worker.

The extent to which clerical homework can provide a real alternative, however, is not fully dependent on the pros or cons of various work-at-home arrangements. Any discussion of clerical homework must take into account several related facts. First, occupational sex segregation is still very high; approximately 97 percent of all secretaries and typists are women. Moreover, women tend to be concentrated in fewer occupations than are men, an indicator of more limited employment opportunities for women. In addition, clerical work as women's work tends to be low-paid and low-prestige. And finally, the domestic division of labor invariably means that women assume the major proportion of housework and child care. Thus, when we speak of homework for clerical workers, we need to frame that discussion in the context of the realities of the structure of clerical work and, more generally, the demands of domesticity and the employment opportunities available for women.

Bibliography

Behr, Marion. "Pros and Cons of Home-Based Clerical Work." Statement submitted for the record. Hearing before a House Subcommittee of the Committee on Government Operations, February 26, 1986.

Behr, Marion, and Wendy Lazar. *Women Working Home: The Homebased Business Guide and Directory,* 2nd edition. Edison, N.J.: WWH Press, 1983.

Berch, Bettina. "The Resurrection of Out-Work." *Monthly Review* 37 (1985):37–46.

Boris, Eileen. "Regulating Industrial Homework: The Triumph of 'Sacred Motherhood.'" *The Journal of American History* 71 (1985):745–763.

———. "A Woman's Place?" *The Nation* (1986):365–366.

Christensen, Kathleen E. "Impacts of Computer-Mediated Home-Based Work on Women and Their Families." Unpublished manuscript. New York: Center for Human Environments, Graduate School and University Center, City University of New York, 1985.

———. "Pros and Cons of Home-Based Clerical Work." Statement submitted for the record. Hearing before a House Subcommittee of the Committee on Government Operations, February 26, 1986.

Costello, Cynthia. "The Office Homework Program at the Wisconsin Physicians Service Insurance Company." Unpublished manuscript. New York: Russell Sage Foundation, 1986.

Elisburg, Donald. "Legalities." *Telematics and Informatics* 2 (1985):181–185.

———. "Pros and Cons of Home-Based Clerical Work." Statement submitted for the record by Representative Barney Frank. Hearing before a House Subcommittee of the Committee on Government Operations, February 26, 1986.

Gerson, Judith M., and Robert E. Kraut. "How Well Off Are Home Workers? Social, Psychological, and Economic Outcomes for Secretarial Workers." Paper presented at the annual meeting of the American Sociological Association. New York, 1986.

Herbers, John. "Rising Cottage Industry Stirring Concern in U.S." *New York Times,* May 13, 1986, p. A18.

Horvath, Francis W. "Work at Home: New Findings from the Current Population Survey." *Monthly Labor Review* 109 (1986):31–35.

Keller, Bill. "Of Hearth and Home and the Right to Work." *New York Times*, November 11, 1984, p. 8E.

Kraut, Robert E., and Patricia Grambsch. "Home-Based, White-Collar Work: Lessons from the 1980 Census." *Social Forces* 66 (1988):410–426.

Leidner, Robin. "Home Clerical Work: A Study of the Interaction of Work and Family Organization." Unpublished manuscript. Evanston: Northwestern University, 1984.

Mason, Karen Oppenheim, and Larry L. Bumpass. "U.S. Women's Sex-Role Ideology, 1970." *American Journal of Sociology* 80 (1975):1212–1219.

Mattera, Philip. "Home Computer Sweatshops." *The Nation* 236 (1983):390–392.

Olson, Margrethe H., and Sophia B. Primps. "Working at Home with Computers: Work and Nonwork Issues." *Journal of Social Issues* 40 (1984):97–112.

Pratt, Joanne H. "Home Teleworking: A Study of Its Pioneers." *Technological Forecasting and Social Change* 25 (1984):1–14.

Ramsower, Reagan Mays. *Telecommuting: The Organizational and Behavioral Effects of Working at Home*. Ann Arbor, Mich.: University of Michigan Research Press, 1985.

Risman, Barbara J., and Donald Tomaskovic-Devey. "The Social Construction of Technology: Microcomputers and the Organization of Work." Unpublished manuscript. Raleigh: North Carolina State University, 1986.

Shabecoff, Philip. "Dispute Rises on Working at Home for Pay." *New York Times*, March 10, 1981, pp. A1, B6.

Toffler, Alvin. *The Third Wave*. New York: Morrow, 1980.

U.S. Congress, Office of Technology Assessment. *Automation of America's Offices*. Washington, D.C.: U.S. Government Printing Office, 1985.

U.S. Department of Labor, Women's Bureau. *Women and Office Automation: Issues for the Decade Ahead*. Washington, D.C.: U.S. Government Printing Office, 1985.

Webb, Marilyn. "Sweatshops for One: The Rise in Industrial Homework." *The Village Voice*, February 10–16, 1982, 22 ff.

4
Corporate Hiring Practices for Telecommuting Homeworkers

Gil E. Gordon

After 100 years of efforts to centralize the workplace since the Industrial Revolution, observers are now seeing serious attempts in the United States to decentralize office work as a way to respond to corporate pressures and employee preferences. There is a wide range of technology available to help make this change, there is growing interest among employees to work at home or elsewhere off-site, and there is a growing list of sound reasons why it should happen.

However, homework for office workers—telecommuting—has not lived up to predictions made for its growth. Although this is disappointing to some, I believe it is an outcome that can be explained and perhaps even welcomed.

Before addressing these issues, however, a definition is in order. The people who are telecommuters are employees of organizations (and thus are not self-employed) and routinely spend between two to four days a week working away from the office. Most often, their time is spent at home, though the home is far from the only type of remote work location possible.

The time spent at home is *in addition to*, not in place of, time spent in the office. Thus, this type of work is not the casual kind done at home during the evening, nor is it work at home done by people who have always worked out of their homes such as salespeople or writers. Here, I am concerned only with the substitution of a remote work location by people who would otherwise commute everyday to a central office location.

This definition is narrow, yet important. Although many people work at home for many different reasons, several of the important policy questions only surface when we look at the routine, ongoing use of the home as a remote work location. For example, questions of adequate remote supervision rarely if ever arise when considering an employee who spends a few hours working at home in the evening after a normal workday in the office.

A Profile of Today's Corporate Homeworkers

The following descriptions of the contemporary salaried home-worker/telecommuter are based on my six years experience in the field, personal knowledge of corporate programs, discussions with corporate managers, and estimates of general activity levels.

Approximately 10,000 salaried employees work at home two to four days a week instead of going to the office. These individuals work for firms that would otherwise have them commute to work; the time these employees spend at home is in place of time in the office.

These telecommuters are employed by approximately 300 organizations, almost all of which are in the private sector, ranging from Fortune 100 companies down to ten-person start-up firms. One should note that many employers have informal and/or hidden programs, and the actual number of firms may be double this estimate.

The employees are fairly evenly divided between professional and clerical workers, although in the past the latter group made up most of these homeworkers. Recently, however, the trend is for more professionals to work at home, although the number of days they spend at home varies because of a more casual approach to scheduling; that is, they might spend one day a week at home one week, four days at home the next, and so on.

The degree of formality in these programs ranges from well-organized, purposeful programs to more casual ones. The former are officially sanctioned by corporate management and generally involve thorough planning; the latter are often implemented by a line manager without guidance from (and sometimes hidden from) top management and/or human resources staff.

In the last three years both informal and formal programs have grown, sometimes, ironically, in the same organizations. In some cases the growth of informal telecommuting spurs the employer to "make it legitimate" by formalizing it; in others, the opposite happens. Once the formal policy or pilot program is in place, telecommuting grows informally because it appears to be sanctioned by management.

My estimate is that 80 percent of professional-level and 50 percent of the clerical-level telecommuters are treated as regular employees with the same benefits and coverage as they would have had in the office. The problem in substantiating this estimate, as has been discussed elsewhere, is that the clerical-level workers are an elusive group to measure. My numbers refer to those telecommuters who had previously been office-based employees of a firm and now work at home; this categorization is different from homeworkers who never were on-site employees. The lack of agreement on how to define these individuals accounts for the wide variations in numerical estimates of clerical homeworkers.

The Growth of Telecommuting to Date

Eight reasons why employers have begun using telecommuters are discussed in turn below.

Improved Recruiting. Anytime there is an imbalance between demand and supply of particular talents, employers are likely to try new ways to attract qualified applicants, thus setting themselves apart from other employers in the labor market. Telecommuting has been offered as an option in order to attract new recruits, especially in the data processing field. Another advantage related to recruiting is the ability to attract people who otherwise could not or would not be able to work in a normal office setting, whether this is due to family needs, health, or simply personal preference.

Improved Retention. It is just as it is important to *keep* good people, once they have been trained, as it is to *find* them. Most employers don't keep accurate records of the costs of losing good employees and finding and retraining replacements, but there have been estimates ranging from $30,000 to over $100,000 to replace a professional (Flamholtz 1985). The motivation to reduce turnover is substantial. Telecommuting lets employers retain a trained, trusted employee who might otherwise have to leave the workforce.

Experimentation. In the early 1980s some trial telecommuting resulted from nothing more than a firm's desire to see how well the innovation would work. As personal computers (PCs) came into the business world, computing power became more portable. If a firm's *only* reason for trying telecommuting is sheer curiosity, however, it is unlikely the experiment will last long or work well. Ideally, telecommuting should be seen as a good solution to a business problem facing an organization; this attitude helps to maintain interest and overcome initial resistance.

Space Savings. Businesses that are growing quickly and need more space, and/or want to pay less for office space, have found telecommuting of interest. As it costs between $1,500 and $6,000 annually for office space and related services for one employee (depending on the city and the type of space), companies have strong incentives to look at ways to cut office space needs.

The real effects of using telecommuting to cut space costs will not be felt until employers begin to factor it into long-term space requirements. If a firm consciously "underbuilds" and then fills the gap via telecommuting, the total square footage saved could be substantial—easily up to 10 percent of a large office building for an information-intensive employer.

Hiring the Disabled Employee. Some telecommuting projects have been designed from the start to address the needs of the disabled. This has been the case for companies that have a strong sense of social responsibility and want to provide jobs for people who otherwise would be unemployable. In addition, several private and government-sponsored agencies have acted as intermediaries, working to find and train the disabled and then placing them for employment. These plans have generally been successful, but the number of people involved is small.

Increased Productivity. Only since the early 1980s have employers begun to be widely concerned about the productivity of office workers. Before that time, productivity was a concept thought to apply only to factory workers. But with the growing percentage of employees—and salary dollars—in the office today, the need to understand and improve office-worker productivity is also growing. One of the most consistent findings from telecommuting programs has been the increase in productivity: Gains in the range of 15 to 25 percent have been typical. However, these gains must be viewed cautiously as office-worker productivity measurement is far from an exact science. Also, the gains are based on relatively little experience—perhaps one or two years, for example—so we have yet to see the long-term effects.

Employee Inquiries. There are two schools of thought about how telecommuting gets started in a company. One says that management initiates it, taking a "top-down" approach. The other says that employers respond to "bottom-up" pressure from employees who want to become telecommuters. A growing number of professional-level workers have purchased PCs for home use and then use them to do after-hours work. They commonly transport diskettes to and from the office, and in some cases telecommunicate with computers in the office. This after-hours work, in some cases, leads to work at home in place of time in the office. The employee begins to ask, "Why should I take the trouble to get dressed in my business suit and commute into the office, just so I can sit at a desk and work at my PC as I am doing now in the comfort of my home?" The purchase of PCs will probably spur growth for homework among professionals, but less so for clerical workers.

Improved Customer Service. Finally, the practice of telecommuting has grown to date because of the benefit to business of providing extended customer service hours. One organization in Chicago, for example, provides 24-hour toll-free telephone service to its customers. The company was having trouble recruiting people to come to the office to work on the third shift starting at 11 P.M. As a result, customers were not always able to have their phone calls answered during the night. Also, the company had to pay for keeping the building open (lights, heating, and so on) for a very small number of workers. The solution was to hire four people to answer phones at home from 11 P.M. until 7 A.M. The result—customer service was maintained, and the costs of keeping the building open during the night hours were eliminated.

The Role of Technology: Driving Force, Catalyst, or Obstacle?

The exact role played by technology in the growth and spread of telecommuting is somewhat difficult to determine, but three explanations are possible.

Technology is a *driving force* in that the spread of PCs and developments in telecommunications require us to rethink how and where office work should be done. The process is analogous to the growth of the automobile; once the population had easy access to personal transportation, the old assumptions about housing, shopping, and recreation were challenged.

Technology is a *catalyst* in that it lets us selectively reorganize and decentralize the office while observing the same basic work procedures and workflow.

Technology is an *obstacle* to the extent that we are overwhelmed by the choices we have in computing and telecommunications. Also, the idea of large numbers of remote workers adds a level of complexity that many data processing managers will not want to consider.

In reality, all three aspects contribute to the overall picture. But I think it is a mistake to assume that there is or will be a causal link between the spread of PCs and the spread of telecommuting.

This kind of technological determinism ignores two factors. First, there are several obstacles, to be discussed in a later section, that are essentially technology-free in nature. Second, there have been and will be many excellent telecommuting applications that only partially rely on technology. These are paper-and-pencil jobs, and perhaps the standard telephone is the highest level of technology that is used.

But we cannot ignore the spread of personal computers as a factor in the growth of telecommuting. We see companies approaching a ratio of one PC for every professional-level employee in the next few years, for example. The more that a job is "contained" in a personal computer, the more that job is made portable to the home or elsewhere. Also, as was noted before, the growing number of employees who purchase PCs for use at home and then begin using them for office work is another example of how remote work is driven by PC growth.

Technology can facilitate remote work by changing some of the assumptions about where certain kinds of work can be done. Here are four examples chosen from very different fields.

Project Victoria

The Pacific Bell telephone company in California conducted an experiment in 1986 that showed how one standard residential telephone line could be transformed into seven digital channels: two for voice, one for medium-speed data transmission, and four for low-speed data transmission. The test was conducted for four months with 200 participants in Danville, California.

This experiment was the first time that such a wide range of data and voice transmissions were possible using one unmodified residential phone line, simply by adding the appropriate "black box" at the central office and within the home. Once this technology is brought to market, employers will be able to set up remote jobs that require high-volume data transmission without incurring the costs of special "dedicated" phone lines. Similar advantages will come with Integrated Services Digital Network (ISDN) technology now being tested by at least two regional Bell operating companies.

Smaller Facsimile Equipment

We are currently seeing a number of small, easily portable facsimile units (machines used to transmit printed materials) with purchase or lease costs that are well within the range of most employers. In some cases these units are integrated with telephones, which is appealing for telecommuters because the units do not require much space on the desktop.

The advantage here is that jobs involving graphics are now more "portable" to the home because images can be transmitted as readily as text. Without this equipment, telecommuters in fields like commercial art or consumer marketing would have to rely on frequent trips to the office, to the courier service, or on more costly PC-based video-to-digital systems.

Portable Microfiche Readers

The relatively old technology of microfiche comes into play in telecommuting because portable microfiche readers, which are much smaller than a briefcase, are available for about $150. This low cost allows a job involving microfiche to be decentralized, as the reader can be moved wherever the worker is. Also, these readers may be a good telecommuting solution for work that relies heavily on paper files (such as accounting or customer service) as the microfiche images of documents can be transported more easily than the documents themselves.

Remote Access–Remote Control Software

Several interesting PC software packages are on the market that are designed to enable a PC user to take control over a PC at another site. These programs work in two ways. First, they allow two PCs to work together so that whatever is seen on one screen is seen on the other. One application is in training or problem-solving; person A is trying to learn to use a word-processing package, and person B (at another location) is acting as tutor. The other application is to run a program on, or gain access to, a PC at another location. If a telecommuter is at home and wants to retrieve information from the hard disk of a PC in the office, or perhaps run an applications program on the office PC because it is a faster machine, this work can be done with these packages *without* anyone having to touch the PC in the office.

The benefit of these packages to telecommuters is clear: There is no need to be physically present with the person or PC with which they interact. All contact can be done over regular telephone lines as needed.

If these and other kinds of technological innovations are available, why is technology an obstacle to telecommuting? Advances in computing have not been matched with advances in telecommunications, and this raises two special concerns. In the rush to buy PCs over the last few years, many companies bought them with little or no thought to standardization and ease of connection.

As a result, one major theme in data-processing circles in the late 1980s is "connectivity"—a fancy word for the attempt to link equipment together that in some cases was never intended to be linked. This occurs from PC to PC and from PCs to minicomputers or mainframes. It creates headaches for data-processing and telecommunications managers who are asked to make these magical connections. What makes matters worse is that the people doing the asking often are nontechnical senior executives who have been convinced by advertising that everything and anything can be done "just by pushing a few buttons."

Telecommuting is in the midst of this connectivity arena, and in some companies there simply has not been enough time to sort out all the combinations and possibilities. Depending on the complexity of the combination and the type of data communications intended, connectivity becomes either an easy task or a technical nightmare to make it work.

One encouraging note is that there have been few reported cases where a company wanted to implement a remote work program and was unable to do so because of technical problems. In some instances the telecommuters may not have been able to perform all the tasks they wanted to with their home PCs (compared to what they could normally do in the office) but were still able to do their jobs.

If connectivity is one technical concern, data security is another. With the publicity given to "hackers" who seek to break into computer systems, there is a concern that the idea of telecommuting in some ways invites problems. There is an added security risk whenever a dial-up system is used to allow remote access. To my knowledge there has been no reported case of computer crime caused by a telecommuter, although companies do not always publicize their security problems.

Security is an interesting part of the technology discussion because it shows how talking about technology alone is only part of the problem. Security experts admit that a determined and resourceful criminal can break into any computer system; however, the security devices currently on the market today are adequate to prevent all but the most determined hackers. But there is often a big gap between the adequacy of the security devices on the market and the computer security practices in large companies, and that is where the problems begin.

Thus, when we talk about the security risks of remote work we have to think about the incremental risks; that is, what if any *additional* risks are there. If a company has lax security procedures to begin with, it is hard to claim that telecommuting should not be implemented because of its presumed security risks.

Also, there are other contradictions between what companies say and what they do in the security field. I have worked with large, sophisticated companies that claim to be very concerned about security risks in telecommuting. Yet in these same firms I have seen terminals in open office areas that have a piece of paper with the current password taped to the terminal, in plain view.

I ask these firms one simple question: Can your employees walk out of the office with a diskette in a briefcase? If the answer is yes, that is a good sign of possible security problems—no matter how much the company *claims* to have strict security.

Nevertheless, one should not minimize the very real possibility that some telecommuters might cause security problems. Also, telecommuting may never be appropriate for some employers, such as banks or hospitals, where confidentiality of the data is essential. No matter how many security systems are in use, management might not ever be convinced that the risk is controlled, and (correctly) will avoid telecommuting or limit it to nonsensitive positions. We simply cannot assume there is a security threat inherent in telecommuting; we have got to look at the whole security picture within a company.

In summary, the role of technology in telecommuting is far from clear. The PC revolution is undoubtedly a part of telecommuting's growth and appeal, but by itself it will not create an explosion of new telecommuting applications. We are fortunate to have the wide range of hardware, software, and telecommunications available from which we can choose, even though the choices can be overwhelming. Technology in its many forms is a necessary part of telecommuting's future, but it is not sufficient in itself to fully decentralize the workplace.

Organizational Lethargy: Obstacles to Telecommuting

If we could have believed what some of the futurists were saying five to seven years ago, we would have expected to see up to 10 percent of the office workforce spending several days a week at home or elsewhere off-site by the late 1980s. The United States is not close to that number, even allowing for a large estimating error.

The question must be asked: "Why not?" If the concept is technologically possible, provides good business benefits, and appeals to many employees, why is it not more widespread? In my experience of the field, old habits last a long time, and the 100-year-old tradition of going to a central workplace encompasses a set of customs and routines based on that daily two-way journey.

What is interesting is that we have lost sight of the cumulative effects and costs of that daily habit. According to survey data from the Hertz Corporation, the car rental company, in 1985 106.4 million people commuted an average of 24.4 miles round-trip to work each day in the United States. Commuting (by any method) in 1985 cost $1,355 per person, per year, and 69 percent of the U.S. workforce commuted to work in their own cars.

If we expand on these numbers and assume that the average 24.4 mile round-trip commute takes 40 minutes per day, that adds up to a cumulative total of 8,119 years the 106.4 million people spend in daily commuting. The total cost of commuting in the United States, using the $1,355 average, was $144,172,000,000 in 1985.

Despite this cost, the weight of tradition still prevails. The unfortunate—but understandable—irony is that if a company with 20,000 employees starts a telecommuting pilot program with ten employees, the company believes it has accomplished something noteworthy. In fact, it has—even though it involves only ten employees, the pilot program is a tangible sign that the company is willing to begin challenging or even breaking the commuting tradition.

The fear of loss of control is perhaps the biggest reason why telecommuting is showing slower progress than some had expected. The philosophy of management prevalent in many organizations goes back to a legacy of factory supervision in which close observation of direct labor was common. Even though we have progressed from the factory to the office, many of our supervisory methods have not changed much.

The challenge is to make the distinction between *observing activity* and *managing results*. The managers who do the best job of managing telecommuters are those who concentrate on the "deliverables," that is, the end-products that an employee must deliver by a certain date and according to certain standards.

Managers of telecommuters almost always say that the process of having to manage from a distance makes them better managers of other employees who remain in the office. The manager is forced to use good management practices such as setting goals and monitoring progress, which is often ignored because the in-office manager substitutes observation for management.

At many companies, the pay level of a job is often determined by the nature of responsibilities, scope of decisionmaking, and other factors. Frequently, these "job evaluation" systems generally do well at measuring the differences in value of different jobs to ensure that managers whose jobs add more value to the organization are paid more.

Interestingly, one of the determinants of a job's value is the size of the organization managed, and in some cases, even the size of the manager's budget. If we put ourselves in the position of a manager, we can see how telecommuting can be threatening if it leads to reductions in the size of the organization. Specifically, the manager might ask, "If some of my people no longer work in the office, and if that means I will be responsible for a smaller work area, will that mean my job will be evaluated lower—and therefore I will be paid less?"

Very few managers would be willing to try an innovation if they thought there was any chance it would lead to a reduction in salary. There is a simple solution to this, however. If we share some of the savings generated via telecommuting with the manager (and even with the telecommuters) who takes the plunge in implementing it, I predict we would see far more pilot programs much sooner.

Worldwide business conditions have become more competitive, and we see many companies reducing staffing levels and taking other steps to control costs. This trend has been developing over the last five years, and there are signs that it will keep growing. With so many managers having to do as much or more work with fewer people and other resources, they are often not willing to pursue something as risky as telecommuting. They see it as a distraction, in the sense that their time for any new project is limited.

This very situation could turn out to be a good reason why telecommuting *will* grow. If managers can see the link between telecommuting and cost-cutting, improved retention of valuable employees, and improved customer service, they will then see telecommuting as a solution to business problems. This change in attitude has been the case in some organizations where telecommuting has worked the best.

One obstacle not discussed thus far is the fear of employee lawsuits, which has made many organizations somewhat hesitant to introduce new programs where there are legal uncertainties, as in the case of telecommuting. This reluctance could affect telecommuting's growth because of the *perceived* uncertainty about several aspects of remote work such as levels of pay, amount of benefits to be paid, and liability for injuries or accidents occurring in the home while the person is working there.

To my knowledge, there has been only one lawsuit to date in these areas, but that one lawsuit is significant. It involves a group of eight telecommuters working for Cal-Western Life Insurance in Sacramento, California. They were among a group of almost 30 telecommuters who had been working at home for over two years doing insurance claims processing. The suit tests the issue of whether they were actually employees of Cal-Western, instead of independent contractors who received no benefits and were paid strictly on a per-unit-of-work basis. As of mid-1987, the lawsuit still had not been heard in court.

The definition of employee status (that is, employee versus independent contractor) is a critical issue in telecommuting. One way the problem can arise is when a person working as an employee in an office becomes a telecommuter working at home. If the employer chooses to convert the person to independent contractor status—even with the person's consent—this conversion may be illegal under various state and federal laws. Such a conversion is very attractive to employers because it lets them eliminate insurance benefits and other overhead expenses that add between 30 and 40 percent to payroll costs.

I believe that it is not only illegal in most cases to carry telecommuters as independent contractors, but that it makes little business sense to do so. Even though there are significant cost savings, these must be compared with the long-term effects of having a nonemployee relationship in which loyalty to the job and company often suffer. Also, when telecommuting is implemented properly, there are enough built-in savings that it becomes somewhat greedy to go for the payroll savings as well.

Future Scenarios for Telecommuting

To Dr. Jack Nilles of the University of Southern California—who is the acknowledged "grandfather" of telecommuting—I owe thanks for telling me that there is no such thing as *the* future. Instead, we have various futures that might develop, which is a better starting point when dealing with innovations like telecommuting.

My experience with the adoption of innovations shows that there are early adopters and late adopters, and the two are very different. Also, how innovations are implemented varies between early and late adopters. These distinctions seem to describe what we have seen in the last five years and what we are likely to see in the next five.

As an analogy, note how the personal computer came into large companies. It is instructive to remember that companies did not always take the PC for granted as they seem to today. If we can remember back to the ancient history of PCs, all the way back to 1980 and 1981, we see that companies were very adventurous if they bought *one* personal computer. That was a very big step in those days. Typically, a company spent a few months experimenting with its computer, trying to figure out how it worked and whether it had a useful purpose.

Once that first hurdle was crossed, the company would then buy perhaps six more PCs, distributing them to departments thought likely to benefit from them. The learning curve was slow at first, the applications were cumbersome, and the time (if not the financial) investment was high. Later, the company bought more PCs, and the microcomputer revolution was underway.

The same is true of telecommuting: This innovation had to start somewhere, and it is likely to have the same incremental pattern of adoption. The difference is that the PC was seen as an interesting "toy" not a fundamental challenge to traditional business practices that characterizes the adoption of telecommuting.

The companies that were the early adopters of telecommuting have generally expanded their programs, as long as two conditions were operative. First, the initial project was set up as a business solution to current or potential business problems and not just as an experiment. Second, the project was planned and managed with at least as much attention to personnel issues as to technical issues. But these initial programs only involved small numbers of people—at the very most, a couple of hundred per company.

The experience of the first adopters forms the basis of the first part of my prediction. We will continue to see slow but steady growth in applications within companies where the initial experiences were positive. The growth will occur in two ways. First, we will see more of the same kinds of jobs being performed remotely. For example, if a department of 50 programmers has two programmers working at home, that number may increase to eight or ten. Second, we will see new jobs being done at home. Other departments that were watching the initial trials from the sidelines will now be more willing to get involved. Also, technological developments will open up new applications; many of these will be based on improvements in telecommunications and/or PC-to-mainframe links.

The second part of the prediction concerns the much larger number of employers who were never involved but who may have been following the field as curious observers. Many of them are in larger or more conservative companies that are never first to try something but are anxious to be among the leaders in the second wave. Now that they see the process can be managed and that it provides real benefits, they will be more willing to set up pilot projects.

Where will all this lead? I think we will see relatively slow growth for the next two or three years, perhaps, and a much faster growth rate after that. This prediction based on the assumption that the novelty of the idea will wear away, and telecommuting will be accepted as a legitimate, practical business tool by most employers. Even though the proportion of office workers for whom telecommuting is suitable may rise to as much as 50 percent by 1990, the practical limit is perhaps 10 percent of the workforce spending two to four days at home or elsewhere off-site.

It is unlikely that the cultural obstacles to work-at-home will disappear quickly, if ever. However, we will probably see parallel growth in the use of remote sites other than the home. One of the strongest forces driving this movement is the tendency for companies to buy services instead of hire workers as they try to control their fixed costs. I can envision departments or functional units being severed from the company and then selling back their services. U.S. employers will probably keep reducing the number of permanent, full-time employees, and remote work in its *various* forms is one way to do this.

Finally, several factors might dramatically increase or decrease the growth of telecommuting. One event that could stimulate growth is another Arab oil embargo like that of the mid-1970s, which was the impetus for the original research on telecommuting by Jack Nilles. One reason his projections did not lead to action was because the idea of remote computing power was fairly new. Compare that situation with the wealth of PCs and telecommunications options in the current marketplace, and it is easy to see how today's response would be different.

A second factor that could cause a big increase would be government incentives. These could include property tax relief for firms that implement telecommuting, for example. This relief would be a reward for those firms causing less traffic congestion and air pollution, or perhaps for employing the hard-to-employ in a satellite work center located in an economically depressed area. Employers are generally very pragmatic; they will be much more likely to implement telecommuting if there's a reward for doing so. This incentive has been shown in programs such as tax credits to hire the disabled or the "hard-core" unemployed.

A third positive factor would be the cumulative effect of pressure from employees who want this option. Their desire could be based on family needs, the growth in numbers of homebound aging parents who need to be cared for by their children, or simply a desire to have a more relaxed, convenient work life. It is unlikely this factor alone will create much change unless employers begin to lose large numbers of valued employees because the remote work option is not available to them.

On the negative side, the biggest potential obstacles are regulatory in nature. If legislators pass laws strictly limiting the terms and conditions of employing telecommuters, most employers would simply abandon the idea in all but a few situations. These laws could be motivated by strong pressure from the labor movement, but this seems unlikely in the near future. A more likely motivation for new laws would be evidence of widespread abuse and poor treatment of telecommuters or homeworkers in general.

The United States is in the middle of one of the most interesting evolutionary changes seen in the workplace. Telecommuting and the decentralization of work is an evolutionary process, not a dramatic revolution. When we consider that it took 20 years for the telephone to achieve a 1 percent market share in the United States, we can see how long it takes for traditions to change. When telephones were first introduced, people said they would never become popular: "We have messengers to deliver our information, and, besides, people will only want to talk to each other in person," was the reaction. Like it or not, today, we could not live without the telephone—and perhaps the same thing will be said about workplace decentralization in years to come.

References

Flamholtz, E. *Human Resource Accounting,* 2d ed. San Francisco: Jossey-Bass, Co., 1985.

5 Independent Contracting

Kathleen E. Christensen

Popular terms for independent contractors are abundant, including freelancers, consultants, homeworkers, and telecommuters. At root, however, independent contracting involves the externalization of the worker from employee rolls, resulting in the worker being hired on a self-employed contracted basis for a finite amount of work, typically by the task, a piece-rate, or an hourly fee. Independent contractors, along with part-time workers, temporary workers, and leased employees make up the contingent workforce—those workers whose ties with their companies are much looser than those held by conventional nine-to-five salaried employees.

A recent survey of 441 U.S. firms conducted by the Bureau of National Affairs (1986) in conjunction with Katharine Abraham of the Brookings Institution, found that nearly two-thirds of both manufacturing and nonmanufacturing firms reported relying on production or administrative support contracts in 1985. Of these companies (which include health care firms) approximately 13 percent reported an increased use of contracting between 1980 and 1985.

Data Collection Problems

Despite data on firms that subcontract, precise numbers for independent contractors do not exist. Part of the difficulty in enumeration rests on definitional issues—who exactly is an independent contractor? Tied to the definitional problems are limitations in data collection procedures by federal agencies. Neither the Internal Revenue Service (IRS) nor the Bureau of Labor Statistics (BLS) of the U.S. Department of Labor (DOL) collect publicly available data on contractors.

The BLS collects employment figures on three groups: the self-employed, wage and salary earners (private and government), and unpaid family workers. Independent contractors are technically self-employed and would fall under that category. But when asked how the BLS defines an independent contractor, Ellie Abramson of their staff was quick to point out that they do not use such a term and that it would be presumptuous to read the self-employment statistics as indicative of the number of independent contractors. Although the Fair Labor Standards Act of 1942 provides a broad definition of employee status, the DOL does not collect this information. According to Ms. Abramson, "the topic is too narrow."

The Internal Revenue Service, although concerned with independent contracting for tax purposes, also does not have publicly available data on these workers. Norm Fox of the Examination Area of the IRS, which audits tax returns and is concerned with contractors for that reason, characterized independent contractors as people who do not have withholding taken from their salaries. He indicated that one way to find demographics on these workers would be to review the 1099 schedule fees form and the 530 tax form. Both forms are used, in addition to a sole proprietorship form by people who consider themselves independent contractors. At this time, the IRS does not as a rule analyze these forms.

Recently, however, the Examination Area of the IRS initiated the SBC 1 Research Study as a strategic initiative to examine employment taxes. Mr. Fox estimated that the research, begun in July 1986, should be completed in December 1987 and would begin to assess how large a problem independent contracting presents for this country. Focusing on the employer, the IRS is attempting to collect data on the *misclassified* independent contractor—that worker who should be treated as a full-time employee and is not. The IRS hopes to discover which industries most commonly use independent contractors, how many contractors they hire, how much money these workers actually earn, and their incidence of nonreported income. Mr. Fox anticipates that this documentation will help the IRS to develop more efficient operations to monitor employers and employees.

Probably the major difficulty encountered in trying to collect data on independent contractors is due to lack of consistency in definition.

Definitional Problems

For federal tax purposes the IRS relies on common law in determining who is an employee, and it draws on a substantial body of case law under the Internal Revenue Code, which supports that practice. The Department of Labor, under the Fair Labor Standards Act (FLSA), does not rely on common law; the courts have made it clear to DOL that the employment relationship is broader than the traditional common law concept would allow. In effect, under FLSA, a worker is an employee if he/she maintains an employee-like relationship with his/her employer.

The common law rules regarding employee status generally rely on the following questions:

1. How much *control* does the worker have over how he or she executes and accomplishes his or her work?
2. Does the worker have the *opportunity for profit or loss?*
3. Has the worker made a *substantial* investment in the enterprise? Does he or she have a place of business and offer services to the public?
4. What is the worker's *skill level?*
5. What is the *permanency* of the relationship?

Generally, a worker is an independent contractor so long as he or she exercises control over the pacing, execution, and timing of work, has the opportunity to gain or to suffer losses from the work, has made an investment in equipment or capital to accomplish the task, has a skill level that allows competitiveness in the marketplace, and is not in an enduring or permanent relationship with the "employer."

The corollary holds true: If the worker experiences little control over work hours, priority, or pacing of work; has no opportunity to gain or lose; uses materials, tools, or equipment from the employing organization; and has an ongoing relationship with the company—then the worker is entitled to the rights and protection accorded by law to company employees. These include the following: The employer contributes an equal amount to the employee's social security account (Federal Insurance Contributions Act or FICA), to his/her unemployment and workers' compensation coverage, and the employee has full right of appeal for discrimination on the grounds of race or sex.

The law, however, is not as simple as it seems on first glance. It provides many outs for an employer who wants to hire a worker as a contractor, not an employee. In 1978, the tax code was amended by a "safe haven" clause that exempts employers from having to hire workers as employees even if the worker has the status of an employee according to the common law concept. Section 530 of the Revenue Act of 1978-3 (Vol. 1) C.B. xi, 119, as amended by Section 269(c) of the Tax Equity and Fiscal Responsibility Act of 1982, 1982-2 C.B. 462, 536, provides "relief from payment of federal employment taxes to persons who did not treat such workers as employees (even though they had such status) if the persons had a reasonable basis for such treatment, filed federal information returns (such as form 1099), and were consistent in such treatment for periods after 1977" (Moore, 1986). The four enunciated safe havens in the Revenue Act, Section 530 include judicial precedent, administrative ruling, prior audit, and industry practice. Where a worker (or a firm) cannot rely on one of these four havens, they likely turn to the more lenient reasonable basis test (Degnan, 1986). In effect, an "employer" can find many ways to skirt the common law regarding employees and thus hire workers as independent contractors. But the safe haven clause has recently been modified and come under controversy.

Section 1706 of the 1986 tax law removed the safe haven provision of the 1978 tax law, so that now computer specialists who meet the common law rules regarding employee status *must* be recompensed as employees not as contractors (Dudek, 1986). In addition, the congressional Subcommittee on Employment and Housing called for elimination of parts of the safe haven clause in their 1986 report on clerical homework (U.S. Congress, July 16, 1986). Based on research and a pending court case in California (Christensen, 1986; MacKenzie, 1986), the subcommittee concluded that there was fraudulent use of independent contracting leading to financial exploitation of home-based clerical workers. These clerical workers were being expected to perform as employees but were not being recompensed as such.

Financial Implications of Contracting Versus Employee Status

Full-time employees typically receive salaries, some job security, opportunities for on-the-job training and promotion, company health and pension benefits, and federal coverage under workers' compensation and unemployment insurance. In addition, employees pay only 7.51 percent of their income toward their social security account. Part-time employees, particularly those working 20 hours or less, typically receive no discretionary company benefits and have more constrained options for advancement or skill upgrading.

Independent contractors have virtually none of the benefits awarded employees. As self-employed workers, they are paid only for the work they produce and not for any lag time between projects. They are given no annual guarantee of money comparable to an annual salary and are entirely outside of their companies when it comes to consideration for skill upgrading, promotion, or other forms of advancement. They receive no health or pension coverage nor are they accorded any federal protections in the event they are hurt on the job, their work is terminated, or they feel discriminated against. Furthermore, the self-employed contractor has to pay the Self-Employment Contributions Act (SECA) tax of 13.02 percent rather than the 7.51 percent FICA tax paid by a company employee.

Some contractors are well-served—both in the short- and long-term—by this financial situation, while others can be severely disadvantaged by the arrangement (Christensen, 1985; 1986). In order to address who wins and who loses by being independent contractors, some fundamental distinctions must be made.

Winners and Losers Among Independent Contractors

Independent contractors vary on several dimensions including the degree of *choice* they have in making the decision to be contractors rather than employees; the *number* of contracts they negotiate; and the *location* at which they do their work, whether it is on-site at the company or whether it is off-site in the workers' homes or in foreign countries.

Choice: Voluntary Versus Involuntary

Choice is a funny word. We all make choices, but what is critical to assess in discussing choice is just what other—if any—alternatives were available when the choice was made. Independent contractors vary as to whether their "choice" was in fact a voluntary one in which they self-consciously chose to be self-employed or whether it was an involuntary one, forced by inadequate alternatives in the marketplace. Voluntary contractors prefer self-employment over employment. Involuntary contractors would prefer to be employed but take contracting work because they see no option for employment that meets their needs. Involuntary contractors parallel involuntary part-timers—those 3.8 million workers who would like to find full-time work but cannot.

Involuntary contractors often come from marginal economic groups that have limited leverage or opportunity in the marketplace. These include mothers with low-wage earning skills; the elderly; the handicapped; and women reentering the labor force after years off to raise their children. A relatively new marginal group include men in their late 40s and 50s who are terminated or prematurely retired—victims of corporate cost-cutting— and who face limited to nonexistent opportunities for other employee-like positions. Some companies, in fact, terminate such employees only to hire them back on a contracted basis and euphemistically refer to them as freelancers or management consultants (Reibstein, 1986).

These involuntary contractors would prefer to be full-time employees if they could. One banker who became a contractor when he was passed over for a major promotion at his company was quoted as saying that while his work is at least lucrative, he would prefer a full-time job.

"When you're consulting, (the company) can follow your advice or not. Frankly, I miss the interaction with peers and the professional recognition, and yes, the power. I'd like to be living with my decisions and not just taking my pound of flesh and moving on" (Forbes, 1986, p. 57).

In contrast to the unknown numbers of involuntary contractors, there are countless others pursuing the arrangement voluntarily. These contractors by preference are business owners. They are typically workers whose skills are in high demand, who can charge more on a contracting basis than they could earn from a salary, and who want more autonomy, control, and flexibility in their work than they could ever have as conventional nine-to-five employees. They often see the uncertainty and instability of their income as a source of challenge and even excitement rather than a source of fear or undue concern (Gross, 1986).

It appears that most of these voluntary contractors have professional or technical skills. However, in recent research, we have also found that some women with clerical skills had a self-conscious identification as business owners and much preferred the true independence of contracting over the security of employment.[1]

The differences between involuntary and voluntary contractors are ones of self-image, confidence, and, most importantly, alternatives. Voluntary contractors are self-consciously self-employed and likely to take full tax advantage of their status, whereas involuntary contractors, who work for only one company, typically do not. Some are not even aware of their self-employment status until they or their husbands take their forms to an accountant at tax time. Because they worked for only one company, they thought they were an employee of that company (Christensen, 1985).

Voluntary contractors can—or at least think they can—obtain an employee position if the need arises, while the involuntary ones believe that if they don't accept this arrangement their only alternative will be unemployment. They feel that accepting work under less than ideal conditions is better than no work. Although the sense of opportunity breeds confidence and leverage, the perceived or real sense of no alternatives breeds the potential for exploitation.

Location of Work

Just as we distinguish contractors on the basis of their degree of choice, we must also distinguish between those who work on-site for the employing company and those who work off-site.

On-site involuntary contractors would prefer employee status and include the growing number of adjunct professors who have become gypsy educators traveling from campus to campus to piece together an income equivalent to one full-time job, as well as researchers in the publishing industry who are expected to be at their desks in the office every day from nine-to-five, yet are hired as contractors. On-site voluntary contractors are often those self-employed people who by the trouble-shooting nature of their business have to go where the work is. These include the highly skilled systems analyst who needs to be on-site to diagnose and solve a problem and the accountant hired for a short-term project at tax time.

Off-site contractors are those who work someplace other than the worksite of the employing organization. These off-site locations can include the worker's home and locations off-shore from the United States.

There is absolutely no way of knowing how many home-based contractors there are. In a national survey (Hirshey, 1985) of home-based working women (in which 7,000 worked at home and 7,000 wanted to), we found that 79 percent were self-employed—but it was impossible to discern the number of independent contractors and whether they were voluntary or involuntary. Part of the problem is one of technical misunderstanding on the part of involuntary contractors. Many of those doing clerical work for one company thought they were employees, only to discover later that they were not. Rather than addressing these particular workers as either telecommuters or homeworkers, we would be more realistic—and in a better position to consider policy—if we characterized them as independent contractors.[2]

Some involuntary home-based clerical contractors are financially penalized by their status compared to office employees or business owners doing similar work. In a small sample, we found that involuntary home-based clerical contractors earned slightly over $7.00 an hour compared to voluntary home-based counterparts who saw themselves in business and who earned over $17.00 an hour (Christensen, 1986). Also, these same types of involuntary home-based contractors often earn less than their office-based colleagues doing the same work. An insurance company programmer earned $25,000 plus benefits as a salaried employee, but earned less than $7,000 without benefits as a home-based programmer for the same company. The difference was due to the switch in her status by her company from an employee to a contractor when she changed her work location.

Not all firms who contract work out contract it to home-workers. Increasing numbers are contracting, particularly their data-entry work, to firms and workers located off-shore. A 1985 Office of Technology Assessment report on office automation estimated that 12 U.S. firms, hiring approximately 2,300 workers, transferred their work off-shore to the Caribbean. These firms were motivated primarily by significant reductions in hourly rates. American Airlines sends its data-entry work to Barbados, where it is 50 percent cheaper than what it would cost to do the same work in the United States. Other companies are shifting their work outside the Caribbean. Mead Data Central, Incorporated, sends clerical work to Southeast Asia, while Dun & Bradstreet Corporation hires workers in Ireland and Mexico (*Wall Street Journal*, 1986, p. 1). Others estimate that the number of companies engaged in the contracting of work off-shore is much greater than available numbers indicate.

In addition to motivation and location, contractors must be explicitly distinguished on the basis of the number of clients they have, indicating the degree to which they may be dependent on only one company for their income.

Single Contracts Versus Multiple Contracts

In principle, a genuine independent contractor has to have control and opportunity for profit or loss. He or she typically accomplishes this by having multiple contracts with different companies over a period of time. A voluntary contractor is more likely to seek out and negotiate multiple contracts. Self-consciously self-employed, this worker wants to ensure as much profit as possible.

An involuntary contractor who prefers to be an employee often has one ongoing contract with one company and depends on the work from that company as the sole source of income. Some of these involuntary contractors are explicitly constrained from taking on additional contracts. A home-based insurance claims processor in California had to sign a contract stating that she would not take comparable work from any other insurance company. Others are precluded from taking on additional work because of the required time commitment to the one company.

These dimensions of choice, location, and number of contracts provide an initial attempt to sort the realities of independent contracting, for the term currently is used to cover a variety of arrangements—some of which may be legal under common law rules, others of which may not. For example, an involuntary contractor who works in her home for one company and is entirely dependent on this one company for work presents quite a different profile than does a voluntary contractor who has other employment alternatives, has multiple clients, and works wherever it is appropriate or convenient. Under common law the first contractor's status is highly questionable (although the situation is made ambiguous by the safe haven provisions), while the latter appears to meet the test of genuine contracting status.

Advantages and Disadvantages to Employers

Just as workers vary with their contracting arrangements, employers vary in their experience in contracting out work. The advantages to an employer vary according to the type of work they contract out and the type of worker they are interested in having as a contractor rather than an employee.

The major advantage has to do with *cost savings*, primarily in the reduction of labor costs. A contractor is paid only for the work done—not for any time between work projects; receives no discretionary company benefits for health and pension; and assumes all responsibility for FICA, saving the employer 7.51 percent on the worker's contribution. The employer is also exempted from having to make any contributions to the worker's unemployment or workers' compensation accounts. The employer can save anywhere between 30 to 40 percent on contractors. Even if the contractor is paid on a higher hourly rate than he or she would be paid as an employee, the savings on benefits and taxes generally offset these increased wage costs. There are also hidden savings such as the company does not pay for any training or skill upgrading of the worker nor do they have to pay for training replacement workers if, for example, the worker is sick or on disability leave.

The second advantage is *attraction or retention of highly skilled workers* who have no interest in being employees. These are without question the voluntary contractors who want more autonomy, flexibility, and money than they could earn as conventional employees drawing salaries.

The third advantage is the company's enhanced ability to *contract, expand, and redeploy their labor force* as demand necessitates. This ability has the secondary advantage of buffering core salaried employees who the company wants to avoid laying off.

The fourth advantage seems particularly relevant to the automobile and construction industries: contracting out work as a way to *avoid the unions*. In fact, the 1986 report by the Bureau of National Affairs (BNA) reported that the use of contracting was higher in highly unionized firms (50 percent or more unionization) than in other firms.

The fifth advantage is attracting a *workforce in rural areas* where people are anxious to do home-based contract work, in order to avoid long or impossible commutes. Again, the BNA found that companies in rural areas were more apt to rely on contracting out than were companies in urban areas. This advantage must be treated with caution for it is possible that employers may take advantage of limited job possibilities in rural areas to garner major cost savings by hiring contractors rather than employees. This practice can lead to exploitation of workers' vulnerability in the marketplace.

Although there are advantages of a contracted workforce, there are also disadvantages. The two major disadvantages are decreased loyalty and reduced control over quality of work.

The contractor is basically a "here today, gone tomorrow" type of worker, never fully brought into the organizational culture and understandably never socialized to identify strongly with the company. The concern expressed by some companies is that such decreased loyalty will result in workers who will not go the extra mile and whose productivity, although acceptable, will not be remarkable.

The second disadvantage has to do with the potential lack or limited control over the quality of work. Contractors are unknown quantities and the companies may be gambling with quality of the product if they have not seen the contractors perform over a period of time in a variety of situations. The BNA found that concern with quality was the leading factor in why companies did not pursue more flexible staffing arrangements. Although they could save money in the short-term, they might reduce quality and productivity in the long-term.

Conclusions

Independent contracting is a staffing arrangement that is pursued for different reasons by employers and is sought or accepted for different reasons by workers. Some contracting practices appear to be fraudulent and must be seen as no more than a ruse to avoid paying the higher wage and compensation costs that would have to be paid to employees. Other practices appear more in the spirit of common law concepts and are pursued as a way to contract, expand, and redeploy a company's workforce to respond to competition and demand.

The language we use regarding independent contracting should begin to be coterminous with the multiple arrangements covered by it—particularly for involuntary contractors. A woman doing clerical piecework at home, with no option of being hired as an employee although expected to perform as one, should not be euphemistically defined as a telecommuter. A 60-year-old man terminated from his job after 35 years should not be glibly referred to as an entrepreneur or a freelance consultant. On the other hand, a person with multiple clients and the autonomy to charge according to prevailing market rates and who assumes the financial risk of his/her employment status could be such an entrepreneur or freelancer.

If companies continue to increase their use of contracting, efforts must be made to explore how these workers can be protected under the law. Just as the U.S. Senate Committee on Labor and Human Resources may consider the provision of benefits to part-time employees, it would be well served to investigate protective provisions for involuntary contractors who have forfeited all of their employment rights under law. Otherwise, the federal government may find that the costs of health and pension coverage will increasingly be shifted to workers and may be indirectly shifted to the government when workers cannot absorb these increased costs.

Another area of concern has to do with the potential de facto segregation of the workplace. It appears that a large percentage of the contingent workforce consists of women who seek these alternative arrangements as a way to earn money and manage their responsibilities at home (Christensen, 1987). It is increasingly possible that women will make up a second-class tier of workers, hired on a part-time, temporary, or contracted basis, with no opportunities for advancement, skill upgrading, or job retraining. The existing gap between male and female median earnings would only grow larger.

Independent contracting, along with part-time, temporary, and leased worker arrangements, signals profound and far reaching changes in how Americans work. Unless adequately addressed, these may also lead to dramatic changes in the culture and organization of work and the adequacy of wage and compensation for workers already marginal in today's economy.

Notes

1. Although these women would be labeled as clerical workers if they worked for someone else, their self-employment status caused them to think of themselves as professionals, prompting us to conclude that employment status overrides occupation at least with regard to women with clerical skills (Christensen, 1985).

2. It must be noted, however, that not all companies who have workers working at home in fact hire them as contractors. Some companies such as Pacific Bell have gone to great lengths to ensure that work location does not affect employment status. They have up to 100 employees in management positions who either work at home or in satellite offices, and these workers receive all of the benefits and protections afforded their colleagues in the centralized workplaces. Contrary to the practices of some insurance companies, Pacific Bell and Mountain Bell do not alter the status of a worker from employee to contractor when that worker moves from the office to the home (Christensen, 1985; MacKenzie, 1986).

Bibliography

Baillie, S. A. "Subcontracting Based on Integrated Standards: The Japanese Approach." *Journal of Purchasing and Material Management* (Spring 1986):17–21.

Berch, B. "The Resurrection of Out-Work." *Monthly Review* (November 1985):37–45.

Bureau of National Affairs. *The Changing Workplace: New Directions in Staffing and Scheduling*. Washington, D.C.: The Bureau of National Affairs, 1986.

Christensen, K. "Women and Contingent Work." *Social Policy* (Spring 1987):15–20.

______. "Pros and Cons of Clerical Homework." Testimony before the House Subcommittee on Employment and Housing, February 26, 1986.

______. "Impacts of Computer Mediated Home-Based Work on Women and Their Families." Contract report to the Office of Technology Assessment for the Office Automation Study, 1985. Available from the Center for Human Environments (1985), Graduate Center, City University of New York. Also published in *Office: Technology and People* 3 (1987):211–230.

Conlon, T. "Contract Pros Fill the Gaps." *Computer Decisions* (November 19, 1985):84–86.

Costello, C. *All the Top Brass Are Men. On the Front: Class, Genre and Conflict.* Ph.D. diss., University of Wisconsin, 1985.

Davidson, J. P. "Minority Business Enterprise: Penetrating the Defense Sub-Contracting Market." *Journal of Small Business Management* (April 1984):67–72.

Degnan, T. E. "Escaping the 'Employee Burden.'" *TAXES—The Tax Magazine* (March 1986):172–178.

Dudek, V. "Tax Law Jars Consultants." *Management Information Systems Week* (December 15, 1986):49.

Forbes, D. "The Growing Ranks of Contract Workers." *Dun's Business Month* (March 1986):56–57.

Gross, J. "No More 9 to 5: Trials and Triumphs of the Freelance Life." *The New York Times Magazine* (November 9, 1986):40.

Hacker, A. "Women at Work." *The New York Review* (April 14, 1986):26–32.

Hirshey, Gerri. "How Women Feel About Working at Home." *Family Circle* (November 5, 1985):70–73.

Journal of Accountancy. "IRS Proposes Real Estate Agent, Direct Seller Rules for Employment Tax Purposes" (March 1986):21–22.

Kirk, M. "To Hire or Contract?" *Business* (August 1984):33-34.

MacKenzie, R. Testimony before the House Subcommittee on Employment and Housing. U.S. Congress, House Committee on Government Operations. *Hearing: Pros and Cons of Home-Based Clerical Work*. 99th Cong., 2d sess., February 26, 1986.

Mellor, E. F. "Investigating the Differences in Weekly Earnings of Women and Men." *Monthly Labor Review* (June 1984):17–27.

Mellor, E. F., and S. E. Haugen. "Hourly Paid Workers: Who They Are and What They Earn." *Monthly Labor Review* (February 1986):20–26.

Moore, R. Correspondence to Representative Barney Frank, Chairman, House Subcommittee on Employment and Housing, April 15, 1986.

Nardone, T. J. "Part-Time Workers: Who Are They?" *Monthly Labor Review* (February 1986):13–19.

Pollock, M. "The Disposable Employee Is Becoming a Fact of Corporate Life." *Business Week* (December 15, 1986):52–56.

Pfeffer, J., and J. N. Baron. "Taking the Workers Back Out: Recent Trends in the Structuring of Employment." In B. M. Staw and L. L. Cummings, eds., *Research in Organizational Behavior,* vol. 10. Greenwich, Conn.: JAI Press, forthcoming.

Reibstein, L. "More Companies Use Free-Lancers to Avoid Cost, Trauma of Layoffs." *The Wall Street Journal,* April 18, 1986.

Soat, J. "The Ins and Outs of Contract Services." *Administrative Management* (February 1986):57–61.

Tarver, H. "Independent Contractors: Know When They Are and When They Aren't." *Personnel Journal* (May 1984):70–72.

Telecommuting Review. "Employee vs. Independent Contractor Status for Telecommuters: A Complex Issue" (May 2, 1985):7–10.

U.S. Congress, House Committee on Government Operations. *Hearing: Pros and Cons of Home-Based Clerical Work.* 99th Cong., 2d sess., February 26, 1986.

U.S. Congress, House Committee on Government Operations. *Report: Home-Based Clerical Workers: Are They Victims of Exploitation?* 99th Cong., 2d sess., July 16, 1986.

U.S. Congress, Office of Technology Assessment. *Automation of America's Offices.* Washington, D.C.: U.S. Government Printing Office, December 1985.

Wall Street Journal. "A Special News Report on People and Their Jobs in Offices, Fields and Factories" (October 7, 1986):1.

PART II

Forces Driving Home-Based Work

6
International Competition: Its Impact on Employment

Roberta V. McKay

> ***Competitiveness is the degree to which a nation can, under free and fair market conditions, produce goods and services that meet the test of international markets while simultaneously maintaining or expanding the real incomes of its citizens.*[1]**

Competitiveness has an abstract yet precise meaning to economists. The definition stresses production costs and market prices. The meaning is rooted in comparative advantage (greater relative efficiency) and ultimately based on relative costs. Simply, in a comparative advantage framework, low-production cost gives a competitive advantage through specialization. By specializing in what a country can produce most efficiently—commodities in which it has the highest productivity—world production is expanded, making it possible to have a rising standard of living, according to a study commissioned by the congressional Office of Technology Assessment.[2]

The United States' international economic leadership was unquestioned in the early post–World War II period. However, with the rebuilding of the economies of Europe and Japan and, more importantly, the rise of newly industrializing Third World countries, the dominant international position of the United States began to erode. Indeed, by the early 1970s, the world economy turned down, triggered by the Organization of Petroleum Exporting Countries (OPEC) energy-price shocks. Fear of inflation kept the world economy slack. As a result, the world market stagnated while world competition continued to grow.[3]

By 1980, the U.S. share of world Gross National Product (GNP) had dropped to about 20 percent from 40 percent in 1950. Similarly, its share of world trade declined to about 11 percent in 1980, from 20 percent in 1950.[4] Significantly, both the rate of productivity growth and real wages dropped, only to recover to 1973 levels by 1979 when the Iranian revolution and the OPEC oil price increase wiped out gains as the United States moved into the recessions of 1980 and 1981–1982.[5]

The perception that U.S. competitiveness in the world economy is lagging is rooted in U.S. industrial performance relative to its world trading partners. Since the 1970s, trading surpluses have become trading deficits; market shares have eroded in many industrial sectors, while profitability has deteriorated, particularly in trade-sensitive manufacturing industries.[6]

Underlying the fall-off in U.S. industrial performance has been the serious slowdown in the growth of labor productivity relative to its foreign trading partners. Other industrialized countries also had sharp declines in productivity growth as well, but their residual growth rates exceeded those of the United States. For example, the average percent change in U.S. manufacturing productivity growth was 3.2 percent in 1960 to 1973 compared with 2.2 percent over the 1973 to 1985 period. However, the comparable rates for the weighted–foreign countries average went from 6.8 percent in 1960 to 1973 to 3.9 percent over the 1973 to 1985 period.[7] Even after the sharp drop in foreign productivity growth, the residual average foreign productivity increase in manufacturing was higher than in the United States. Productivity measures the real value of goods and services per hour of labor, therefore, it is the source of rising real wages and a rising standard of living.[8]

Clearly, the challenge today is to maintain and enhance the U.S. standard of living in an increasingly competitive international marketplace.[9] The competitive question relates to relative changes in unit labor costs that involve changes in both productivity and compensation—wages and salaries, supplements, and employer payments for social security and other employee benefit plans. Thus, productivity and wage rates interact to determine unit labor costs. For example, increases in productivity growth that offset increases in compensation result in lower unit labor costs, providing there is no shift in shares between labor and capital. Such interaction allows for greater competitiveness because of greater efficiency of production factors and, thus, relatively lower costs. Similarly, decreases in compensation growth that offset declines in productivity also result in reduced unit labor costs and increased competitiveness. Competitive strategies that aim at lower unit labor costs by optimizing compensation/wage and productivity efficiencies make it possible for real economic improvement.

Taking into account the appreciation of the U.S. dollar adjusted for exchange rate changes, the United States and Canada were the only countries to post rising unit labor costs over the 1979 to 1985 period.[10] It is anticipated that, with the current depreciation of the U.S. dollar relative to foreign currencies, U.S. unit labor costs will fall relative to foreign labor costs, making the United States more competitive.

Restructuring U.S. Industry: The Problem

The seriousness of the international competitiveness problem is highlighted by the growing dependence of the U.S. economy on international trade. By the late 1970s "(1) one out of six manufacturing workers produced for export; (2) one out of three acres of U.S. farmland produced for export; and (3) nearly one out of three U.S. dollars of U.S. corporate profits were derived from international activities, exports, and investments of U.S. corporations."[11]

Exports as a percent of Gross Domestic Product (GDP) have doubled since 1973 to about 14 percent in 1985. The falling dollar is expected to increase exports by lowering prices as U.S. goods and services become more attractive to foreign buyers. At the same time, imports as a percent of new supply increased substantially in some of the long-term declining trade-sensitive industries such as leather, apparel, primary metals, electrical machinery, and miscellaneous manufacturing.[12]

An important source of competitive advantage is superior technology—making a good product at an attractive price. Superior manufacturing or process technology as well as product technology are ways of achieving low costs. For products and commodities that are technologically similar, cost and price are the primary determinants of competitiveness.

Nonetheless, public policy and the closing technology gap can confound simple cost/price measures of competitiveness. Most obvious is when governments subsidize high-cost producers or create trade barriers so that producers can charge high domestic prices. On the other hand, although U.S. firms have long been technological innovators, it is becoming more difficult to safeguard technological innovations for very long. Within shorter and shorter periods of the introduction of a new product, clones of the new product are on the market. Research and development must be a continual process for firms today. The closing technology gap creates even greater pressure on firms to maintain their competitiveness and, in doing so, the international competitiveness of the United States.

In the end, it is the capability of individual firms that determines a nation's competitiveness.[13] Their ability to create and develop, manufacture and market (including sales, service, and customer support) determines a nation's competitive position in the world economy. A *New York Times* article cites several firms that illustrate the successful adaptation to foreign competition including an innovative semiconductor firm.[14]

Improving U.S. international competitiveness, with its related employment trade-offs, is a complex issue. International competition is also affected by the more general restructuring of the U.S. economy. Changing consumer demographics and demand patterns, the pervasiveness of computer-based technologies incorporating advanced electronics and telecommunication, and lowered transportation costs are the other major forces facilitating U.S. industrial restructuring. Along with increased international competitiveness, the foregoing forces are changing the workplace expectations of both employers and workers.

Against these structural changes, U.S. competitiveness is further being challenged by traditional European trading partners and, even more aggressively, by newly emerging trading partners from East Asia (Pacific Rim countries of South Korea, Taiwan, Singapore, Hong Kong), Latin America, and the Caribbean, as well as industrialized Japan. The competitive challenge from these nations, particularly the Pacific Rim, comes not from favorable natural resource endowments but, largely, from comprehensive national strategies that mobilize and shape productive capabilities to promote the health of industries that produce for export.[15]

More specifically, studies have found that both traditional high-volume, standardized production systems and low-wage, labor intensive production is shifting to the newly industrializing countries in East Asia, Latin America, and the Caribbean. East Asia, particularly, is outperforming all of the North Atlantic countries. On the other hand, U.S. comparative competitive advantage is shifting to more sophisticated, technology-driven, precision-engineered, and/or customed-tailored commodities or products manufactured with rapidly changing technology. Leading edge firms are implementing more flexible production systems utilizing more flexible employment arrangements in response to changing competitive conditions.[16]

The Changing Workplace

The decline in U.S. international competitiveness is relative to that of its trading partners. Individual firms or industries may become noncompetitive, but an entire country cannot.[17] In a dynamic economy, change is continual. To improve their international competitiveness, firms and industries are continually adjusting their production and job requirements to reflect consumer demand. Firms go in and out of business, depending upon the degree to which they can efficiently meet the demand for their product. Thus, the corporate restructuring, leveraged buy-outs, and downsizing, while necessary to keep business competitive, can produce casualties. When the adjustments are pervasive and rapid because of fundamental technical or structural change, worker displacement may develop. There is evidence that in the United States the pace and pervasiveness of long-term structural changes are accelerating.[18] Nonetheless, the U.S. economy continues to have a strong capacity to generate employment.[19]

In the postrecession period, there has been a sharp upturn in U.S. economic activity. Increased productivity, lower inflation and interest rates have contributed substantially to improved industrial performance and the sustained economic recovery the United States has experienced since November 1982.[20] While employment in some trade-sensitive manufacturing industries has declined, total output has remained at about 20 to 21 percent of GNP since the 1970s.[21] Manufacturing output has actually posted increases since 1979, reflecting gains in productivity that helped to maintain its share of GNP.[22] In addition, the introduction of newer, more efficient technologies as well as changes in the manufacturing industry-occupation mix also contributed to productivity gains.

Meanwhile, aggregate U.S. employment has continued to expand, reflecting the continued increase in service sector employment. Although manufacturing output remains an important contributor to the value of GNP, employment expansion underscores the growing dominance of the service sector as employer. Like manufacturing, the service sector is diverse, having both high- and low-wage employment. The service sector includes professional, technical, managerial, and administrative positions that include high-wage and fast-growing occupations, as well as clerical and service occupations that also include lower wage and higher wage jobs.

It is also important to realize the considerable interdependence between the goods and service sectors. The restructuring and downsizing that has occurred in manufacturing has been accompanied by growth in services industries to support manufacturing. Some of the work previously done in-house can be supplied at lower cost and more efficiently by outside firms specializing in business services, the fastest growing division within the services industry. More important, U.S. manufacturing is not finished, it will continue to provide good, if different, jobs.

Although the U.S. economy is competitive, improving its competitiveness relative to its foreign trading partners needs to be a national priority.[23] Lower cost is the operational watchword in international competitiveness. The push for an increased share of international markets is an important driving force behind employer-initiated, more flexible labor markets and human resource management. Many flexible human resource arrangements have been characterized as peripheral or contingent, reflecting part-time, temporary, and other workers, and work arrangements usually associated with secondary labor markets. These employees may have applied directly to the employer for employment;

may have been leased to employers by leasing agencies; may have been sent by temporary help service agencies; or, may have worked for the firm as an outside contractor or subcontractor. More flexible arrangements reflect the drive for lower costs to obtain larger international product market shares. Greater flexibility in work arrangements has been assisted by technologies incorporating advanced microelectronics and telecommunications.

The pervasiveness of computer-based technology and telecommunication allows for greater productivity by lowering unit labor costs, if attendant increases in compensation do not outpace overall productivity gains. Thus, superior technology, alone or through telecommunications, can facilitate the changing workplace as well as the drive for international competitiveness.

In the workplace, the organization of work is changing. There is a growing emphasis on teamwork, decentralization, streamlining, and human-resource oriented work. Both workers and firms can be more flexible and mobile, allowing greater options for work/leisure tradeoffs. At the same time, to maintain and gain a larger share of world markets, U.S. firms are beginning to implement a variety of cost-cutting/flexibility strategies, supplementing their "lean staffing" with contingent workers who can move in and out of firms as needed and at a lower cost than permanent workers. Costs can also be lowered by the internationalization of production processes as domestic firms develop off-shore manufacturing and service operations.

These options remain controversial to some observers. Although the above mentioned cost-cutting strategies are accepted standard operating procedures by firms in their drive for competitiveness, other interested groups see contingent work and off-shore production as both a move to undercut the hard-earned benefits of U.S. workers and a move to export U.S. jobs. Thus, the public debate focuses on the potential for a growing sector of "unprotected" workers who are likely to have little job security, health, medical, and pension benefits or employee representation. At the same time, the data to determine with validity and reliability the potential size and characteristics of contingent workers is not now available on a consistent basis. Such measures promote an informed public debate.

Indicators That Affect Competitiveness

International competitiveness is comparative and dynamic over time; thus, its indicators vary over time. Indicators that most frequently impact a firm's ability to compete include relative trends in labor productivity, wage rates, profitability, import penetration ratios, process

Figure 6.1
Productivity and Related Measures in Four Sectors of the Economy, 1973 to Second Quarter 1986

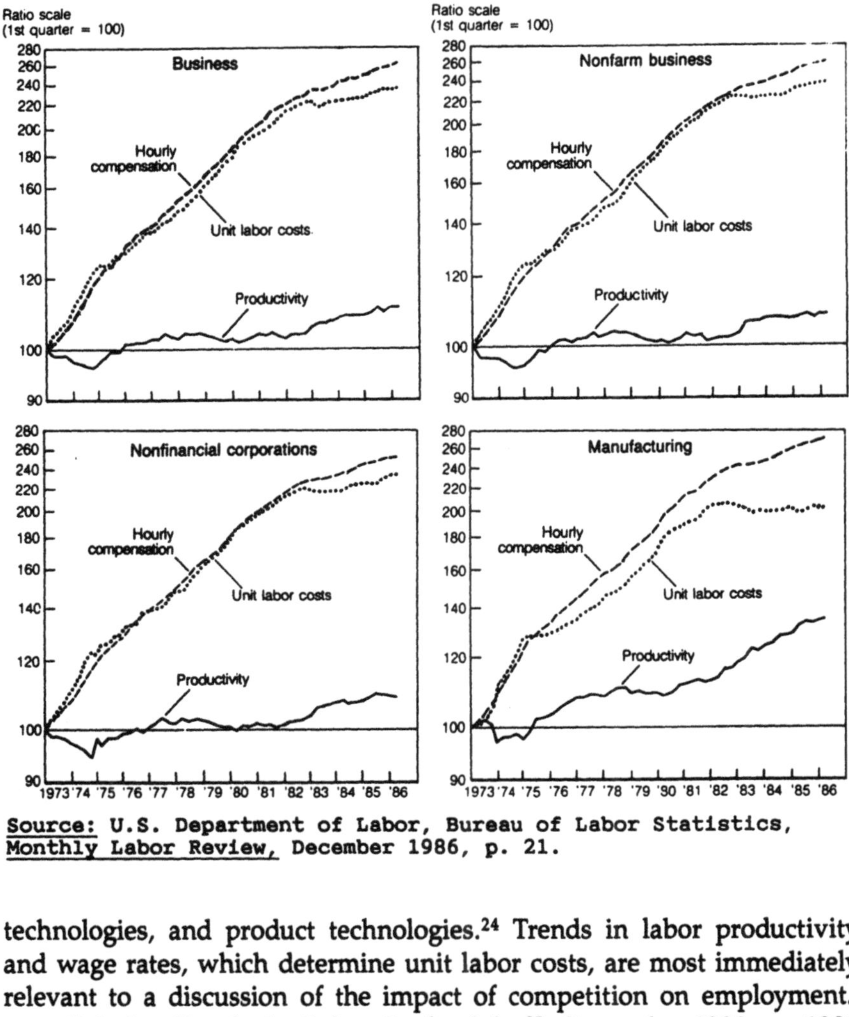

Source: U.S. Department of Labor, Bureau of Labor Statistics, Monthly Labor Review, December 1986, p. 21.

technologies, and product technologies.[24] Trends in labor productivity and wage rates, which determine unit labor costs, are most immediately relevant to a discussion of the impact of competition on employment.

Relative Trends in Labor Productivity.[25] Since the 1980 to 1982 recession, there has been a sharp pickup in U.S. labor productivity in manufacturing, although productivity in the business, nonfarm business, and nonfinancial sectors have not done as well (see Figure 6.1).

Significantly, by 1985, the U.S. growth rate of output per hour in manufacturing reached 4.4 percent. This rate was above the weighted index for 12 foreign countries but below the rates of 5.0 and 5.6 percent posted by Japan and West Germany, respectively, as shown in Table 6.1. Because of the continued trade surpluses among U.S. trading partners, the *Economic Report of the President* (1987) anticipates that the dropping

Table 6.1
Annual Percent Changes in Manufacturing Productivity, 12 Countries, 1960-85

Year	United States	Canada	Japan	France	West Germany	Italy	United Kingdom	Belgium	Denmark	Netherlands	Norway	Sweden	Foreign Countries (weighted)[1]
Output per hour:													
1960-85......	2.7	3.4	8.0	5.5	4.8	5.4	3.5	6.5	4.8	6.2	3.2	4.7	5.4
1960-73....	3.2	4.7	10.3	6.5	5.8	7.3	4.3	6.9	6.4	7.4	4.3	6.4	6.8
1973-85....	2.2	1.9	5.6	4.4	3.7	3.5	2.7	6.0	3.0	5.0	2.1	3.0	3.9
1973-79....	1.4	2.2	5.5	5.0	4.3	3.3	1.2	6.2	4.2	5.5	2.1	2.6	3.9
1979-85....	3.1	1.7	5.7	3.8	3.2	3.7	4.2	5.7	1.9	4.4	2.0	3.3	3.9
1984.......	4.1	3.7	7.0	3.9	3.7	5.4	4.5	3.5	1.0	10.7	2.6	4.4	5.0
1985.......	4.4	3.2	5.0	3.3	5.6	3.1	3.4	4.6	.7	3.1	.9	2.7	4.1

[1]A trade-weighted average of the 11 foreign countries. See description of weights in text, referenced in the source note.
Note: Rates of change based on the compound rate method.

Source: U.S. Department of Labor, Bureau of Labor Statistics, *Monthly Labor Review*, December 1986, p. 13.

value of the U.S. dollar will cause U.S. exports to be more attractive (lower cost) to U.S. trading partners.

With the resurgence and restructuring within manufacturing industries, attention is shifting to productivity improvements in the service sector, the source of most of the expansion in employment since November 1982. The products/commodities and services produced by these industries are a growing source of U.S. international trading. As with manufacturing, strong labor productivity will be needed to sustain real earnings and a rising standard of living. Yet consistent measures of productivity in the service sector are difficult to develop. Nonetheless, according to a Bureau of Labor Statistics *Monthly Labor Review* (June 1982) article, the earlier slowdown in labor productivity is not primarily (or importantly) the result in shifts in employment to service-producing industries. Indeed service industries include both labor- and capital-intensive industries, and the range of output per hour growth in service industries is not significantly different from that found among goods-producing industries.[26]

Moreover, some researchers find that "lagging productivity is not a symptom of technological innovation lag, but derives more from managerial and broader economic and cultural factors."[27]

Relative Wage Rate Trends. Economic theory holds that real wages (wages adjusted for inflation) should not rise faster than overall productivity (unless there is a shift in shares between capital and labor) if a rising standard of living is to be maintained. Today, controversy characterizes the discussion of whether real earnings have declined over the 1973 to 1986 period. Several studies have been shaping the debate and are at the center of ongoing research, particularly the work of the Bureau of Labor Statistics and Barry Bluestone and Bennett Harrison.[28]

Part of the confusion lies in the selection of the relevant tools of analysis. Depending upon the price deflator used—Consumer Price Index (CPI), Personal Consumption Expenditures inflation index (PCE), or the BLS's experimental CPI-X index—and whether fringe benefits (which are a large and growing proportion of labor costs) are included in the wage measure, real earnings over selected time periods can rise or fall. Moreover, the 1973 to 1979 period was characterized by sharply rising inflation, while in the post–1980 to 1982 recession period economic conditions were quite different. Combining these periods can confuse the underlying economic trend. It is clear that care must be taken in searching for a final conclusion to this complex issue.

The Impact of Competition

The impact of competitiveness on employment has been to increase the flexibility of the U.S. labor market in response to the quickened pace and pervasiveness of structural change facilitated by technology and other factors. The responsiveness (flexibility) of the U.S. labor market to changes in the economic variables of unemployment and price has increased since the mid-1970s. The Conference Board developed measures of responsiveness related to changes in wages and unemployment by proposing a set of questions on labor market responsiveness to econometricians at Chase Econometrics, Data Resources, and Wharton. The econometricians translated the questions to input variables measuring wages/compensation, prices, and unemployment, and then ran the data through their respective models of the economy. They concluded that U.S. labor markets were more flexible in 1986 compared with 1976.[29]

Richard S. Belous, a senior research associate at the Conference Board noted in his remarks on "Labor Market Flexibility" that real compensation is in the mid to late 1980s, at least, 20 percent more responsive to changes in economic conditions than in the mid-1970s. Although the U.S. labor market is 50 percent less rigid than in Western Europe, it is not as flexible as in Japan.[30] In addition to greater labor market responsiveness to unemployment, wages, and prices, worker dislocation and off-shore employment are other responses to the impact of competitiveness on employment and other labor market conditions.

Educational Attainment and Occupation. The demand for skilled and educated workers is increasing, while the demand for the unskilled continues to decline. The U.S. labor force reflects these increased demands. More than six out of ten U.S. workers have completed some post–high school education or training. Moreover, about 44 percent of all workers completed one or more years of college in March 1986, up from 29 percent in 1973. The increase in college training has occurred among both younger (25 to 44 years) and older (45 to 64 years) workers. The proportion of younger workers who had completed one or more years of college increased to 48 percent in March 1986, while the proportion for older workers was 44 percent.[31]

Similarly, the shift in U.S. competitive advantage is also reflected in the occupational distribution of its workers. The growing employment trend is shifting from large numbers of low-skilled employees to a growing number of middle and upper level workers needed to sell and develop new products. Moreover, with the computerization of routine and repetitive jobs (in both offices and factories), clerical occupations are becoming more skilled as firms seek to customize the service/product to the needs of individual customers. Nearly 44 percent of all workers are employed at jobs in precision production, craft, and repair occupations or in technical, sales, and administrative support occupations. An additional 25 percent work at jobs in professional specialties, executive, administrative, and managerial occupations. Continuing education and retraining is at the center of worker adaptability to a changing workplace.

Moreover, in the context of competitiveness, the growth in labor market flexibility, supported by rising educational attainment, suggests the leading edge of a more permanent change to new or nontraditional work arrangements. Although the growth in part-time and temporary work may have been largely cyclical in the past,[32] their continued growth, after nearly five years of sustained economic recovery, indicates a small, but significant, more permanent change in work arrangements. More important, much of the growing body of literature and statistical information concerning emerging work arrangements has been developed from case study or anecdotal sources[33] with the exception of part-time workers. The growth of more peripheral or contingent labor force attachment needs more study and monitoring, not only to sort out the tradeoff, but also to develop a consistent and ongoing data series.

Employment Level. Since 1973, total U.S. nonagricultural payroll employment increased at a slower pace (30 percent, 1973–1986) than in the earlier 1960 to 1973 period (40 percent), although an impressive 23 million rise in private nonagricultural employment was posted. Of the increase, just about all was realized in the service sector.[34] The absolute decline in manufacturing employment contrasts with the growth in service jobs in response to changing demand. As of the late 1980s, the service sector accounted for 75 percent of total nonagricultural jobs, up from 59 percent in 1950. Within the service sector, business and professional services have shown, and are projected to continue to show, strong employment growth.[35] The Organization for Economic Cooperation and Development (OECD) tabulation of the top ten industries gaining or losing employment are shown in Table 6.2.

Significantly, the relative gains and losses in employment in some individual manufacturing industries reflect the changing competitive advantage of the United States as it has moved from the production of goods that intensively use unskilled labor and/or high-volume, capital-intensive, standardized production to those using highly skilled and educated labor, using rapidly changing technology, and more flexible production systems.[36] Table 6.3 presents the projected changes in employment for selected industries posting the greatest employment gains, fastest rates of growth, and the most rapid rates of decline, 1984 to 1995.[37]

Dislocated Workers. An outcome of fundamental and pervasive structural change in the U.S. economy is worker displacement because of the closing or moving of a plant or company, slack work, or the abolishment of jobs or entire shifts. Although white men account for the majority of all adult dislocated workers (57 percent), a far from

Table 6.2
Top Ten Industries Gaining or Losing Employment, 1985

Gainers	Losers
Health services	Primary metals
Retail eating and drinking	Textile mill products
Business services	Apparel and other textiles
State and local government	Railroad transportation
Wholesale trade (durables)	Fabricated metals
Retail food stores	Retail general merchandise
Hotel and lodging	Stone, clay and glass
Banking	leather and leather products
Miscellaneous services	Miscellaneous manufactures
Special trade contractors	Local transit

Source: Organization for Economic Cooperation and Development (OECD), Economic Surveys 1985/86, United States, November 1985, Table A-3, p. 107.

insignificant proportion of women (35 percent) and minorities (11 percent) were also classified as dislocated workers. (Minority women are included in the totals for both women and minorities.)

Moreover, women and minority workers were more likely than white men to have been dislocated from lower wage and declining trade-sensitive industries, particularly nondurable goods, steel, and automobiles. This points to the fact that not all displaced workers were displaced from high-paid jobs. In addition, dislocated workers were last employed about equally in manufacturing—durable goods (33 percent), nondurable goods (17 percent)—and service (50 percent) industries, according to Bureau of Labor Statistics survey information.[38]

The Bureau of Labor Statistics' special survey of dislocated workers conducted in January 1986 found that 10.8 million adult workers (20 years and over) were displaced from their jobs during the January 1981 to 1986 period.[39] Of the 10.8 million, 5.1 million adult workers had been at their jobs for at least three years before becoming displaced. In January 1986, an estimated 3.4 million (56 percent of the 5.1 million) were reemployed; 900,000 were unemployed; and nearly 800,000 had left the labor force. In addition, about 330,000 who had lost full-time jobs were working part-time when surveyed. Among those who returned to full-time work, 56 percent were earning as much or more than they had on their former jobs. Although an earlier survey found that most displaced workers received unemployment benefits, 60 percent of formerly

Table 6.3
Projected Changes in Employment[1] for Selected Industries, 1984-95

Most New Jobs	Employment Gain (in thousands)
Business services	2,633
Retail trade, except eating and drinking places	1,691
Eating and drinking places	1,203
Wholesale trade	1,088
Medical services, n.e.c.	1,065
Professional services, n.e.c.	1,040
New construction	558
Doctors' and dentists' services	540
Hotels and lodging places	385
Credit agencies and financial brokers	382

Fastest Growing	Average Annual Rate of Change (percent)
Medical services, n.e.c.	4.3
Business services	4.2
Computers and peripheral equipment	3.7
Materials handling equipment	3.7
Transportation services	3.5
Professional services, n.e.c.	3.5
Scientific and controlling instruments	2.9
Medical instruments and supplies	2.8
Doctors' and dentists' services	2.6
Plastics products	2.5

Mostly rapidly declining	Average Annual Rate of Change (percent)
Cotton	-4.2
Wooden containers	-3.6
Leather products including footwear	-2.8
Iron and ferroalloy ores mining	-2.7
Sugar	-2.7
Leather tanning and finishing	-2.6
Railroad Transportation	-2.6
Nonferrous metal ores mining, except copper	-2.6
Dairy products	-2.3
Blast furnaces and basic steel products	-2.2

[1]Includes wage and salary jobs, the self-employed, and unpaid family workers. n.e.c. = not elsewhere classified.

Source: U.S. Department of Labor, Bureau of Labor Statistics, Monthly Labor Review, November 1985, p. 31.

covered displaced workers were no longer covered by health or medical benefits.[40]

Workers with continuing difficulty were those who had been displaced from blue-collar jobs, minority (black) workers, and persons formerly employed in manufacturing. (Blue-collar jobs can be found in both goods and service industries.) In addition, when women were permanently displaced from their jobs, they experienced a longer spell of unemployment, had fewer employment options, and obtained lower earnings from subsequent employment, according to an econometric study commissioned by the Department of Labor's International Labor Affairs Bureau (ILAB).[41] The ILAB study further found that workers displaced from import-sensitive manufacturing industries included a slightly higher share of black and female workers than was true for all workers displaced from manufacturing industries. More important, the study found that the problem of worker dislocation was more widespread than previous studies indicate, and not necessarily confined to declining industries, occupations, or regions. This once again suggests the introduction of newer technology, restructuring, and downsizing for better productivity and lower unit labor costs to obtain greater global competitiveness.

Off-Shore Employment. Some U.S. firms have adapted to the changing patterns of comparative advantage by integrating production operations across national boundaries. Unskilled assembly is done in low-wage areas, while more highly skilled operations are done in developed countries that have an abundance of skilled labor and technological and scientific resources.[42] By internationalizing, U.S. competitors can take advantage of the abundance of low-wage, unskilled workers in the Caribbean Basin, Latin American, and Pacific Rim countries. Some U.S. firms cite high worker productivity and dedication to the job, while the population explosion in newly industrializing nations makes rising wages unlikely.

U.S. firms do the largest amount of foreign assembly because other developed countries have a greater degree of protection against foreign imports.[43] Foreign assembly is also used as a way of penetrating foreign markets.[44] The principal industries are electrical machinery, transportation equipment, and metals; the principal products include semiconductors, textiles, television sets and components, and motor vehicles. Although wages are lower than in developed countries, some participants (such as Singapore) have decreed higher wages in an effort to gain higher skilled work.[45]

It is not surprising that the industries and products that figure most prominently in foreign assembly are also industries of declining domestic employment. "Although they are still only a small part of total

U.S. output and trade, more than half of all U.S. sales of certain products in textiles and electronics are assembled abroad. . . . The import of products assembled abroad have reached a level of almost a sixth of total U.S. imports of manufactures and about a quarter of imports of manufactures from developing countries."[46] The effect of the internationalization of production on U.S. workers is the trend toward greater investment in human capital (on the part of both employee and employer) in response to the shifting U.S. competitive advantage to more sophisticated and skilled production. Moreover, a recent study done for the Department of Labor by the Hudson Institute says the key to domestic economic growth is increased productivity, particularly in the rapidly expanding service industries. It calls for better education and job training for an American workforce that will include more women, minorities, and immigrants.[47]

Conclusion

Contingent work arrangements are at the center of the U.S. move to more flexible production systems to enhance its national and international competitiveness. These work arrangements will include both high-skill and low-skill work and will have an important role in shaping tomorrow's labor force. Although the benefits to employers and employees of contingent work arrangements—mobility and flexibility—are more easily understood, the context and potential outcomes of a more flexible environment is less easily understood. The following questions, derived from Richard Belous's work on labor market flexibility, should provide points of research and study for those interested in shaping the public debate:

- Are flexible labor markets characterized by shifts in employee compensation: Do they create income inequality and/or inequality of opportunity?
- Do flexible labor markets produce more jobs without basic benefits?
- Do flexible labor markets create "dead end" jobs and/or segmented labor markets?
- What is the role of public policymakers to sustain basic health, safety, and "fair" labor standards, other work and family issues, including child care and parental leave, in a more "flexible environment?"

Notes

This chapter benefited from comments from Jerome A. Mark, Associate Commissioner, Office of Productivity and Technology, Bureau of Labor Statistics,

U.S. Department of Labor (DOL); Robert W. Bednarzik, Senior Economist, Division of Foreign Economic Research, Bureau of International Labor Affairs, DOL; and David Demers, Senior Economist, Office of the Assistant Secretary for Policy, DOL. I am grateful to them for their comments. However, none of these individuals is responsible for anything contained in this chapter. Any error is the fault of the author.

1. President's Commission on Industrial Competitiveness, *Global Competition: The New Reality*, vol. 1 (Washington, D.C.: Government Printing Office, January 1985), p. 6.
2. U.S. Congress, Office of Technology Assessment, *U.S. Industrial Competitiveness—A Comparison of Steel, Electronics and Automobiles* (Washington, D.C.: Government Printing Office, July 1981), p. 25.
3. Frank Levy, "We're Running Out of Tricks to Keep Our Prosperity High," *Washington Post*, Outlook Section, December 14, 1986, p. 1.
4. Bruce R. Scott and George C. Lodge, eds., *U.S. Competitiveness in the World Economy* (Boston, Mass.: Harvard Business School Press, 1985), p. 18 and pp. 1–40.
5. Frank Levy, "We're Running Out of Tricks."
6. Ibid.
7. Arthur Neef, "International Trends in Productivity, Labor Cost in Manufacturing" (Washington, D.C.: Government Printing Office, U.S. Department of Labor, Bureau of Labor Statistics, *Monthly Labor Review*, December 1986), Table 4, p. 31.
8. Frank Levy, "We're Running Out of Tricks."
9. President's Commission on Industrial Competitiveness, *Global Competition*, p. 2.
10. Arthur Neef, "International Trends in Productivity," p. 15.
11. Robert J. Gordon, *Macroeconomics*, 3d ed., "Policy in an International Setting" (Boston, Mass., and Toronto, Canada: Little, Brown and Company, 1984), p. 596.
12. Gregory K. Schoeffle, special tabulation, U.S. Department of Labor, Bureau of International Affairs; and Council of Economic Advisers, *Economic Report of the President* (Washington, D.C.: Government Printing Office, 1987), pp. 108–128. Also see *U.S. Industrial Outlook* (Washington, D.C.: Government Printing Office, U.S. Department of Commerce, International Trade Administration, 1987).
13. Office of Technology Assessment, *U.S. Industrial Competitiveness*, p. 25.
14. Steven Greenhouse, "Revving Up the American Factory," *New York Times*, January 11, 1987, Section 3, p. 1.
15. Scott and Lodge, *U.S. Competitiveness in the World Economy*, p. 2, and the "East Asian Challenge," pp. 49–63.
16. Robert B. Reich, *The Next American Frontier* (Harrisonburg, Va.: R. R. Donnelley and Sons, 1983), pp. 127–133.
17. Office of Technology Assessment, *U.S. Industrial Competitiveness*, p. 25.

18. Report of the Secretary of Labor's Task Force on Economic Adjustment and Worker Dislocation, *Economic Adjustment and Worker Dislocation in a Competitive Society* (Washington, D.C.: Government Printing Office, U.S. Department of Labor, Office of the Secretary, December 1986), p. 11.

19. Janet L. Norwood, statement before the Senate Finance Committee, U.S. Congress, July 16, 1986 (Washington, D.C.: U.S. Department of Labor, Bureau of Labor Statistics, Office of the Commissioner), and "The Job Machine Has Not Broken Down," *New York Times*, February 22, 1987, Business Section 3, p. 3.

20. Frank Levy, "We're Running Out of Tricks." At the same time, the substantial U.S. recovery is rooted in strong consumer demand. Although multiple family earners allowed continued spending despite stagnant wages, increased spending was also buttressed by a sharp increase in credit spending (indebtedness).

21. Council of Economic Advisers, *Economic Report of the President* (Washington, D.C.: Government Printing Office, 1986), Table B-11, p. 265.

22. Janet L. Norwood, Senate statement, July 16, 1986, p. 4.

23. President's Commission on Industrial Competitiveness, *Global Competitiveness*, pp. 173–174.

24. Office of Technology Assessment, *U.S. Industrial Competitiveness*, pp. 173–174.

25. Arthur Neef, "International Trends in Productivity," pp. 12–17; and Lawrence J. Fulco, "U.S. Productivity Growth: The Post-Recession Experience" (Washington, D.C.: Government Printing Office, U.S. Department of Labor, Bureau of Labor Statistics, *Monthly Labor Review*, December 1986), pp. 18–22.

26. Ronald E. Kutscher and Jerome A. Mark, "The Service-Producing Sector: Some Common Perceptions Reviewed" (Washington, D.C.: Government Printing Office, U.S. Department of Labor, Bureau of Labor Statistics, *Monthly Labor Review*, April 1983), pp. 21–23; and Jerome A. Mark, "Measuring Productivity in Service Industries" (Washington, D.C.: U.S. Department of Labor, Bureau of Labor Statistics, *Monthly Labor Review*, June 1982), pp. 3–8.

27. Harvey Brooks, "Technology as a Factor in U.S. Competitiveness," in *U.S. Competitiveness in the World Economy*, p. 341.

28. Barry Bluestone and Bennett Harrison, *The Great American Job Machine* (Washington, D.C.: A study prepared for the Joint Economic Committee, December 1986), and "The Grim Truth About the Job Miracle," *New York Times*, February 1, 1987, Business Section 3, p. 3; Janet L. Norwood, Senate statement, July 16, 1986; Rudy Boschwitz, "Misreading the Jobs Machine" (Washington, D.C.: Government Printing Office, *Congressional Record*, January 16, 1987), p. S-879; Warren T. Brooks, "Low-Paying Jobs: The Big Lie," *The Wall Street Journal*, March 25, 1987; Neal H. Rosenthal, "The Shrinking Middle Class, Myth or Reality?" (Washington, D.C.: Government Printing Office, U.S. Department of Labor, Bureau of Labor Statistics, *Monthly Labor Review*, March 1985), pp. 3–10; Patrick J. McMahon and John Tschetter, "The Declining Middle Class: A Further Analysis" (Washington, D.C.: Government Printing Office, U.S. Department of Labor, Bureau of Labor Statistics, *Monthly Labor Review*, September 1986), pp. 22–27; Robert Z. Lawrence, "Sectoral Shifts and the Size of the

Middle Class," *Brookings Review*, (Fall 1984):3–11; Scott and Lodge, *U.S. Competitiveness in the World Economy*, pp. 34–40.

29. Richard S. Belous, The Conference Board, "Remarks on Labor Market Flexibility," *Daily Labor Report* (December 29, 1986):E 1–4.

30. Ibid., pp. E 1 and 3.

31. Department of Labor, Bureau of Labor Statistics, Current Population Survey.

32. Thomas J. Plewes, "Understanding the Data on Part-Time and Temporary Employment," paper prepared for the Conference on the Contingent Workplace: "New Directions for Work in the Year 2000" (New York: U.S. Department of Labor, Women's Bureau, January 15–16, 1987).

33. Kathleen Christensen, "Women and Contingent Work," *Social Policy* (Spring 1987): 15–25. Based on paper presented at the Israel-American Symposium on Women and Work, November 12, 1986, U.S. Department of Labor, Women's Bureau.

34. U.S. Department of Labor, Bureau of Labor Statistics, Current Population Survey.

35. Janet L. Norwood, Senate statement, July 16, 1987 pp. 5–6.

36. C. Michael Aho and James A. Orr, "Trade-Sensitive Employment: Who Are the Affected Workers?" (Washington, D.C.: Government Printing Office, U.S. Department of Labor, Bureau of Labor Statistics, *Monthly Labor Review*, February 1981), pp. 29–35; also see Robert Z. Lawrence, "Is Trade Deindustrializing America? A Medium-Term Perspective," in *Brookings Papers on Economic Activity*, Vol. 1 (Washington, D.C.: Brookings Institution Press, 1983), pp. 129–159; and Robert B. Reich, *The Next American Frontier.*

37. Valerie A. Personic, "A Second Look at Industry Output and Employment Trends Through 1995" (Washington, D.C.: Government Printing Office, U.S. Department of Labor, Bureau of Labor Statistics, *Monthly Labor Review*, November 1985), p. 31 and pp. 26–41.

38. U.S. Department of Labor, Bureau of Labor Statistics, NEWS 86-414, October 14, 1986, p. 1. Also see U.S. Department of Labor, Office of the Secretary, *Economic Adjustment and Worker Dislocation in a Competitive Society.*

39. Ibid., Figure 1, "Characteristics of Displaced Workers."

40. Paul O. Flaim and Ellen Sehgal, "Displaced Workers of 1979–83: How Well Have They Fared?" (Washington, D.C.: Government Printing Office, U.S. Department of Labor, Bureau of Labor Statistics, *Monthly Labor Review*, June 1985), p. 9.

41. Michael Podgursky and Paul Swaim, *Labor Market Adjustment and Job Displacement: Evidence from the January 1984 Displaced Worker Survey*, Final Report for the U.S. Department of Labor, Bureau of International Labor Affairs, January 1986, p. 51; and Richard M. Devens, Jr., "Displaced Workers: One Year Later" (Washington, D.C.: Government Printing Office, U.S. Department of Labor, Bureau of Labor Statistics, *Monthly Labor Review*, July 1986), pp. 40–43.

42. Joseph Grunwald and Kenneth Flamm, *The Global Factory, Foreign Assembly in International Trade* (Washington, D.C.: Brookings Institution Press: 1985), pp. 2–8.

43. Ibid., p. 32.

44. For example, the joint ventures with German and Japanese automobile and electronics firms.

45. Joseph Grunwald and Kenneth Flamm, *The Global Factory,* p. 232.

46. Ibid., p. 12.

47. Hudson Institute, Inc., *Workforce 2000: Work and Workers for the 21st Century* (Indianapolis, Ind.: Hudson Institute Press, June 1987).

7
Office Automation Technology and Home-Based Work

Vary T. Coates

Home-based clerical work and off-shore data entry are alternative and partly competitive techniques for reducing the labor component of the costs of business services.[1] Both have been around for some time, but both have been made newly feasible and economically attractive by advances in telecommunications and computer technology. Neither activity has affected any significant portion of the clerical workforce as yet, but both could increase dramatically over the next decade. Although some technological trends may encourage the spread of either or both home-based work and off-shore work, other trends could well limit or even abort that growth. The development of both home-based clerical work and the off-shore transfer of data entry is tied to a larger employment trend, sometimes referred to as contingent work.

Forces Driving Contingent Work

In the United States and in most other highly industrialized nations, there is a pronounced trend toward greater use of part-time, temporary, or contract workers—some of whom work in offices, some at home. The driving forces behind this trend are economic and demographic factors. But technological changes are at least encouraging and facilitating the trend and, with regard to clerical and professional work, may be a major factor.

The greater use of contingent workers is probably stronger than is generally realized. It seems to be accelerating faster than can be reflected in conventional employment data, if one can judge by the statements of human resources specialists in major corporations. By 1990 it is likely that at least 8 percent of all U.S. employees will be temporary workers,[2] and another 20 to 24 percent will be working part-time.

In the United States, the shorthand term for this trend is "lean staffing." Companies plan to keep the minimum workforce necessary (or even somewhat smaller than necessary) to handle their minimum daily workload. They will depend on temporaries, contract workers, and part-timers not only for unexpected peaks but also to handle normal seasonal or cyclical fluctuations. A conservative pattern, for example, is one in which at any one time, 10 to 15 percent of the workers are temporary or contract workers, and another 5 to 10 percent are permanent part-time employees.[3]

Clearly, the central force behind this move is competitive pressure to cut operating costs, especially labor costs. Even if temporary and contract workers receive higher wages than permanent employees doing the same work (which is likely to be the case for professionals and the more specialized support workers, but not for lower level clerical workers), temporary and part-time workers are usually a bargain for the employer. This is not the case because secondary labor costs (overhead and benefits) add an estimated 100 to 150 percent to the cost of a permanent employee, but because the employer pays only for actual, productive workhours and only those when the worker's output is essential. Use of a contingent workforce is usually a "load-leveling" strategy for the employer.

A second economic factor is the volatility of the economy or, more exactly, the uncertainty that many U.S. firms feel about both the outlook for growth or recession and the long-range competitive position of their company or their industry in the global marketplace. In this situation they wish to minimize their obligations (legal, contractual, financial, and social) to a permanent workforce.

In government employment, this economic pressure is greatly reinforced by political pressure to reduce the federal workforce and by the conservative position that government services should be "privatized," or contracted out, to the greatest extent possible. In this case, office automation technology is explicitly viewed as a substitution for labor, but also as a means of standardizing the handling of information and, thus, some government operations and the delivery of some government services, so that they can be done by contractors or by seasonal temporary workers. The Internal Revenue Service, the Census Bureau, the Social Security Administration, and other agencies that process huge volumes of data electronically depend heavily on temporary and part-time hires, and are probably increasing the proportion of nonpermanent employees.

On the labor-supply side, demographic trends are clearly important—specifically, the surge of mothers into the workforce. In the United States, half of women with children under three years old are working, 60 percent of those with children from 3 to 5 years old, and 70 percent of those with school-age children.[4] Increasing numbers of retirees and working students add to the supply of part-time or temporary workers.

The increased number of women seeking work is a global phenomena, as is the trend toward use of contingent workers. In Japan, where a long-range shortage of labor is anticipated, the number of working women has doubled since 1960; they now make up 35 percent of the workforce. There is still cultural resistance to married women working, and although only 20 percent of them are working part-time, they make up 80 percent of the part-time labor pool.[5] Both the International Labour Organization and a study being conducted for the Organization for Economic Cooperation and Development (OECD) report that part-time and temporary work are increasing in most European and Scandinavian countries as well as Japan, with the larger proportion of these workers being women, especially women clerical and sales workers.[6]

Technology and Contingent Work

If economic pressure and demographic forces are the dominant factors in the trend toward a contingent workforce, technological factors are nevertheless clearly important. The technology of office automation strongly encourages and facilitates the shift. Automating equipment is a nice complement for the load-leveling strategy, and both contribute to cutting labor costs.

The sweeping and pervasive automation of office work with computers and telecommunications increasingly affects professional and managerial work as well as clerical work. Clerical occupations, however, account for over 60 percent of assignments in the temporary services industry, which has been growing at a rate about 20 percent per year in recent years.[7] Part-time work in financial services and retail trade is now growing faster than part-time work in construction, which has traditionally been the leader. The increase in part-time or temporary work in the last ten years has been greatest in banks, insurance firms, retail trade, and food sales, those industry sectors where computerization of services has proceeded most rapidly.

Historically, automation was assumed to have the opposite effect, that is, to discourage contingent work. By increasing the firm-specificity, task-specificity, and system-specificity of the skills that were required, new technology supposedly forced an employer to invest some specific training in each employee and reduced the hiring of casual untrained labor. Even in office work, it was feared at first that employers would lose the option of bringing in temporary workers because there were so many different kinds of word processors and software systems. But this barrier quickly disappeared. Manpower, Inc., the largest supplier of temporary office workers, reportedly trained 100,000 people in 1986 on most of the major word processing systems currently in wide use, and most temporary agencies supply both diverse training and a hot line to assist any temporary who finds herself (and in clerical jobs, the overwhelming majority are female) trying to cope with an unfamiliar procedure.

Office automation has gone through three major waves since the late 1950s. "Back-office functions," the high-volume processing of data, was first automated with large mainframe computers controlled by centralized processing centers. Typically, this work is rationalized, simplified, routinized, and nearly always associated with computer sequencing of tasks and computer monitoring of performance. This form of computerization of data handling appears to facilitate or encourage the use of contingent workers for a number of reasons:

- When back-office work (the routine processing of standardized data or text) is rationalized and deskilled, investment in training is minimal, and the value of experience and continuity is also minimal.
- Capitalization encourages the addition of nighttime or weekend shifts or longer hours, often filled by part-timers. For example, suburban banks began staying open longer for the convenience of commuters; automation made this economically feasible because fewer workers are needed to provide the necessary services.
- Computer monitoring depersonalizes supervision and tends to make workers more interchangeable.
- The convergence of systems and the widespread use of some systems such as IBM or Wang reduce the importance of knowing the idiosyncracies of firms. The format of letters or the name of a file can be corrected with the push of a few buttons; computerized bookkeeping software packages are quickly mastered. The value of long experience in the firm tends to be eroded.
- When work is depersonalized and standardized, employers are more likely to accept job-sharing, part-time work, or work at unconventional times and locations.
- At the same time, tasks within an organization may be specialized, so that it is harder for regular employees to substitute for each other due to illness or vacation.
- For high-level work—specialized computer programming, software development, systems analysis, and so forth—employers often seek contract workers whose training is more recent or specialized than that of permanent employees. Contracting may

be cheaper than investment in frequent skill upgrading or mid-career retraining for employees.

- Computers and telecommunications have made it newly feasible and attractive to both employers and employees to shift work to the worker's home. Home-based clerical work, recently estimated at about 5,000 to 10,000 jobs, could increase rapidly.[8]

Something of the same kind of deskilling and rationalizing of work occurs with the use of computer systems at the "front-end"—the customer end—of retail trade in food stores, department stores, and other chain store operations. Knowledge about the product, the inventory, and the prices is embedded in the computer; the salesperson can be less knowledgeable and is often required only to accept merchandise from the would-be buyer and pass it over a magic eye or under a magic wand. Experienced clerks can be replaced over time with less trained part-time workers who will not demand regular pay increases and promotions.

The custom-design, implementation, and maintenance or upgrading of such systems has created many demanding, well-paid, specialized jobs. The organization may, however, need these services only sporadically and thus contract them out. In addition, an organization may prefer to use mostly contract or project-duration people in many of these tasks as an alternative to permanent staff, whose skills and knowledge of new technologies would tend to become stale and outmoded over time.

The second wave of office automation began in the mid-1970s with the rapid spread of stand-alone word processors, personal computers, and packaged software. These do not usually supercede but are added to a large organization's centralized automated data processing (ADP) operations. The third wave of office automation—networking—is already well underway. It is not clear whether decentralized or distributed computer capabilities have any significant effect on demand for contingency workers. What is clear, however, is that they did not for long constitute a barrier to the use of temporary and part-time workers as had been anticipated. The convergence and growing compatibility of small computers, and the emergence of large temporary services companies willing to train their workers, effectively removed the barrier.

Without a doubt, one type of contingent work is, however, newly feasible and attractive because of advances in office automation technology—home-based performance of office services, especially data and text entry.

Technology and Home-Based Clerical Work

Americans have a long tradition of working in the home to supplement family income. Home-based production work has been highly controversial at times and was banned in a few industries in the 1930s.[9] Some kinds of clerical work are often done at home—for example, typing or envelope stuffing—at piece-rates. The clerical tasks that can be done manually or mechanically at home are routinized tasks that require little or no supervision, can be easily measured, are not time sensitive, and can be done in isolation. How much home-based clerical work is done is not known. Much of it may be part of the underground economy, never reported to the IRS. It is likely, however, that relatively few employers have found it worthwhile to farm out this work and relatively few employees have found such low-paid work attractive.

Computers and telecommunications technology have made home-based clerical work more attractive to both employers and employees. At least in theory, these technologies free employment from the restrictions of time and distance. The data or text that is to be generated or processed, the instructions for doing the work, the supervision or monitoring of the work, and the delivery of the product can be electronic. Computers in the home can be used at any hour of the day and the results communicated to the central office computer at any time.

At present most home-based workers are probably using a stand-alone word processor or personal computer. Raw data is delivered to them on paper or in the form of a cassette from a dictating machine, and the product is returned to the employer on tape, disk, or paper. But some home-based clerical workers use dumb terminals connected to an employer's mainframe computer, usually by a modem and an ordinary telephone line. An additional line may be installed to avoid interference with, or by, the calls of other family members. In a few cases a dedicated leased line is necessary for data security. This is the most sophisticated form of home-based clerical work, and the technology is available, reliable, and cheap. There have been very few problems with equipment, according to most reports.

Telephone companies are placing great emphasis on upgrading equipment and services to meet the needs of industry, and rate structures are also changing rapidly. Improved equipment will make home-based work with a direct electronic link to the office even more attractive. How rate structures in the future may affect home-based work of this kind is more uncertain.

At present, the equipment may be owned and installed by the employer and either lent or rented to the worker. For example, Blue Cross clerical workers pay the employer a yearly rental for the equipment.[10] Or the worker may own or lease her own equipment, especially if she accepts work from more than one source.[11]

Technology is not in the late 1980s a major barrier to home-based clerical work, and it will be less so in the immediate future. There are strong economic and social incentives for employers to move toward greater use of home-based workers. The strongest incentive is cost-cutting. The employer saves money in terms of floor space and other facility costs, equipment and energy costs, direct labor costs, and worker's benefits or indirect labor costs.

The savings in equipment costs can be important, even if the employer is supplying the equipment. For example, in a pilot program run by the U.S. Army Materiel Development and Readiness command, when three employees shifted to home-based work and began to work in off-hours as a second shift,[12] there was a 64 percent increase in computer usage without additional costs.

The big savings for the employer, however, are clearly in direct and indirect labor costs. The employer usually pays only for actual work time—not preparation and set-up time, not time for coffee breaks or office gossip, not time spent learning from or tutoring other workers, not time for bathroom trips. In most cases, home-based clerical workers are considered independent contractors, or at best part-time workers, and are not covered by benefit packages or guaranteed a minimum number of hours of work. Thus the employer avoids the cost of "slack time," while the worker's income may fluctuate widely. Because the benefits typically add up to 30 to 40 percent of wages, this is clearly a strong economic incentive to convert workers to home-based independent contractors. As hardware costs continue to decline—or even if they stabilize at 1988 costs—we would expect home-based clerical work to increase.

Technology and Off-Shore Clerical Work

Alternatively, employers may choose to send their data-entry work to be done in Third World nations. Advances in communications technology make it increasingly attractive to move data-entry operations off-shore. Data-entry clerks in Caribbean countries may earn weekly wages that are about 15 to 20 percent of U.S. wages; in some countries the gap is even wider. Even with transportation, communication, and other costs, there is a powerful economic incentive to send work off-shore. Two kinds of U.S. firms are involved: companies that have moved some of their own operations off-shore, and vendors or intermediaries who provide off-shore services for client firms.

Currently, there are probably 12 to 15 U.S. firms with data processing operations in the Caribbean; there are others in India, Singapore, the People's Republic of China, Ireland, and Mexico. At present there may be no more than 5,000 or 6,000 jobs involved, but off-shore data entry could expand rapidly in the next 5 to 15 years. The plans and expectations of practitioners and vendors point in that direction.[13]

There are three principal methods of linking off-shore data-entry operations with data sources and data users in the United States. In the simplest form, paper documents, cards, ticket stubs, or other sources of data are collected; the data are shipped overseas by air freight or overnight courier, entered on magnetic tapes or disks, and then shipped by air back to the United States for use, storage, or further processing. In many cases, off-shore processing consists of converting text or data in hard copy into digital form so that they can be used by computers in this country. The source documents sent abroad include, for example, manuscripts, insurance forms, subscription forms, ticket stubs, mailing lists, sweepstake entry forms. With the low wages prevailing in developing nations, data may be keyboarded by two or more workers and compared by computer to detect and eliminate errors.

A second mode is to air-ship source documents, cards, and so forth overseas, where they are processed and electronically transmitted back to the end users. The data processing sites may be linked by telephone lines to satellite earth stations or to submarine cable facilities.

Finally, electronic links may be used in both directions. Documents are facsimilied in the United States, transmitted off-shore, keypunched or processed, and transmitted back by satellite or cable. This method has the shortest turnaround time and is used for very time-sensitive information such as financial data. Facsimile clarity is a significant problem, and facsimile transmitters are too slow for much time-sensitive work. Improvement in this technology would further increase the attractiveness of off-shore operations.

There are a number of factors that will influence the future growth of off-shore data processing: future demand for data processing services, relative costs of domestic and overseas labor, corporate attitudes, the availability and cost of international communications, regulatory barriers, government policy, and further technological development.

Growth in demand for information processing, and particularly for converting existing paper-based data to digital form, is potentially almost unlimited. The more computerized information handling becomes in the future, the more need there will be to convert historical data to digital form to avoid a break in the continuity of organizational and societal records.

The gap between domestic labor costs, including secondary labor costs, and overseas wages will continue to favor off-shore data entry, even when compared to relatively low-cost home-based work in the United States. Although wages in this country are not likely to rise as steeply as in past decades, the gap will probably remain attractively large, at least in many Third World countries, for the foreseeable future. As wages rise in one developing nation, off-shore operations can shift to other less-developed nations with lower wage rates.

Institutional inertia and outright management resistance to change are perhaps the biggest barriers to the rapid spread of both off-shore and home-based work. Most companies simply have not considered either of these innovations in employer-employee relationships and are unlikely to do so unless some entrepreneur outside or inside the company decides that one or the other of these strategies should be adopted and begins to actively champion it. Even then, there is likely to be resistance to trying something that challenges or changes traditional mechanisms and techniques of management. Strong economic pressures, however, can eventually wear down even strong resistance.

The future availability and cost of international communications services and infrastructure will be a major factor. But both availability and cost are improving and even now are not generally considered high barriers, although they influence the choice of overseas sites. Future trends in communications services are expected to favor the expansion of overseas data transmission. Microwave and cellular telephone systems, for example, are under consideration in several developing nations. These technologies may play an important role in Third World countries in the future. They would provide additional links between off-site offices and international communications terminals.

Regulatory impediments to the exportation or flow of data across international borders are few or nonexistent. At present there are almost no regulatory or customs barriers. U.S. customs laws allow U.S. companies keying their own data overseas to import these records duty free. In general, recorded data from any off-shore operations are regarded as returned U.S. goods and not subject to duties. At worst, duties imposed are those related to the physical media (for example, a few cents per square foot of magnetic tape). The information embedded on the physical media is not regarded as added value. A few countries regulate the operation of data banks and transborder data flows in the interest of privacy or national security, but there are no such laws in the Third World nations that are likely sites for off-shore office work.

U.S. government policy presently encourages off-shore operations in the interests of economic development in friendly Caribbean or other Third World nations. Because of the low volume and low visibility of this activity there has been no strong pressure to reverse this encouragement, although such pressure could emerge suddenly and strongly if white-collar unemployment rates rose significantly.

The governments of Third World countries generally favor this kind of investment in their economy. It generates employment rapidly, it is environmentally clean, and it provides rudimentary training for a workforce that can potentially later be a valuable resource for indigenous computer-related industries. Foreign workers like the data-entry jobs because they are clean, physically light, and relatively well-paid jobs that in a developing country may carry considerable prestige.

Technological Limits on At-Home and Off-Shore Clerical Work

The growth of these nontraditional forms of clerical work is basically driven by two factors: (1) the increasing demand for data and text entry and, therefore, for keyboarding; and (2) the pressure to take advantage of information technology in order to reduce labor costs. Information technology may, in the long run, drastically reduce the demand for keyboarding and thus the economic incentive for home-based and offshore work.

In the 1980s, a major portion of office work consists of keying data and text into computers—even when that data and text are generated with another computer, sometimes even one in the same organization or physical location. Secondary data entry of this kind is sure to decline precipitously. More and more, computers are able either to communicate with each other directly or to exchange floppy disks, and, where they are not yet compatible, services to translate between systems are increasingly available and affordable.

In the future, the following scenario may be commonplace. A manufacturer's computer that tracks and controls inventory will automatically transmit an order for materials to a supplier's computer (possibly after comparing continually updated bids from competitors), the supplier's computer will automatically generate a shipping order, and both will interact with one or more bank computers to adjust accounts—all of this with oversight and supervision, but not necessarily any keyboarding, by corporate workers. Most information will be created in machine-readable form from the beginning and will be passed from computer to computer with transitory appearances on paper for specific uses.

Primary keyboarding is also likely to decline significantly for several reasons. First, more data will be captured at the source, as a customer keys information into an automated teller machine or a point-of-sale terminal or purchases tickets from electronic machines. Secondly, major advances are now occurring in optical scanning or character recognition technology. It is this development that most dramatically may affect the need for keyboarding; human fingers will not be necessary as the bridge between paper and computer memory. Much further down the road, there should be breakthroughs in the development of speech recognition as still another method for communicating with computers.

Technology, then, may drive the growth of home-based and offshore clerical work for some years to come, but eventually it is likely to abort that growth by providing an even cheaper method of data and text entry.

Notes

1. Although this chapter draws on Office of Technology Assessment (OTA) reports, it has not been reviewed by the OTA or the Technology Assessment Board and is solely the responsibility of the author.

2. "The Use of Temporaries: A Way to Control Costs and Increase Productivity," *Small Business Report* (December 1984):52.

3. Ibid.

4. Bureau of Labor Statistics, as reported by Sharon Cantor of Manpower, Inc., August 20, 1986.

5. Marc Beauchamp, "Problems of a Part-Time Workforce," *PHP Intersect* (February 1985):35–37.

6. International Labour Organization, Advisory Committee on Salaried Employees and Professional Workers, *The Effects of Technological and Structural Changes on the Employment and Working Conditions of Non-Manual Workers*, eighth sess. (Geneva, 1981). The OECD study was reported informally at a working seminar at the Bureau of Foreign Economic Analysis, U.S. Dept. of Labor, December 4, 1986, by Larry Hirschhorn and Thierry Noyelle.

7. National Association of Temporary Services, September 1985.

8. "Home-Based Automated Office Work," in U.S. Congress, Office of Technology Assessment, *Automation of America's Offices* (Washington, D.C.: U.S. Government Printing Office, December 1985), chapter 7.

9. The prohibition on home knitting of women's outerwear was ended in November 1984; bills have been introduced to amend the Fair Labor Standards Act to lift the ban on home sewing, knitting, and other industrial homework so long as the employer complies with wage and hour laws.

10. "If Home Is Where the Worker Is," *Business Week*, May 3, 1982, 66. In most formal corporate programs studied by Margrethe Olson, the employer paid for installation of equipment and monthly telephone charges; in one program employees rented equipment from the company. See Olson, "Working at Home and Telematics: Myths and Realities," presentation at the Office Automation Conference, (Los Angeles, February 20–22, 1984), p. 10. Also see Olson, *Overview of Work-at-Home Trends in the United States* (New York: New York University, Center for Research on Information Systems, August 1983).

11. The distinction between home-based clerical employees and home-based entrepreneurs providing business services for more than one client at rates set by the market is an important one for most analytical purposes, especially those related to public policy, but it need not concern us here. Whether clerical workers own their equipment does not determine whether they may be considered

as "independent contractors" as opposed to employees, according to IRS rulings. See Internal Revenue Service Technical Advisory Memorandum 845 1004, August 1, 1984, Index nos. 3121.04-00, 3306.05-00, 3401.04-00.

12. Mary T. McDavid, "The ALMSA Work-at-Home Prototype," presentation at the National Executive Forum: Office Workstations in the Home, National Academy of Sciences (Washington, D.C., November 10, 1983).

13. This portion of the chapter is based on chapter 8, "Off-Shore Work," of the OTA report, *Automation of America's Offices.* That chapter, in turn, was based largely on the work of OTA contractors, Christopher P. Astriab and Anne Posthuma, who conducted many interviews and drew on documentary sources both in the United States and abroad. See the OTA report for more detailed information and additional references and citations.

8
Corporate Culture and the Homeworker

Margrethe H. Olson

The scope of this chapter is corporate culture and its effect on white-collar home-based employment. The specific question explored is, How does the organizational culture of the employer affect employees and their ability to structure their work at home? The general perspective taken is that of organizational management rather than that of the employee. In addition, the chapter addresses the following questions: What is the degree of corporate interest in work-at-home as an employee work option and why? What is the current level of activity among corporations in experimental or formal work-at-home programs? What will organizations likely be doing in the future regarding flexible work options for employees?

Much of the publicity about work-at-home carries the notion of "telecommuting" and that the computer and telecommunications link are the primary drive behind the trend. For several reasons I contend that, today at least, technology is not a major driving force behind the trend (if there is one) to work at home.

Ultimately, when all of the tools that people need to perform their "office" work are either in their computers or accessible via telecommunications, the nature of work will change dramatically. These tools, however, include other people—a key ingredient. In the 1980s, most organizations do not have the technological infrastructure that allows people to depend entirely on technology to accomplish their work and communicate with others. In particular, substitution of electronic forms of communication for face-to-face interactions are not yet common. Thus, employees who telecommute are typically working with a set of tools that is different from and not as powerful as those available on-site.

Furthermore, I contend that even when such tools are inevitably in place, management adaptation to using those tools in powerful and flexible ways will take a very long time. Basically, after the threshold of technological penetration and integration is reached, the physical constraints of time (nine-to-five) and place (central office) will be removed. The potential exists not only for increased employee flexibility, but also for management flexibility in utilization of scarce human resources (for example, project assignment not limited by employee location). However, management culture changes slowly and presents a barrier to innovative and creative uses of technology even when it is available and cost-effective.

Corporate Interest in Work-at-Home

Although many companies spend modest efforts "studying" work-at-home as an employee work option, few have such programs. In the 1980s, at the professional level at least, virtually no U.S. company has a formal program for employees to apply to work at home on a regular basis several days a week. And it is virtually impossible to document the extent of informal arrangements between a single employee and his or her manager.

This chapter will address the issue of corporate interest in work-at-home as an employee work option. The observations are based on my survey of pilot programs in 19 Fortune 500 corporations in the insurance, banking, and computer industries. I also completed intensive longitudinal case studies of three of these pilot programs. The number in the individual pilot studies ranged from 4 to 15.

Employers are primarily interested in work-at-home because of their need to attract and/or retain qualified personnel in certain key areas, particularly technical specializations such as programming and word processing. This is the main reason that many pilot programs originate in data processing.

In some cases, a pilot project is begun in order to respond to a very specific and immediate need to attract or retain qualified personnel. Frequently, informal arrangements are made to accommodate a valued employee during a special situation such as a maternity leave when the employee would otherwise be absent. Typically, this arrangement is carefully set up under circumstances that gradually bring the employee more and more frequently into increased responsibilities requiring on-site attendance.

One formal pilot project I studied was set up explicitly to retain a few key personnel when a department of approximately 30 employees was moved from a metropolitan to a suburban location, significantly increasing most commute times. The key employees were data processing specialists whose skills were in demand and who had expressed dissatisfaction with the move. When management proposed that these employees be permitted to work at home two days a week to alleviate the stresses of a long commute, the employees agreed to be relocated rather than leave the company. After the move was completed, however, the employees' project assignments and responsibilities made it more and more difficult for them to work away from the office. Their days working at home gradually tapered off, and after six months the telecommuting pilot project was terminated.

In other cases, management has recognized a long-term opportunity to tap an otherwise unavailable labor force (for example, mothers of young children) who have training and experience but who have dropped out of the labor force either permanently or temporarily. Many of these workers are anxious to keep their skills up-to-date if the work can be performed conveniently, given their nonwork schedule and location. Management typically begins with a small pilot program of regular, carefully selected employees, in order to "sell" the idea that work can be performed at home successfully. Usually the performance goals are modest; as long as performance does not decrease and the employee's supervisor feels comfortable with it, the pilot project is deemed a success. Often, however, even if the program is successful, the long-term plan to shift the program to a permanent workforce of employees specifically hired for the work-at-home arrangement is not carried out. Frequently, management decides to terminate the pilot program after the specified number of months for reasons further elaborated on in this chapter.

A third reason for short-term corporate interest in work-at-home is simple faddism and a sense of competition. Many human resource "experimental programs" are studied and watched by personnel departments; if they do happen to "take off," the company needs to be in a position to implement them or it may lose valued employees to companies that do offer the programs. This is true of many flexible work options such as job sharing and part-time work.

A fourth reason some corporations are interested in telecommuting is their concern with the market potential of the technologies to support it. For instance, several telephone companies have recognized that if telecommuting were to become widespread, there would be an expanded market for telecommunications services in the home. The Mountain Bell and Pacific Bell telephone companies, for instance, have fairly extensive telecommuting programs. Although the programs are targeted toward benefitting their own employees, the companies are also gaining valuable knowledge about the technological support required for a telecommuter. Presumably, this accrued knowledge of market needs will feed into new product development.

Some organizations have used work-at-home as a demonstration of the corporation's service to society. Two pilot projects in particular involved the severely physically disabled. The projects received a considerable amount of publicity and misled some people into thinking that they were very large programs, when, in fact, they involved ten or fewer workers who were on special contract status.

Some enlightened managers recognize the potential for a significant productivity gain for employees working at home. Some employees have estimated as much as a 100 percent improvement in their work output on the days when they are at home; a more typical estimate is a 20 to 25 percent gain. Managers consistently estimate productivity gains to be considerably less than employees do, typically estimating between 1 and 10 percent gains (a 10 percent gain is still quite impressive).

The real issue is, To what can these productivity gains be attributed? The general management claim is that employees are less distracted when they work at home; this assertion assumes that employees are not managing nonwork responsibilities at the same time (for example, children). Another hypothesis has it that they simply work more hours, and there is anecdotal evidence to support this assumption. Based on self-report diaries of people working at home compared to an on-site control group, I found that the average number of hours reported worked is about the same for both groups. However, interviews reveal different definitions of "hours worked." For on-site employees, hours worked are defined by hours in the building, including all social interactions that are not directly work-related. When an employee works at home, hours worked are determined by clock time spent at the desk or in front of the terminal; breaks for doing the dishes, chatting with a neighbor, or taking a telephone call regarding school activities are conscientiously subtracted from hours worked.

In the long run, companies foresee financial savings in facilities costs as well as in overhead expenses for maintaining parking lots, cafeterias, fitness centers, and so forth. As facilities are such high fixed-cost items, significantly large numbers of employees would need to be shifted into their homes before these payoffs would occur, however. One company turned to a work-at-home program when it both ran out of space in its facility and faced a shortage of potential employees who would be willing to come to a central facility; within its suburban region the company successfully recruited qualified individuals to work at home and solved both problems.

Implementing a Pilot Program

Typically, the idea for a pilot program within a corporate structure is generated by someone in a functional area, such as data processing, who has hiring responsibility. If it is to be a formal experiment, it needs approval by corporate management, the human resources department, and frequently the legal department. In one company whose goal was to run a six-month pilot project with four employees, approvals from these departments took over two years to obtain.

Once the pilot program is approved in concept, an effort is launched to identify appropriate candidates. Management seeks volunteers who must meet fairly stringent criteria. Frequently, these criteria for selection are primarily based on the nature of the work performed. In data processing (for example, system development), employees typically must be assigned to program coding rather than system specifications or system testing. Commonly, an employee who is on a "management track" may not be considered; in several cases studied by the author, an employee had to formally switch career paths from the management to "technical" track in order to qualify to participate in a pilot project. Frequently, the employee is made to understand explicitly that promotion is not possible while he or she participates in the pilot.

The most important criterion, however, is support of the employee's supervisor. No matter how formal the pilot program, the supervisor must agree to the participation; frequently management approval at the next level is also required. This approval must be explicit and active rather than passive; the supervisor must agree to certain changes in his or her own activities (special monitoring and reporting) in order to support the homeworker. Furthermore, the supervisor is really making a statement of trust in the employee's abilities and self-motivation; frequently this is considered a strong message that is withheld for all but the ablest candidates. Of course, as these are also the very people who would most likely be management material, they can be turned down for the program because they are considered too valuable.

Employees are usually required to sign a document that explicitly details the conditions of their employment under the arrangement and the terms they have agreed to, such as waiving of promotion. The document is generally drafted to protect the employer's rights against the employee.

Once the pilot program begins, criteria for its success are usually conservative and nonsystematic. Typically, the explicit criterion is that productivity will not decrease. However, the implicit criterion is that supervisors maintain control. This is usually more important in judging the ultimate fate of the pilot program. Supervisors are given the right to terminate the arrangement at any time without explicit cause, and often do. Furthermore, during the course of the pilot program, some of the few participating employees are transferred to a new project and/or manager (despite the employee agreement to give up the right to such changes) who disapproves of the arrangement and requires the employee to terminate it.

What happens at the end of the pilot period? First, the pilot program is judged to be a success or failure, based on the limited explicit criterion defined. Second, it is either terminated or allowed to continue on a curtailed basis for one or two "special case" employees. Occasionally the pilot program is extended to a new group; often it is a special case social program for the "functionally limited" or severely physically disabled. In no case the author studied was the next stage a formal option for employees to apply for work-at-home status.

How Is Organizational Culture Imposed?

It is clear that the corporate managers I surveyed were not overwhelmingly in favor of having employees work at home. Subtle signals of management culture tend to work against the arrangements. In general, organizational culture is geared around the "place"; when an employee walks in the door of the building, he or she is "owned" by the organization until the end of the day when he or she leaves. In corporate culture, working nine-to-five is subordinate in importance to "being there."

There are many organizational symbols manifested throughout the day that teach the employee accepted norms of behavior in terms of how much one can "goof off," when coffee breaks take place, how punctual one should be at a meeting, what clothes are appropriate. All these symbols create norms of acceptable behavior that go far beyond getting by in day-to-day performance. They constitute conformity to organizational norms—playing by the rules is rewarded. In a typical bureaucracy, consistency of behavior (predictability) is rewarded above acceptable performance.

For the employee, the reward for consistent behavior is promotion. No matter how much it is stated that good performance is rewarded, the real key to promotability is visibility. One does not only have to conform to organizational norms, one must also demonstrate conformity to those that count. This often entails demonstrating punctuality at meetings, wearing the right clothes, speaking at the right times, and so forth. Obviously, it cannot be done at home.

Signs of status and position abound in the organization and are important mechanisms for transmitting culture. Many organizations have systematic rules for the furniture in an employee's office, so that his or her hierarchical level is immediately communicated. In one organization, the joke is that "only those with wooden desks make decisions." It is important who goes to lunch with whom, whom one speaks to in the elevator, what time one comes in and leaves. In many companies, a whole contingent of "up-and-comers" may compete with one another in getting to work first in the morning.

Management resistance to work-at-home programs is the first-line cultural resistance to work-at-home. Often managers show resistance by putting extreme constraints on the participant, giving conservative evaluations of performance outcomes, and terminating arrangements. Typical constraints on the employee include eliminating opportunities for consideration for management or general promotion and limiting task assignments.

Another form of management resistance is the tendency to create reasons for the employee to be on-site—increasing the number of meetings or client contacts, for example. Middle management tends to rely heavily on direct observation for employee control, regardless of how ineffective that method might be. They rely on this because of a lack of other adequate performance criteria, but also, more importantly, because they often lack trust in their employees. For an ineffective manager, having an employee work at home is threatening precisely because it exposes that manager's lack of trust and ineffectiveness.

All of these mechanisms of management resistance and corporate culture operate strongly against work-at-home as an employee work option. If one does work at home, this culture must be negotiated.

Negotiating Corporate Culture for the Homeworker

Most often, when an employee is granted the opportunity to work at home, the corporate culture is moved to the home basically intact. For the most part, after an initial experimental period employees settle down to a regular routine of hours that tend to approximate nine-to-five. For some, this schedule is imposed by nonwork (family) constraints. To some, the work schedule is forced by habit and guilt. But for many it would be more convenient to work different, more flexible, hours. Subtle signals also emanate from the corporation. Reports are frequently given of a supervisor calling an employee in mid-afternoon and responding as if it were a crisis situation if the phone is not answered. In many pilot programs, core hours when the employee must be reachable by telephone (typically 10:00 A.M. to 2:00 or 3:00 P.M.) are required.

Do employers take into account the employee's nonwork constraints? From the pilot programs studied, the resounding answer is no. This is true even if the employee explicitly requests the work-at-home arrangement in order to accommodate child care. Employers assume that there will be plenty of volunteers to work at home because of their child care needs, but employers are not concerned with how these employees work out their child care arrangements. Furthermore, employers do not want the lack of child care for these workers to intrude on their daily availability for work. Some companies may explicitly consider work-at-home options as an alternative to corporate daycare, but I have not come across any such cases. In general, employees' needs for flexibility in their work lives are not addressed in either a general or specific (case-by-case) way by an organization.

Despite core hours, surveys indicate that employees who work at home arrange their work around their nonwork constraints. Across the pilot programs evaluated here as well as in many other pilot programs, work time was found to spill over into nonwork time.

The overlap, psychological as well as physical, between corporate culture and the home has not been examined systematically. Some employees have expressed concern about the organization invading their privacy. Some corporations, on the other hand, have expressed concern, often excessively, about protection of corporate hardware, software, and data. Letters of agreement frequently contain statements regarding employee liability if machines are stolen or damaged, and employees must take responsibility for altering their home insurance to cover these issues. In some cases, there is great corporate concern about accessing data over telephone lines and displaying it or printing it at home. This concern also seems excessive when compared to the typical lack of company security measures, which never challenge what employees take home from the office on computer printouts.

In summary, there are many messages of corporate culture that constrain the employee's work behavior at home. Frequently, these become so burdensome as to force the employee to return to the office full time.

Predictions for the Future

The corporations I surveyed, as should be clear from the above discussion, were not at all anxious to provide work-at-home as an employee work option. The primary cause was overt management resistance, which was fueled by the more subtle corporate culture. Currently, technology is also a constraint. When a certain threshold of technology is reached, "office" work organization most probably will begin to change dramatically. But that does not mean that corporate offices will be replaced by "electronic cottages" overnight.

As technology softens organizational boundaries, it will first serve to more closely link multiple sites of the same organization. This will result in significantly more remote collaboration, where organization members in separate locations work closely in teams. There are many subtle changes in management style required with remote supervision, but as more and more remote collaboration occurs, managers will discover that, despite their resistance, they *are* supervising remotely.

At that point, there may be a sideways shift of work into the home. However, there will also be many other ways that technology can support greater flexibility in work for employees, as nine-to-five and physical location constraints will be removed. My contention is that the only way truly flexible work options (facilitated by technology) will occur is if employee demands, as well as skill shortages, are significant enough that organizations *must* pay attention to them in order to acquire and retain qualified personnel.

9
Clerical Home-Based Work: A Case Study of Work and Family

Cynthia B. Costello

Relatively little is known about the actual experience of clerical homeworkers.[1] An analysis of the clerical homework program at a medium-sized insurance firm can provide insights into the advantages and disadvantages of homework as a solution to women's household and child care duties. Based largely on interviews with managers and homeworkers presently or formerly employed by the Wisconsin Physicians Service Insurance Corporation (WPS), this chapter traces the consequences of home-based employment for the women hired to work at home.[2]

The Clerical Homework Program at WPS

Starting in the winter of 1980, WPS began to recruit women for part-time work processing insurance claims in their homes. The company required that homeworkers be housebound women with preschool-age children; "[the company] wanted people who could not go out to work," explained one supervisor. By 1984, the company had hired approximately 100 women to work as clerical homeworkers.

From the company's point of view, the homeworkers provided a cost-effective method for adding staff to process high-volume medical and dental claims without having to expand the physical plant in an industry with peak and slack periods. WPS could hire part-time homeworkers and adjust their hours to the flow of insurance claims at the company. In addition, homeworkers were less expensive than their in-company counterparts. Hired at a rate ranging from $3.35 to $3.75 an hour, homeworkers received no paid vacation, sick leave, or medical and pension benefits. Finally, the substitution of nonunion homeworkers for union employees allowed management to circumvent the union that represented the in-company clerical workforce, Local 1444 of the United Food and Commercial Workers.

Once hired, homeworkers completed a two-week training program at the company. In groups of five to ten, new recruits were assigned to supervisors who instructed homeworkers in the skills of claims processing—the interpretation and coding of medical diagnoses and procedures; the application of insurance guidelines; and the determination of insurance payments. These workers then returned home to begin their new jobs. Between 4 and 7 P.M., four afternoons a week, a truck delivered a bucket of claims to the homeworker. The amount of work varied from day to day and week to week, depending on the workflow at WPS's main office buildings. The homeworker had 24 hours to complete the work except in the case of the Thursday-night delivery, which left the homeworker with the weekend.

Some homeworkers addressed envelopes, pulled staples from insurance claims, and typed correspondence. The majority were either coders or adjusters. Coders transferred the appropriate codes for medical diagnoses and procedures from insurance manuals to insurance claims. Back at the company, a keypuncher entered the coded claims into the computer and the computer "paid" the claim. Homeworkers who adjusted insurance claims checked the diagnosis for each claim to make sure it matched the medical procedure and consulted insurance manuals to determine the cost of the service performed.

Until 1984, all of the homeworkers processed insurance claims manually, using code sheets, pencils, and calculators. Beginning in 1984, WPS began to introduce personal computers to a handful of homeworkers. Computer homeworkers entered data from insurance claims directly onto computer disks, eliminating the intermediary step of transferring information from the insurance claim to a codesheet.

The homeworker had only sporadic contact with WPS management. Supervisors communicated with homeworkers through memos outlining any procedural changes and sent homeworkers monthly audits reporting their productivity and error rates. Personal contact with supervisors was rare. Periodically, supervisors called meetings to update homeworkers on new procedures for processing claims.

Supervisors assigned homeworkers rate expectancies that represented the number of claims a homeworker was expected to process in an hour. For the first three months, homeworkers were on probation; supervisors closely monitored their productivity and error rate through frequent audits. After the probationary period, raises depended on favorable audits, as well as the homeworker's availability and attitude. The maximum raise was 8 percent. The highest paid homeworker had worked at home for five years and received $5.00 an hour; most of the homeworkers earned $4.00 an hour or less.

Homework and Family Life

Women adapted their homes to the requirements of homework with varying degrees of success. Those with extra space transformed a spare bedroom or basement into a home office. Women with a separate room for claims adjusting could leave claim forms, calculators, and reference books out without worrying that a family member would disturb them. Those with little space utilized a kitchen table to process claims, which required the constant packing and unpacking of homework materials for meal preparation. "When I started out," stated one homeworker, "I had a little area where I worked and I could put work aside and leave it out. By the time I left [the company], I had a large box full of information and paper. It [the work area] was completely cluttered with all sorts of manuals and supplies. [It] was cluttering up the family environment."

The privatized aspect of homework affected women differently. Some homeworkers appreciated the solitude of the work, particularly at first. "I like regulating my hours," reported one homeworker. "You do your work and nobody is hassling you or watching you." Another homeworker characterized the appeal of working at home: "Being able to do it at my own time, setting my own hours. No one was watching over me . . . over my shoulder all the time making sure I was doing it correctly." At least one homeworker also underscored that homework allowed her to claim privacy in relation to her family: "I thought, this was one time of the day I can be alone, no one will bother me."

But for other homeworkers, the feeling of detachment, of "being cut off from the mainstream," was disconcerting. Women missed the social interaction of the office and looked forward to returning to an organizational work setting. "The isolation was awful," reported one homeworker. "I had always worked with lots of people. I liked being out in the office . . . I felt out of it. I was like a recluse. I didn't know how women were wearing their hair. . . . That part was real hard." A second homeworker agreed: "At first, it was great. I thought this is really it. This is fun. I can finally be home with my kids. And I enjoyed being a domestic person for awhile. After a while, I think I started talking like the kids. I missed the interactions with other people. I missed doing what I like doing best, that is being a secretary and being able to work with other people."

One problem encountered by homeworkers was the invisibility of their work. Presuming that homeworkers "weren't really working," friends and neighbors did not hesitate to call for a social chat, drop in for a visit, or send their children over to play. "Other women outside the home didn't look at you as working," reported one homeworker, "so they think of calling you any time of the day. It is so frustrating. People think it isn't work, [but rather] a hobby." Even spouses sometimes failed to regard homework as "real work." "It is hard because [my husband] doesn't see it as a job because I am home," stated one homeworker. "A lot of men in this world think that just because you are at home, you aren't doing anything. I think they should have their heads looked at." In a few cases, homeworkers themselves downplayed their work. When friends asked her if she was working, one homeworker responded, "no."

Women differed as to the ease with which they juggled household, child care, and homework responsibilities. Some women integrated the homework into their lives with little difficulty. "I don't mind homework," one woman with a preschool daughter explained, "because when I'm home, I can have the laundry going when I am doing my homework." A second homeworker expressed a similar assessment: "You really can't ask for more [than] to have the work actually brought to you and still be able to raise your children." And a third woman concurred: "On the whole, I didn't think you could beat it because you were getting minimum pay or just a little above, but you were still able to be at home with your kids and you could work it around your schedule."

Other women encountered difficulties balancing the demands of homework and family. Some women received help from husbands who cleaned or cared for children so that the homeworker could complete claims adjusting. But most homeworkers retained primary responsibility for the household. The job of claims adjusting was added onto their housework and child care tasks, resulting in a lengthened workday. Women with children in public school could complete most of their claims adjusting during school hours. Those with preschool children at home worked around their children's schedules. Many homeworkers processed the simpler claims when children were awake, leaving the more difficult ones for naptime, evening, and early morning. One homeworker's allocation of her time typified their strategies:

> When I get the claims at night, I try to put in an hour while the kids are watching TV. Then I get up at 4:30 A.M. to work before the kids get up. . . . It is easier when nobody is around so my mind isn't wandering. . . . During the day, I turn on the TV and tell my preschooler to watch . . . then, when she takes a nap, I can work.

A second homeworker described a similar work pattern:

> I would get up at 8:00 A.M., feed the girls, and try to straighten up a little bit. . . . At 11:30, I would feed the kids and then at 12:00, they'd

> nap. The entire time until 3:30, I would do claims. I'd do claims I hadn't finished the night before [while] getting ready for that day's pickup. I'd go for a ride with the kids. At 5:00, we would eat. At 6:00 sharp, my husband would take them downstairs and I would work. At 7:00 P.M., I would stop and get the kids in bed. Then, I would work until 10:30 or 12:30 at night. It was exhausting. I was never so drained. It hit and never went away.

Some homeworkers had no alternative but to let some of their housework go. "As far as housework, the house was never in such bad shape," reported one homeworker. For women whose primary identity was bound up with home and family, this caused distress. "The [homework] is always on my mind at home," reported another homeworker. "Doing homework is real difficult for me because I think I should be doing homework when I'm doing the laundry and then I think, 'No, this comes first.'" In particular, many homeworkers found the demands of homework antithetical to the requirements of children. "I'd just get a claim done and [the baby] would get into something or he needed to be fed or held," stated one homeworker. "It is hard to hold a baby and do your work at the same time."

Particularly frustrating for many homeworkers was the negative effect of children's interruptions on productivity. Minutes spent responding to children's needs cut into the time allotted for each claim. "You are working at home with small children," reported one homeworker, "and you are always interrupted for, 'Mommy, can I have a snack? Can I have this?' You have to write down the time you stop and the time you start up again. I have time sheets a foot long [at] times." A second homeworker underscored the difficulty balancing child care and homework: "Contrary to public opinion, it is not easy [to do homework] because you have your kids that you have to work around. If children interrupt me, I have to start all over again, and I have to absorb that time."

In some cases, children registered their own discontent with the homework. "Mom is always at the claims," complained the child of one homeworker. "She can't take me anywhere because she's always at the bucket." When he saw the delivery truck arriving, the two-and-a-half year-old child of another homeworker stated, "Here comes your stupid P.S. [WPS] work." This woman concluded that the costs of homework were too great: "I was treating my children like they were getting in my way. . . . The main reason I quit my job at the bank was to be home with the children. [But] I was treating the job at WPS like a big career." Another homeworker summed up the contradiction inherent in homework: "The advantage is being able to stay home and the disadvantage [is] not being able to keep up with your parenting responsibilities."

One of the ironies of homework was the cost it exacted on family relationships. Most homeworkers chose the work so that they could care for their children. But for homeworkers to complete the work, their children had to at least be occupied if not ignored. Over time, homeworkers realized they were snapping at their kids, and homework was cutting into their family time. "I feel real bad I took so much time away from the family life," stated one homeworker. "There were playgroups and there were swimming lessons I would like to have gone to. In the morning, I couldn't go because I was so exhausted from working." The stress this caused was summed up by one homeworker: "It was stressful being interrupted and going back and forth to work and children. I would say, 'Don't bother me now, mama is working.' That was not fair to my children because if anything comes first, my family does."

Sometimes, the homework caused conflict with spouses as well. In one instance, a husband resented the homework because it prevented him from returning to the office after dinner. This husband urged, "It's not worth it, just quit." A second husband who initially endorsed the homework option asserted, "I don't care, the money is not worth it. I can't stay down in the family room [with the children] one more night." Spouses sometimes objected to the time that homework took away from their marriage. Several men demanded that the homework be completed before they arrived home for dinner.

Homeworkers drew different conclusions about the effect of homework on their family lives. Some women emphasized that it would be difficult to give up homework because it integrated so smoothly with their lives. For these homeworkers, there were sufficient hours when their children were sleeping, playing, or occupied to complete the work. But others underscored the difficulties encountered trying to separate "homework" from "family" responsibilities. Women resented the intrusion of homework into their households. "You can't leave your home-based problems behind," emphasized one homeworker. In the words of another homeworker, "The work was always hanging over your head. . . . I was always exhausted." And as a third homeworker concluded,

> I felt that I was working full-time between doing the claims and, even when my work was done, having to wait for the delivery. . . . The disadvantage to it for me personally was the feeling oftentimes of being trapped. . . . I would say to myself, 'I'm only working 18 hours a week, but I feel like I am doing this stuff all the time.' . . . It was constantly hanging over me. . . . Even when my work was done there was this new pile facing me for the next day. . . . I felt really tied down with it.

Homeworkers' Job Satisfaction

The women's (dis)satisfaction with the home as a work environment was integrally tied to their assessment of the working conditions associated with the WPS homework program. Many homeworkers appreciated the employment offer from WPS. Some women felt devalued in their status as housewives. By hiring them, WPS was placing a "value" on the homeworkers' time. "There was somebody out there who was willing to hire us," stated one homeworker. "We're not just housewives—people with no minds—that are sitting home raising children. Somebody was giving us a chance to use our minds again and paying us to do it. Yet we were all able to stay home." A second homeworker reiterated, "You really felt kind of privileged because they were allowing you to do the career you chose to do instead of putting the kids in daycare and yet they were saying, 'Gee, you've got something to offer us.'"

For many women, the homework earnings had a positive effect on their input into family decisionmaking. As housewives without an income, women were reluctant to ask their husbands for money. But with the earnings from homework, women became more assertive in relation to their husbands. As one homeworker put it, "This job has given me my own independent power to make decisions, to make financial decisions." A second homeworker echoed, "I was always asking for money from my husband, and I felt left out of everything. Then I thought, with homework, at least I'd have my own paycheck and I could do what I wanted to do with it." And for a third homeworker who would have preferred to work outside the home, the income earned from homework provided a degree of independence and autonomy: "My husband's preference is for me to be at home . . . I would prefer to work out just for myself to get out. I first started working as a homeworker because I hated asking for ten dollars. I don't have much income, but it is nice not to always have to be asking."

Homeworkers expressed mixed feelings about the daily work of claims adjusting. Particularly in the beginning, many homeworkers enjoyed their work. "I like the work," stated one homeworker, "sometimes there is variety. Some [claims] are easy and others are difficult." A second homeworker concurred: "Work was a challenge. I would think, 'gee, I can get these all done tonight and I think I got them all right . . . these claims are easy and I can get them done in no time.'" But after mastering the skill of the job, many homeworkers found the work monotonous. "Once you get it," stressed one homeworker, "it is like a factory or assembly line worker." One woman explained that, at times, she would think, "what am I doing in this job?" And then at other times, she would think, "I really like this job."

Among homeworkers, dissatisfactions surfaced over wages and working conditions. Many women felt they deserved higher wages. "For a while, I rationalized [the low pay] by saying, 'I am saving money. They are saving money. It's a good deal for the company and it's a good deal for me so it balances out.' But I really think the company does get the better end of the deal. They are saving a lot more money than I am saving by staying at home." A second woman believed that WPS had a captive labor force in homeworkers: "They get a lot of work done for little money. And they know that. They are at an advantage because they don't have to pay benefits and they don't have to give any kind of decent raises. The women who stay have to stay and they know they've got them. . . . A lot of these women have no alternative because for what they make, the babysitting is expensive. But the main thing is that being home with the kids is more important than material things."

The rate expectancies, which varied depending on the type of claim a homeworker processed, were another source of dissatisfaction. Some of the homeworkers had no problem meeting the rate. One woman reported that she always performed at 200 percent of the expectancy. But others concluded that the rates were unfair. "They make it sound that it is the offer of a lifetime," explained one homeworker, "but after you're hired, they are going to squeeze everything out of you and then ask for more." Another woman characterized the employment situation as a "sweatshop": "It seemed to me they were more interested in speed than anything else. They wanted to know how many claims you could process in a day. And the more you processed, the more they sent you."

Frustrations arose over other issues as well. One was the requirement that homeworkers be home (but not paid) for the delivery of the claims bucket. In general, homeworkers could predict within an hour the arrival time of the delivery truck, but sometimes the truck arrived late, preventing the homeworker from participating in a family activity. The erratic amount of work caused additional problems. Although some homeworkers received a consistent amount of work from week to week, for others, this was not the case. "If they got behind in-house, we went without work," stated one homeworker. "If they needed to get those claims, it was always a call out. . . . 'Can we deliver some more?' and they loaded us up." Homeworkers felt pressured to process all of the claims or else attach a note to the claims bucket explaining why the work was unfinished. This caused stress for one woman: "If you'd get six hours of work someday and you have two little kids at home and you only have three hours worth of TV, when are you going to get the rest of the work done? And you may have made plans. One of the advantages of being at home was the flexibility. And yet, you weren't really flexible when you had planned on getting three hours of work and all of a sudden they gave you six hours of work. . . . That really limited your flexibility."

In the assessment of some women, supervisors were unnecessarily rigid. There were instances where supervisors made adjustments for the homeworker's family responsibilities. If a sick child prevented a homeworker from processing more than an hour or two of claims, the supervisor accepted it. But on other occasions, supervisors expressed irritation with homeworkers whose children interfered with their work. At one point, WPS sent homeworkers a memo offering suggestions for the scheduling of household responsibilities around the requirements of homework. In an extreme emergency, the memo stated, women can send claims back. But this ought not to happen on a regular basis. Supervisory pressure to complete the work added to the stress experienced by homeworkers. One homeworker concluded,

> You are always meeting the deadline. You cannot live your life that way if you've got kids. I mean they get sick or they want to do things. . . . It is very stressful because you have double duty. You have to take care of the kids and try to make these deadlines. . . . If you have more than one kid, it is incredible the pressure. . . . I found that with homework I was always doing something and not doing anything for myself. . . . It would have been much simpler for me to go out during regular working hours and then come home to my kids than what I've gone through.

Conclusion

Like other homeworkers, the women at WPS welcomed the opportunity to combine wage-earning, household, and child care responsibilities. These were women who identified strongly with their family roles. Through homework, they sought to fulfill their family commitments—particularly child care—while also earning an income and retaining their ties to the labor market. For some homeworkers, the reality of homework matched their expectations. By adjusting their homework time to their children's schedules, these women found homework a satisfactory arrangement for earning an additional income. But for others, the day-to-day requirements of homework undermined their ability to meet their family responsibilities. Rather than integrating smoothly into their lives, homework led to conflict and stress.

For the women who experienced dissatisfaction with homework, the reasons lay in the relative *inflexibility* of both family members and WPS management. Children—especially young children—felt proprietary toward their primary caretakers and adapted poorly to the competing demands of homework. Nor were husbands necessarily amenable to making adjustments for homework. When the demands of homework upset the traditional division of labor in the family, tension sometimes resulted.

The rigidity of WPS's policies exacerbated the difficulties encountered by some homeworkers. The women hired by WPS anticipated a flexible work arrangement readily adaptable to their family situations. What they found instead were rigid procedures and regulations that governed their workday. The pick-up time, the rate expectancies, and the variability in workflow all made it difficult for women to plan their schedules. As a result, the homeworkers found themselves increasingly adjusting their family lives to the homework rather than the other way around.

This case study suggests that home-based employment is most likely to offer women a solution to household and child care responsibilities when (1) the workload is consistent so that women can plan their schedule from day to day; (2) the evaluation system is positive rather than punitive to diminish the stress level; (3) a good communication system is established between managers and homeworkers to allow problems in the system to be worked out; (4) spouses support the homework arrangement by increasing their contribution to housework and child care; and (5) supplemental child care services (daycare, babysitting, after-school care) are available for at least part of the day.

These recommendations are consistent with the conclusions reached by other researchers. Most of the research on home-based employment demonstrates that the major impetus for women to work at home is to care for their children.[3] But contrary to popular assumptions, homework does not, in many cases, satisfactorily substitute for supplemental child care services. McLaughlin found that the availability and quality of alternative child care services were major determinants of a woman's satisfaction with home-based work.[4] And Christensen concluded that when homeworkers "have primary responsibility for child care, they report the combination as isolating and stressful. Furthermore, they express resentment that their hours are defined in response to the demands of their family or employer."[5]

Many women prefer to stay at home when their children are young. In the absence of acceptable quality, inexpensive daycare, homework expands women's options. But as the WPS case demonstrates, the "choice" to work at home generates costs for the homeworker as well. For homework to provide women with real benefits, "flexibility" must be built into the corporate design and home setting from the start.

Notes

1. The research for this chapter was supported by the Russell Sage Foundation. I wish to express my appreciation to Cynthia Fuchs Epstein, Patricia

Gurin, Joanne Miller, and Harold Benenson for comments on an earlier version of this chapter.

2. Most of the data for this chapter was drawn from interviews with 5 current homeworkers, 21 former homeworkers, and 3 former managers involved in the clerical homework program at the Wisconsin Physicians Service Insurance Corporation (WPS). There is undoubtedly some bias in the data because the homeworkers were contacted through newspaper advertisements and recommendations from other homeworkers. Most of the homeworkers were paid for their interview time.

The interviews with homeworkers covered the following topics: work history, motivations for seeking employment as homeworkers, attitudes toward work and family, experience of working as homeworkers, friendship networks, attitudes about the homework program, and strategies for responding to their work and family situations. The interviews with former managers included questions on managerial responsibility for the homework program, advantages and disadvantages of homework from the managerial perspective, and perceptions of management-union relations.

3. Kathleen E. Christensen, *Impacts of Computer-Mediated Home-Based Work on Women and Their Families* (report prepared for the Office of Technology Assessment, 1985); U.S. Congress, House Committee on Government Operations, *Report: Home-Based Clerical Workers: Are They Victims of Exploitation?* 99th Cong., 2d sess., July 16, 1986; U.S. Congress, Office of Technology Assessment, *Automation of America's Offices* (Washington, D.C.: U.S. Government Printing Office, 1985); Margrethe H. Olson, "New Information Technology and Organizational Culture," *MIS Quarterly* 6 (December 1982):71–92; Joanne H. Pratt, "Home Teleworking: A Study of Its Pioneers," *Technological Forecasting and Social Change* 25 (1984):1–14.

4. N. M. McLaughlin, *Physical and Social Support Systems Used by Women Engaged in Home-Based Work* (Master's thesis, Cornell University, 1981).

5. Christensen, "Impacts of Computer-Mediated Home-Based Work," p. 68.

PART III

What Role Should the Government Play in White-Collar Home-Based Work?

10
The Government's Role in Regulating Home Employment

Kristine Iverson

Experience should teach us to be most on our guard to protect liberty when the government's purposes are beneficent. . . . The greatest dangers to liberty lurk in insidious encroachment by men of zeal, well-meaning, but without understanding.

—Justice Louis Brandeis

This chapter examines the issue of home employment in the broader context of political philosophy. Research on the psychology, legal implications, history, and economics of homework is, of course, essential to the making of public policy, but statistics, surveys, and observations must be evaluated by policymakers within the strictures of their individual views concerning the role of government.

The fundamental question to be addressed is whether the government is justified in using its police powers to restrict or prohibit individual endeavor, and if so, to what degree. Government has tried to "establish justice" out of the pragmatism and self-interest inherent in any society and has set limits to freedom when the result of its exercise is beyond the bounds of what a civilized society will tolerate. The challenge to policymakers in a free society is to determine where that boundary lies and to enact laws that will deter and punish excesses without inhibiting the people's activities and opportunities within it.

The Philosophical Context and Debate

The current debate over regulating home employment is illustrative of the ongoing friction between two schools of thought about the role of government in a sophisticated, complex world. The "protective" view holds that a major function of government is to promote both the physical and economic security of individuals, protecting them from potential harms and ensuring equality in the distribution of benefits. The "responsible choice" view is that government's purpose is to safeguard the right of individual initiative and equality of opportunity, giving individuals full freedom to reap the fruits of their activities as well as bear the consequences of them. A policymaker will identify with one of these views more than with the other, thus providing the philosophical milieu for his or her evaluation of the research.

We know from the existing studies that there are many pros and cons to homework.[1] Person A enjoys the freedom of movement and familiar surroundings; person B feels isolated and out of touch. Person A appreciates the flexibility in scheduling; person B prefers structure as protection against extraneous demands. Person A does not want the children in daycare and enjoys lunches and informal time with them; person B finds the children an interruption to work and appreciates time away from them in an adult setting. In some cases, person A finds that intangible benefits and reductions in commuting, clothing, child care, and other expenses offset wages and benefits that may be higher in a traditional work setting; person B is more concerned about working for the best possible wages and benefits. When all of these factors are taken together, we may conclude that some people prefer working at home and some do not.

The adequacy of the evidence on any given issue is itself a point of difference between the protective and responsible choice schools. Subscribers to the former tend to place more of the burden of proof on opponents of governmental intervention to demonstrate that such intervention is unnecessary or ill-advised. For example, although it is acknowledged that research on the effects of homework is inconclusive and primarily anecdotal, individuals who desire to work at home in the six industries where it is currently prohibited (women's and children's apparel, button and buckle manufacture, the making of gloves and mittens, sewing of handkerchiefs, embroidery, jewelry-making) still find themselves unable to do so despite legislative and administrative efforts to permit such arrangements. Those of the responsible choice school argue that these individuals are, at the least, the victims of policy double standards. On the basis of the scientific evidence, a better case can be made for outlawing cigarette smoking, a habit research clearly shows to be injurious to one's own health and to the health of others.

To what extent is government responsible for individual decisions and the ramifications of those decisions? Adherents to the protective school argue for a strong affirmative government role for several reasons. First, they maintain that government has an obligation to protect workers not only from actual violations of the Fair Labor Standards Act (FLSA) and other labor laws, but also from potential violations. Sol Chaikin, president of the International Ladies Garment Workers Union (ILGWU), testifying before the Senate Labor Subcommittee in 1984 on legislation proposing to lift the 1942 ban on industrial homework, stated:

> The AFL-CIO has called for a ban on computer homework. We cannot afford to wait for a history of exploitation . . . in that field.
>
> The legalization of homework, in conjunction with a decreased enforcement capability, invites [employers] to continue breaking the law and victimizing their employees. . . . [It] will lead not only to violations of the FLSA, but to violation of child labor laws and established sanitary and safety standards for workplaces and consumers.[2]

Sharing this assessment, Barbara F. Warden wrote on behalf of the National Consumers League: "The legislation . . . is an ill-conceived proposal that would undermine some of the fundamental protections available to the public while relegating countless numbers of workers to government-sanctioned exploitation."[3]

Her comment is noteworthy because it indicates sympathy for protective laws and regulations beyond a single constituency. Coalitions are based not only on shared benefits from a government action but also on a common view of government's regulatory limits and responsibilities.

Second, some are concerned with the impact of home labor beyond strict enforcement of the FLSA. Donald Elisburg, assistant secretary of labor for Employment Standards during the Carter administration, posed such a question in a letter to Representative Barney Frank, chairman of the House Subcommittee on Employment and Housing: "What are the economic consequences to a class of employees who aren't eligible for company-sponsored health insurance or pension plans? Will society have to assume the burden that would otherwise fall on the employer?"[4]

Additionally, the subcommittee cited other downsides to home employment that are more subjective in nature: isolation, loss of opportunities for career advancement and networking.[5] The subcommittee acknowledged the desirability of the homework option for some individuals but also recommended adequate protections, particularly clarification of the homeworker's status as an employee or independent contractor for income tax purposes.[6]

Without affirming or denying the validity of these findings, responsible choice advocates do not believe they constitute sufficient cause for government-imposed limitations on homework. A government restriction on home employment for the purpose of preventing workers' exploitation, stress, and isolation, or of guarding their career advancement and business-social networks, reflects very narrow thinking about the intelligence of homeworkers. Such government intervention assumes that homeworkers do not know their own interests. On the contrary, testimony presented to congressional committees in both the House and Senate by homeworkers indicates that they are astute and independent. Mrs. Audrey Pudvah, a homeworker from Vermont, testified before the Senate Labor Subcommittee: "I just feel that we are sophisticated enough to know our rights, and we are educated and informed enough to protect those rights from someone attempting to deny a fair wage for our work. More importantly, we have made a conscious choice not to go out to work, but to stay in the comfort of our own homes."[7]

During a hearing before the House Subcommittee on Employment and Housing, Mrs. Mary Dworjan, a homeworker from New York, testified to the many pitfalls of home employment, but she concluded her statement by saying that she and her husband were expecting their second child and that she intended to continue typing at home until their child reached school age.

> *Representative Nielson:* After you have done this work, and been through all that you have, the work arrangement, losing the benefits, et cetera, if you have 20–20 hindsight, would you do the same thing again?
>
> *Mrs. Dworjan:* Well, I hope to do it after my second child is born and after it is a bit older and I can send it to a nursery school or something, until he goes to full-time school.
>
> *Representative Nielson:* So, in spite of the fact that you earn less wages; in spite of the fact that you have to take FICA and everything else out of it, in spite of the fact that you had to work until 3 in the morning on occasion, you would still do it again?
>
> *Mrs. Dworjan:* Yes; I would be home with my child [sic], which is important to me, to take care of them.[8]

Mrs. Pudvah and Mrs. Dworjan bear out the theory that when we make choices we also accept the ramifications of those choices. Harvard University Professor Harvey Mansfield put it this way: "To choose responsibly, therefore, we take account of things that necessarily accompany our choices. In doing this we assume responsibility not only for actions we have chosen, but also for their consequences, which we have not chosen . . . Thomas Aquinas [said] that if you choose to walk in the hot sun you choose to perspire."[9]

Laws and regulations restricting home employment also provide an advantage to labor unions. Working conditions are a factor in whether workers choose a union as well as a possible issue for the union during collective bargaining. If employees are working at home, their working environment is not by itself a reason for them to support a labor organization, nor does the demand during collective bargaining for a new employee lounge or other workplace improvements matter much. Moreover, if workers are all in one place, unions have a much easier task of selling their points of view or of informing their members; and, of course, the more workers in an industry who are union members, the greater the power of the union to influence wages and benefits throughout the industry. In short, prohibiting or restricting home labor is, at the least, a convenience for organized labor. What is wrong with this? Nothing, except that government policy should not favor institutional rights, such as those of labor unions, over those of individuals, such as homeworkers.

It should be emphasized, however, that the freedom to join a union need not be sacrificed to the freedom to work at home. Mr. Elisburg points this out in his statement to the House subcommittee: "However, any idea that homeworkers are exempt from collective bargaining protections is incorrect. Such employees have the same rights as any to organize. To the extent that such employment is under exploited conditions, it is likely that unions will make every effort to sign up these workers for their own protection."[10]

The responsible choice view is that labor unions, like any free market entity, must adapt to the needs and wants of buyers. A labor union need not wait for employers to exploit homeworkers, as Mr. Elisburg suggests, before developing outreach programs to encourage the association of this growing part of the labor force with organized labor. If labor unions choose to continue old-fashioned methods of worker representation, they may also suffer continued membership losses.

Some individuals, however, such as recent immigrants or the illiterate, *are* vulnerable to exploitation, and it is for them that protected avenues of redress under law or collective bargaining contracts should be available. Such procedures are not open to individuals working in an industry where home employment is prohibited since claiming their rights would put their very livelihoods at risk.

This problem raises the issue of the degree of government regulation. Should government take the extreme position, as it has done with the six industries in which home labor is totally prohibited? Is it not possible to protect the rights of workers under the Fair Labor Standards Act (FLSA) without resorting to absolute prohibitions? Government's administration of other laws suggests that it is. For example, every community in the United States enforces its traffic laws without prohibiting driving or automobile ownership. The protective theory—which holds that government must protect individuals from all potential injury and which would be used to support either current or future prohibitions on home employment—if applied to traffic accidents, would be ludicrous. Mrs. Mary Clement, a homeworker from Wisconsin, likened the current six-industry ban on home employment to "banning football because an occasional player gets hurt."[11]

A ban on driving or football is also an absurd proposal politically. In the case of driving, every driver, automobile dealer, garage, and gas station owner in the United States would be indignant that his or her freedom was to be legislated away because some drivers violated the laws. No member of Congress who wished to be reelected would support such extreme protective action. Unfortunately for the home sewers, embroiderers, jewelry makers, and others, they do not outnumber those who benefit from the current prohibition. It is easier for politicians and bureaucrats to restrict freedom when the group affected by such a restriction is small.

Government's Role and Citizens' Control

What, then, should be the government's role in regulating home employment? First, government must enforce the FLSA's wage, hour, and child labor provisions, and take steps to ensure the adequacy of information upon which individuals can base their choices and judge the lawfulness of their employment situations. No advocate of expanding opportunities for home employment endorses a return to the sweatshop era. In a letter to Secretary of Labor William E. Brock supporting Labor Department proposals to overturn the 1942 homework prohibition in the six garment industries, Senator Orrin Hatch stated:

> I want to emphasize that it was not my intent in introducing S. 665 to absolve business from their obligations under the FLSA. Wage and hour as well as child labor provisions must be enforced. I am convinced, however, that the establishment of an effective enforcement program permits the Department of Labor to do away with prohibition as a means of FLSA enforcement in these six industries. It is reasonable to expect that requirements for homeworkers to be provided with accurate information regarding their rights under the Act would be a part of such a program.[12]

Second, government can clarify the definition of "independent contractor" as it pertains to home employment. Doing so would better delineate the responsibilities attendant to both employers and homeworkers who are parties to such a relationship as well as remove a hefty tax burden from the shoulders of homeworkers who choose to be "employees."[13]

Finally, inasmuch as the United States was built and is sustained on the concept of free choice, which is embodied in both our political and economic systems, policymakers should reevaluate the 1942 prohibition on industrial homework in light of the peoples' demand for workplace flexibility in the 1980s. The current ban remains an extreme example of government paternalism. As the late Professor G. Warren Nutter put it: "There is a big difference between meaning well and doing well."[14]

The question remains, however, of what control citizens actually have over policymakers' collective interpretation of government's responsibility, that is, what determines the propensity of government to "do well." Professor Nutter went on to state: "The one power a facile mind holds over others is its unlimited ability to rationalize. Having decided in advance what to do . . . the intellectual can always prove, to himself as well as to others, that it is the right thing to do."[15] If Nutter is correct, the basic challenge to the electorate in a representative democracy is to discern a candidate's place on the continuum between the protective and responsible choice philosophies. The research on home labor or any other issue will be assessed and utilized by a policymaker based on that position a good deal of the time—unless the individual falls exactly in the middle, a condition that should cause a voter some concern about the candidate's values or vision.

The best way of influencing a policymaker is as a political consumer in his or her state or district. Policymakers may consider themselves "intellectuals" as Nutter describes, but they are also political entrepreneurs who must every few years seek renewed licenses at the ballot box. It is this process that ultimately determines the degree to which the government's power is used to protect people per se or to protect their freedom of choice.

Notes

Though the views represented in this chapter draw on the author's experience, they are solely the responsibility of the author and should not be attributed to any official agency.

1. For the purposes of this chapter, home employment is a subset of homework; the term "homework" includes both independent contractors and entrepreneurs who work from their homes as well as employees who perform tasks for an employer for compensation. The distinction is often fuzzy, and some home employees may be improperly classified as independent contractors.

2. Senate Committee on Labor and Human Resources, *Hearing: Amending the Fair Labor Standards Act to Include Industrial Homework*, 98th Cong., 2d sess., February 9, 1984, pp. 102, 105.

3. Ibid., p. 141.

4. House Committee on Government Operations, *Hearing: Pros and Cons of Home-Based Clerical Work,* 99th Cong., 2d sess., February 26, 1986, p. 4.

5. House Committee on Government Operations, *Report: Home-Based Clerical Workers: Are They Victims of Exploitation?* 99th Cong., 2d sess., July 16, 1986, p. 7.

6. Ibid., pp. 8–9.

7. Senate Labor and Human Resources Committee, *Hearing,* p. 28.

8. House Government Operations Committee, *Hearing,* pp. 47–48.

9. Harvey C. Mansfield, Jr., "Choice and Consent in the American Experiment," *The Intercollegiate Review* 22 (Spring 1987):20.

10. House Government Operations Committee, *Hearing,* p. 7.

11. Senate Labor and Human Resources Committee, *Hearing,* p. 26.

12. Orrin G. Hatch, unpublished letter to William E. Brock, October 20, 1986.

13. Several of the chapters in this volume (see especially the chapter by Joy Simonson) provide a more complete discussion of the independent contractor/employee issue.

14. G. Warren Nutter, "For a Free Economy: The Need for Our Time," in Jane Couch Nutter, ed., *Political Economy and Freedom* (Indianapolis: Liberty Press, 1983), p. 32.

15. Ibid., p. 33.

11
Protection of Clerical Homeworkers: From What, by Whom?

Joy R. Simonson

With the increasing number of home-based clerical workers, it is important to consider whether they are in need of the same kinds of protection that our society provides for office-based workers. Over the past 50 years the United States has developed an extensive network of protective or supportive legislation and employment benefits for employees:

- *The Fair Labor Standards Act (FLSA),* administered by the U.S. Department of Labor, governs the payment of minimum wages, requires overtime wages for work beyond specified hours, and prohibits or limits the employment of minors.
- *The National Labor Relations Act (NLRA),* administered by the Labor Department, gives workers the right to organize for purposes of collective bargaining and prohibits unfair labor practices by employers or unions.
- *The Occupational Safety and Health Act (OSHA),* administered by the Labor Department, protects workers against some of the illness and injury hazards in the workplace.
- *Title VII of the Civil Rights Act of 1964,* administered by the Equal Employment Opportunity Commission (EEOC), prohibits discrimination in employment on the basis of race, sex, religion, or national origin. Section 504 of the Rehabilitation Act of 1973 and the Age Discrimination in Employment Act (ADEA) similarly prohibit discrimination on grounds of handicap and age.
- *The Equal Pay Act (EPA),* administered by EEOC, requires equal pay for work of substantially equal value performed in the same establishment.

- *The Social Security Act,* which includes Medicare benefits, is a contributory program administered by the Social Security Administration of the Department of Health and Human Services.
- *The Employment Retirement Income Security Act (ERISA),* administered by the Labor Department and the Internal Revenue Service, regulates many provisions in private pension programs.
- *Unemployment insurance* is an employer-funded federal-state program to provide income during relatively short periods of unemployment.
- *Workers' compensation* for injuries on the job is the subject of state legislation.

In addition, there are various programs for workers in specific industries such as mining and railroads and for certain categories such as employees of federal contractors. Such contractors are subject to Executive Order 11246 that requires employers to undertake affirmative action to achieve an equitable and representative workforce.

Following a public hearing and additional research by its Employment and Housing Subcommittee, the House Committee on Government Operations issued a report, *Home-Based Clerical Workers: Are They Victims of Exploitation?* on July 16, 1986 (hereafter, the committee report). It concluded that "All home-based workers are entitled to full protection of the laws which cover on-site workers." But enforcement of such laws is all too often inadequate or absent.

Homeworkers as Contractors or Employees

Problems of enforcement that result from the very nature of home-based work, with individual workers scattered over wide areas, are greatly exacerbated, according to the committee report, by confusion over the status of such workers as "employees" or as "independent contractors." There are, of course, bona fide entrepreneurs or small businesses that provide clerical services from offices located in private homes. Such operations are properly classified as "independent contractors" subject to laws affecting other employers.

But many homeworkers who consider themselves to be independent contractors are, through the nature of their relationship to an employer, actually employees. Clearly, an office employee who transfers to home-based work for the same employer does not thereby become an independent contractor. Likewise, workers hired to perform work at home are not contractors simply because they never appear at the employer's worksite. Nor does payment on a piecework basis rather than through hourly wages or weekly salaries determine a worker's status.

The definition of "employee" for the purpose of FLSA coverage has been the subject of frequent litigation. According to the Employment Standards Administration of the Labor Department, in a letter to Representative Barney Frank, chairman of the subcommittee:

> The Supreme Court has said that there is "no definition that solves all problems as to the limitations of the employer-employee relationship" under FLSA; it has also ruled that the determination of the relation cannot be based on "isolated factors" or upon a single characteristic or "technical concepts," but depends "upon the circumstances of the whole activity" including the underlying "economic reality." See *Rutherford Food Corp v. McComb,* 331 U.S. 722 and *United States v. Silk,* 331 U.S. 704. The factors which the Supreme Court has considered significant although no single one is regarded as controlling are: (1) the extent to which the services in question are an integral part of the employer's business; (2) the permanency of the relationship; (3) the amount of the alleged contractor's investment in facilities and equipment; (4) the nature and degree of control by the principal; (5) the alleged contractor's opportunities for profit and loss; and (6) the amount of initiative, judgement, or foresight in open market competition with others required for the success of the claimed independent enterprises. Generally, the Department has found that homeworkers, when measured against the foregoing criteria, do not meet the definition of "independent contractor." (Meisinger 1986)

The Internal Revenue Service (IRS) is concerned with the classification of workers because it affects the payment and collection of Federal Insurance Contributions Act (FICA) taxes that finance social security benefits, of federal unemployment taxes, and the withholding of income taxes. IRS operates under the common law definition of employee. In a Technical Advice Memorandum, IRS stated that

> for purposes of the FICA, the term "employee" means any individual . . . who performs services for remuneration for any person as a home worker performing work, according to specifications furnished by the person for whom the services are performed, on materials or goods furnished by such person which are required to be returned to such person or a person designated by him. This provision applies if the contract of services contemplates that substantially all of such services are to be performed personally by such individual; except that an individual shall not be included in the term "employee" under this provision if such individual has a substantial investment in facilities used in connection with the performance of such services (other than in facilities for transportation). (IRS National Office, 1984)

In the case that was the subject of this memorandum, the IRS determined that transcribers preparing transcripts from court reporters' recordings cannot be considered independent contractors even though they have invested $3,000 or more in equipment.

From a worker's standpoint, being classified as a contractor has both advantages and disadvantages. Coverage by protective federal or state laws—most importantly the FLSA, pension, and unemployment insurance coverage—is not available. Concerning taxes, a contractor has no income taxes withheld and no FICA tax deducted. On the other hand, a contractor is required to pay the Self-Employment Contributions Act (SECA) tax. Until 1990 this tax is lower than the combined employer-employee FICA payments but larger than the employee's share (13.02 percent vs. 7.51 percent in 1986). Contrary to widespread opinion, the rules governing income tax deductions for use of home–office space are not significantly different for contractors and employees.

Advantages for a homeworker of being *properly* classified as an independent contractor are the control over one's work schedule on an hourly, weekly, or yearly basis, and over other aspects of employment that characterize a business owner, whether based at home or elsewhere.

For an employer there are clearcut financial advantages to treating a homeworker as a contractor rather than an employee. An employer has no obligations to pay FICA or unemployment taxes, to withhold income taxes, to maintain the wage and hour records required by FLSA, or to be concerned with health and safety provisions or workers compensation and unemployment claims. Nor is an employer subject to equal pay, antidiscrimination, equitable pension, and other protective laws in relation to bona fide contractors. "With regard to the Internal Revenue Service's policy and enforcement program, we can assure you that all available resources are applied in enforcing the Code and regulations. We share your concern that in many situations, workers are not being properly classified for federal employment tax purposes" (Manfreda, 1986).

However, even when the IRS finds that an employer has improperly treated workers as nonemployees, Section 530 of the Revenue Act of 1978, as amended in 1982, permits continuation of such treatment if the employer had a "reasonable basis" for that treatment. Congress directed that "reasonable basis" be liberally defined, including several "safe havens" and a catch-all provision. (The 1986 Tax Reform Act exempted from Section 530 technical service workers such as computer programmers, systems analysts, and engineers.) An employer who meets the test of Section 530 is relieved of obligations to pay employment taxes past, present, and future for both current and subsequently hired workers.

Such workers, although treated for employment tax purposes like contractors, maintain their employee status for other purposes. They are required to pay only the employee share of the FICA tax, but are entitled to full social security benefits even though no employer tax has been paid on their wages. The Social Security Administration informed the House Government Operations Committee that until 1990 the social security trust funds' revenue losses are made up from federal general revenues (McSteen, 1986). Based on reports made by the IRS, the Social Security Administration deems the problem to be too small to warrant special administrative procedures to account separately for workers under Section 530 (Hardy, 1986).

Home-based workers, even if under Section 530, are eligible for participation in their employers' pension plans under ERISA if they work at least 1,000 hours a year. The IRS examines qualified pension plans for coverage through a pension examination program. Also, when tax audits reveal misclassification of employees as contractors, that information is referred to the pension section. No statistics are available concerning the number of cases of improper exclusion of home-based workers from qualified pension plans.

The IRS apparently does not routinely notify homeworkers who are found to have been misclassified as contractors when Section 530 permits their continued tax treatment on a contractor basis. Therefore, such employees may be unaware of their eligibility for pensions and unemployment insurance and that they need pay only the employee share of the FICA tax. The committee report recommended that the IRS notify such employees that they have been misclassified as independent contractors and inform them of the implications of such findings.

The committee also recommended that the IRS expedite a proposed three-year study of the effect of Section 530 on employers, workers, and the government, particularly because Section 530 affects more than home-based workers and certainly other than clerical workers.

Homeworkers and the Minimum Wage and Hours Law

Enforcement of the wage and hour law for homeworkers—even apart from the question of their classification as employees—presents special difficulties for the Employment Standards Administration (ESA). In a May 9, 1986, letter to Representative Barney Frank, the Deputy Undersecretary of Labor stated: "In 1981, the Department began a concentrated enforcement program focused on employers of homeworkers. . . . the Department has maintained an active homeworker enforcement

Table 11.1
FLSA Enforcement of Clerical Homework, FY 83-86

	Total Homework Investigations	Homework Investigations with Clerical Homeworkers	Clerical Homework Inv. with Monetary Violations	Clerical Homework Inv. with Minimum Wage Violations	Clerical Homework Inv. with Overtime Violations
FY 83	313	35 (11%)	16 (46%)	5 (14%)	13 (37%)
FY 84	377	27 (7%)	8 (30%)	4 (15%)	4 (15%)
FY 85	335	57 (17%)	35 (61%)	12 (21%)	30 (36%)
FY 86	364	45 (12%)	21 (47%)	3 (7%)	20 (44%)
TOTALS	1,389	164 (12%)	80 (49%)	24 (15%)	67 (41%)

Source: U.S. Congress, House Committee on Government Operations, Report: Home-Based Clerical Workers: Are They Victims of Exploitation? 99th Cong., 2d sess., July 16, 1986.

program in . . . industries, including those involving home-based clerical work. For the fiscal years 1983–1985, 11% of all homework investigations involved clerical workers." The ESA forwarded the statistical data as presented in Table 11.1. Additionally, the ESA reported that for the same period homework investigations represented one-half percent (0.5 percent) and clerical homework investigations totalled 0.06 percent of the total workload.

The ESA described to the committee what it termed "active efforts" to seek out home-based clerical workers, identify firms that employ them, and enhance enforcement. Nevertheless, the committee report criticized the program and recommended that the ESA "markedly improve its enforcement" of the program. In reply, the Labor Department said that it had investigated all complaints received involving homework and

> actively sought, through a variety of information sources . . . to make sure that homework activity, wherever it occurs, is in compliance with the FLSA. . . . In the period from October 1, 1981, through July 31, 1986, a total of 1,530 investigations of employers utilizing homeworkers were conducted, as compared with only approximately 75 to 80 such investigations during the previous six-year period. This increase, of almost 2,300 percent, in the number of homework investigations conducted annually, is tangible proof of the Department's resolve to ensure that employees working in their homes receive the same FLSA protections as those working at their employers' places of business. (Brock, 1986)

However, of the 164 clerical homework investigations made in FY 1983 to 1986, 47 percent were initiated by complaint, leaving only 87 investigations based on routine or special outreach efforts in four years.

Homeworkers are required to maintain Homework Handbooks issued by the ESA in which they are to record detailed information about the work they perform, time worked, rate of pay, wages paid, and so forth. Employers are to keep records of the information maintained by their homeworkers. This recordkeeping may be difficult for a mother of young children who must snatch odd hours—minutes, even—to work at her typewriter or computer. The committee learned that home-based workers may have to work very late or long hours to meet the demands of both employers and families. They may have to adapt to the availability of employers' computer time. Some clerical workers have found that their "flexible" homework situation adds up to more hours and more pressure than their previous on-site jobs.

A special problem in computing the hourly wage (and thus both total income and compliance with FLSA) for clerical homeworkers is the fact that they are usually paid on a piecework basis, in contrast to the weekly or monthly salary basis of most on-site workers. In assessing compliance for industrial homeworkers, ESA normally verifies the time required to complete a product and compares it to the piece-rate paid. In measuring their time and output, however, clerical homeworkers tend to omit the time spent in setting up, correcting, printing, and collating, although such essential tasks obviously are part of an office worker's regular day. Nor can they include the time spent by office workers on personal business and interaction with fellow workers.

Homeworkers frequently must buy their own equipment or rent it from the employer (a committee witness reported paying $32.50 every two weeks for her typewriter), as well as pay for their own telephone and other utilities. Such expenses reduce the net hourly earnings (possibly below the statutory minimum wage, although this would not be apparent from the Homework Handbook) and may easily outweigh the savings on commuting, clothes, and lunches that are considered to be advantages of home-based work. There is no evidence that the Department of Labor considers these factors in its compliance investigations involving home-based clerical workers.

There is also no information about possible child labor violations by homeworkers, although it is quite likely that they use their minor children to help them on computers or in such tasks as assembling and collating.

Other major factors affecting the earnings of home-based workers are employer-provided benefits: vacation, sick, and emergency or administrative leave; training; health, disability, and life insurance; and other benefits occasionally offered on so-called cafeteria plans, such as child care, legal services, and tuition aid. Benefits may be offered on the initiative of an employer or negotiated with unions. Although relatively few in-office clerical workers are organized, almost no home-based clericals belong to unions. Benefit packages add up to as much as 30 percent or more of salary costs, so that employers have a major inducement to utilize homeworkers who do not receive such benefits either because (1) they are not under union contracts; (2) they are piece-rate and not hourly or salary workers; (3) they are part-time workers and thus ineligible for benefits; (4) the accepted practice is not to award any benefits to home-based employees; or (5) they are considered (correctly or not) to be independent contractors.

Irregularity and uncertainty about the flow of work can also reduce homeworkers' earnings and are a serious problem for them, especially for women supporting their families.

For all these reasons, there is a consensus that, although exact comparisons are difficult, clerical homeworkers (who are not entrepreneurs) earn considerably less than their office counterparts. For example, Robert E. Kraut and Patricia Grambsch (1988) found that such workers are almost twice as likely to live in households below the poverty line as are conventional workers. The Office of Technology Assessment report, *Automation of America's Offices* (1985) states that: "clerical home workers almost always earn less than their peers in the office, even within the same firm. Sometimes the pay rate is technically the same, but those at home are shifted to part-time or piece-rates without fringe benefits. They usually work fewer hours than those in offices, either because work is not regularly available, because of the home-related duties, or by choice."

Employment Discrimination

Questions of employment discrimination in violation of federal or state laws are rarely if ever raised, although the EEOC acknowledged that home-based employees are protected by Title VII and the Equal Pay Act (EEOC, 1987). There is no information about allegations of discrimination being filed by homeworkers, would-be homeworkers, or in-office workers who believe that they are disadvantaged by their employer's selection of home-based employees.

Discrimination against homeworkers is likely to extend beyond hiring. It may take the form of excluding them from the opportunities available to in-office workers for upward mobility through training, details to other jobs, and both formal and informal access to promotions.

The committee report recommended that the Equal Employment Opportunity Commission ensure that employers include homeworkers on the quarterly EEO-1 report that they must file. These reports serve as an indicator of potential discrimination on grounds of race, sex, or national origin. The EEOC replied that it believes " . . . that information currently required will effectively disclose situations which merit investigation" (EEOC, 1987).

Although not as hazardous as most industrial employment, clerical work has potential dangers, such as faulty electric wiring, ergonomic problems, and possible hazards of video display terminals. The jurisdiction of OSHA extends to home workplaces, but inspections are quite unlikely unless complaints are made. Presumably it would be only a disgruntled employee who would make such a complaint.

Compensation for workplace injuries is governed by state laws, but clearly there are complex questions when accidents occur in the home. Proof of an employer's responsibility is likely to be much more difficult.

Conclusion

In considering policy recommendations—whether legislative, administrative, or other—one must first decide whether home-based clerical work, with its numerous pluses and minuses, should be encouraged, discouraged, or ignored.

The House Committee on Government Operations weighed the testimony of union opponents, of homeworkers reporting benefits and drawbacks, and of experts. It concluded that: "The potential and even the known dangers of exploitation of the vulnerable group of clerical homeworkers are not sufficient to justify a total ban on home office work. The mixed blessing which homework provides for thousands of women at some stages of their lives is a legitimate option, but one which requires protection through legislation, enforcement programs and enlightened employer attitudes and practices."

The problems associated with clerical homework should not be ignored. Nor should government policies *advocate* such work as a desirable option. Rather, they should provide an environment in which individuals can make unforced and well-informed choices. The committee report stated: "A critical shortage of affordable, accessible, quality childcare services is forcing many women into home-based work, many aspects of which are unsatisfactory and inequitable. However, home-based work is not an ideal solution to the dual problem of childcare and need for income. Lack of other forms of supportive service such as daycare for infirm elderly or invalids increases the pressure on women to accept homework as a 'better than nothing' choice."

Perhaps the development of home-based careers should now lead to a new basis for legal protection against employment discrimination: location of work. Just as discrimination on grounds of race, sex, religion, national origin, age, and handicap is prohibited, so should discrimination against workers because of where they work be prohibited. The broad definition of what constitutes employment discrimination under Title VII could be applied so that homeworkers would not be second-class citizens in matters such as training, promotion, leave, and other benefits.

There is an urgent need for information concerning the pros and cons of home-based work, the legal rights and obligations, the financial, practical, and even emotional/psychological aspects of such employment. The Women's Bureau of the Department of Labor could stimulate and coordinate such an information campaign. Other arms of the Labor Department, including the Employment Standards Administration, the state employment services, labor unions, and women's and employers' organizations should all participate in such efforts. The purpose would be to ensure that both current and potential homeworkers are apprised of all possible factors affecting home-based employment so that they receive any benefits or protections to which they are entitled, avoid exploitation, and make informed and appropriate decisions about such a work arrangement. This could be considered a homeworker's right-to-know, analogous to an industrial worker's statutory right to know about occupational hazards.

Employers have an interest in dissemination of such information in order to reduce unfair competition by employers who avoid payment of benefits, minimum wages, and so forth to improperly classified or protected homeworkers.

Finally, it is clear that better enforcement of existing laws that protect home-based as well as in-office workers is urgently required. It is unrealistic to expect that government agencies will—or should—ever investigate conditions in every home where paid employment occurs. However, if homeworkers are well informed about their legal rights, we can expect that there will be complaints filed with government offices and pressure on employers to treat home-based employees more equitably. Government agencies charged with enforcing minimum wage and hour, tax, pension, social security, safety, antidiscrimination, unemployment insurance, and workers' compensation laws must be alert to the special problems of home-based workers and devise methods of extending their protective umbrella to those who perform clerical work in their homes equally with those who work in commercial establishments.

References

Brock, William E., secretary of labor. Letter to Representative Barney Frank, attachment, October 28, 1986.

Equal Employment Opportunity Commission. Letter to Representative Frank, January 5, 1987.

Hardy, Dorcas R., commissioner, Social Security Administration. Letter to Representative Barney Frank, November 16, 1986.

Internal Revenue Service National Office. *Technical Advice Memorandum 8451004*, August 1, 1984.

Kraut, Robert E., and Patricia Grambsch. "Home-Based White-Collar Employment: Lessons from the 1980 Census," *Social Forces* 66 (1988):410–426.

Manfreda, Richard A., chief, Individual Income Tax Branch, IRS. Letter to Representative Barney Frank, April 15, 1986.

McSteen, Martha A., acting commissioner, Social Security Administration. Letter to Representative Barney Frank, June 13, 1986.

Meisinger, Susan, deputy undersecretary for Employment Standards. Letter to Representative Barney Frank, May 9, 1986.

U.S. Congress, House Committee on Government Operations. *Report: Home-Based Clerical Workers: Are They Victims of Exploitation?* 99th Cong., 2d sess., July 16, 1986.

U.S. Congress, Office of Technology Assessment. *Automation of America's Offices.* Washington, D.C.: U.S. Government Printing Office, 1985.

12
Blue-Collar, White-Collar: Homeworker Problems

Dennis Chamot

After more than four decades of government bans on several forms of industrial homework, a major effort has been under way during recent years to remove all restrictions on employees working at home. Unfortunately, the push may be coming about for all the wrong reasons.

Conservative ideologues seem to believe that "a woman's place is in the home." On the other hand, some businesses recognize the enormous economic advantages that could accrue if a substantial part of their current costs could be shifted to the employee, including rent, health and retirement benefits, vacation and holiday pay, even equipment purchase and operating costs. More subtle cost-shifting also occurs. For example, paying homeworkers by the piece eliminates pay for set-up time, rework and rest breaks.

There is also an element of cynical manipulation. The labor force participation rate for women has been increasing rapidly. Some of this has resulted from economic pressures since 1970—a period of very strong inflation, substantial job loss among men and, hence, the necessity for wives to work, and the increase in the number of single women and female-headed households leading to an increasing need among women with small children to support themselves and their families. Unfortunately, under the Reagan administration, the debate has focused on reducing government restrictions and on encouraging women to work at home and care for their children at the same time (thus requiring them to try to do two jobs at once, to the possible detriment of both). Rather, working mothers should demand, and government officials should concentrate on developing, truly acceptable alternatives such as decent, affordable daycare and improvements in social and medical services for the elderly or infirm. Only then would the decision to work at home truly be based on free choice.

Figure 12.1
Homeworker Classification Scheme

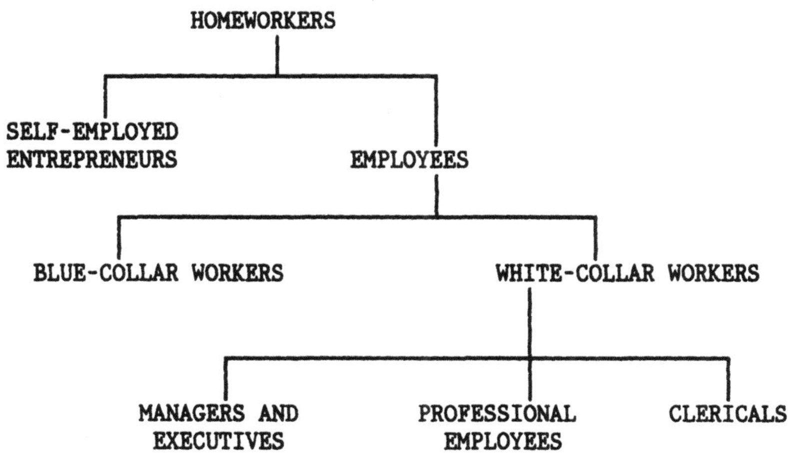

Classification of Homeworkers

All homeworkers are not alike, just as all homework is not the same. I find it useful first to divide the potential home workforce into two groups. This major division places blue-collar, manufacturing workers in one group, and white-collar and service workers in the other (see Figure 12.1). The latter group is then further subdivided into managers and executives, professional employees, and clericals (for the purposes of this discussion, clericals are defined as all nonsales white-collar workers who are not in the other categories).

This scheme is a qualitative one for the purpose of policy analysis and is not dependent upon the number of people in each category. It is necessary because the potential for abuse, and actual experiences, are considerably different for each group.

This discussion, and indeed, the whole question of restricting homework, applies only to *employees*. This point is important because the public debate in the media sometimes glosses over this distinction, causing unnecessary concern among self-employed people. Those who are properly described as self-employed are not covered by the Fair Labor Standards Act (FLSA), and thus are not subject to either a ban on a particular kind of homework, nor to various recordkeeping requirements that deal with minimum wage and overtime provisions. Although a major problem today is the improper classification of many homeworkers as independent contractors rather than employees, in this essay I will assume that employees are correctly designated.

Referring back to the classification scheme, the only employees covered by the regulations against homework issued in the 1940s were blue-collar workers. They were people who worked with their hands in seven light industries: knitted outerwear, women's apparel, jewelry-making, gloves and mittens manufacturing, buttons and buckles fabrication, handkerchief sewing, and embroidery.

These were industries that, *at the time*, were found to have the most frequent and serious abuses. Previous experience with attempts at regulation over many years, including extensive efforts at the state level, failed to control the problems that existed.

In fact, the passage of the FLSA, with its minimum wage and overtime provisions and its prohibition of the use of child labor, made the difficulties of regulating homework even clearer. Ruth Crawford, of the U.S. Department of Labor, noted in 1944 that

> (t)he basic difficulty . . . was the fact that homeworkers were under compulsion to falsify the records, for if they could not earn the minimum wage they would lose their employment. What resulted was a system of record keeping by which outward conformity was obtained, primarily for the manufacturer's protection. The workers were told how many hours should be required for the work and this was shown on the records kept. . . . Obviously, there was no way of knowing how many persons did the work for which a single individual was paid, for what was done in the privacy of the home could be only a matter of conjecture. This uncertainty frequently led to a violation not only of the Fair Labor Standards Act, including its child labor provisions, but also of the Social Security Act, for no records existed for many who were entitled to benefits under the latter statute.[1]

Violations of employee protection laws continue up to the present day. Former Labor Secretary Ray Donovan helped to demonstrate the existence of sweatshops in well-publicized raids in New York City in 1981.[2] Furthermore, Department of Labor investigations of homeworkers both in restricted and unrestricted industries revealed many violations. Even so, the department went ahead and removed the ban on home knitting in 1981, eventually establishing a system of certification instead.

The Department of Labor has proposed removing the restrictions in the remaining six industries, although this is currently under challenge. Many would argue that there is continued violation of the law in home knitting. For example, the AFL-CIO recently noted that

> (t)he Department of Labor's own finding that over three-quarters of the certified knitted outerwear employers are in violation of the Fair Labor Standards Act is a forceful condemnation of its 1981 decision. Record-

> keeping violations are not minor infractions, they are the very substance of homework wage and hour compliance. . . . There are fewer than 500 compliance officers to enforce all the elements of the Fair Labor Standards Act in all of the 50 states. To pretend that this little band of investigators can protect the rights of thousands of new homeworkers in six newly deregulated industries does not reflect any great respect for the intelligence of the American people.[3]

All of the above seeks to demonstrate, first, that the historical experience with industrial homework indicates that homeworkers have been seriously mistreated, and second, regulation of homework is exceedingly difficult and has never been fully successful.

What does all this mean for white-collar employees who may work at home? This is the key to understanding the current debate. As has been noted by many observers, only seven industries have been subject to homework bans, and similar kinds of work were permitted to be performed at home. Yet there was neither a strong effort to rescind these bans, nor a loud call to expand them to other kinds of work. Only in recent years, with the possibility of greatly expanding the number of *white-collar* homeworkers, has there been active and widespread concern on both sides.

Do White-Collar Workers Need Protection?

Recent technological advances centered around the development of inexpensive yet powerful personal computers, associated software, and the easy availability of electronic communications systems have made feasible a mass movement of office work to other locations, including homes. The economic advantages to employers of such a shift are enormous. There are also advantages to some employees (although the benefits may be enjoyed by people other than those who suffer the problems), thus the pressure for greatly expanding the pool of homeworkers is increasing.

Many of the elements that existed in the past, which contributed toward the potential for exploitation of homeworkers, are present today in the area of electronic homework: wide availability of worker-owned equipment; a large labor force with the requisite skills; highly competitive product and labor markets; and the difficulty facing many homeworkers to organize or achieve control over their work.

Do white-collar employees need the same kinds of protections offered to button and handkerchief manufacturers? To answer that question, we have to return to my classification scheme and look at each group separately.

For the most part, the current policy debate does not deal with managers and executives, and the reasons for that are instructive. Most managers work at home as a matter of personal convenience. They have offices at regular workplaces, they usually have good salaries and benefits, they have a great deal of control over the work itself, which, indeed, is what permits them to arrange their work in such a way as to take some home. Many managers and executives have routinely brought work home with them for various reasons. The availability of personal computers simply places a new tool into a well-established pattern.

Professional employees present a more complex problem. Many kinds of professional employees are already using computer systems in their work, for example, engineers, journalists, accountants. As the price of personal computers has dropped, more and more professionals began using them for such routine activities as typing and file management, in addition to job-specific applications. It is probably safe to say that in the foreseeable future, most professional employees will find themselves doing their work on computer terminals, and, just as with managers and executives, some professionals may welcome the flexibility of being able to do some of their work at home. Completely voluntary work of this nature, done for no other reason than personal convenience, should not present a problem. However, the *availability* of homework may become the *necessity* for doing homework, as managers increase part of the work (case loads for social workers, for example), expecting many of the administrative tasks to be done at home.

Clerical homeworkers present the most clearcut case, bearing many similarities to industrial homeworkers, both in the routine nature of the work and the lack of control over many aspects of the job. Even though the number of full-time electronic clerical homeworkers is still small, abuses have already surfaced.[4]

> For the past five years, (Ann) Blackwell has been working at home . . . as a participant in what Blue Cross calls its "cottage keyers" program. Blackwell puts in an average of 50 hours a week at the terminal, mostly while her two children, aged 7 and 13, are at school; but when she is behind quota she works at night as well. She is paid 16 cents per claim, each of which requires about 90 seconds to process. By completing about 2,000 claims a week (the company requires a minimum of 1,200), she nets about $100—after deductions for taxes and equipment rental charges paid to Blue Cross. That is for a 50-hour week, with no paid vacation time, no paid sick leave, and no fringe benefits.[5]

It is my understanding that at the time, at least, all of the "cottage keyers" were spouses of full-time Blue Cross employees, and therefore were covered by the spouses' medical insurance.

More recently, graphic testimony was presented to a hearing of the Employment and Housing Subcommittee of the House Committee on Government Operations by a woman who typed at home. After listing some of the advantages she saw with home-based work—no extra clothing expense, no commuting time or expenses, and flexible hours—she went on to describe the disadvantages:

> You never see anybody except your family . . . nobody takes you very seriously. They don't seem to think you are really working . . . there are no benefits, no sick pay, insurance, pension, etc. . . . I believe you put in more hours than at an outside job . . . physically, it is very taxing. There are many back, neck, and shoulder problems . . . there is no time to slow down. . . . In an office environment, if you are finishing a project, or would just like to leave something off to begin fresh in the morning, you just slow down a bit and take your time. . . . At home, you are always under pressure . . . if you don't type, you are just not paid for it. There is absolutely no pay for the time you have to collate, staple, count, put together all your work you have typed, or for the time you spend making out your tally sheets or inventory forms.[6]

In addition, the witness indicated that the company for which she typed regarded her as an independent contractor, which meant that she was responsible for the full social security contribution, relieving the company of the requirement to contribute to unemployment insurance funds. Questioning of the witness by Representative Barney Frank, the subcommittee chairman, revealed that her classification as a self-employed contractor was probably erroneous.[7]

Anecdotes do not necessarily prove that exploitation among clerical homeworkers is widespread, but problems have already arisen that seem more predominant in this group than among other white-collar workers. Steven S. Kawakami, in a review of the literature on electronic homework and in a survey of companies and government agencies, has noted that

> (t)he traditional differentiation between clerical workers and managers/professionals in conventional offices is apparently being repeated in home-based teleworking projects. Managerial and professional homeworkers tend to be highly paid, possess high status, enjoy payment on a salaried basis and substantially all fringe benefits, are subjected to a low to moderate amount of supervision, and are usually provided with all necessary equipment and materials by employers. By comparison, the clerical homeworkers studied here receive considerably lower pay and less status, are paid on an hourly or incentive basis, sometimes lack certain insurance benefits, may be supervised much more closely (including through on-

line computer monitoring), and sometimes are required to pay for some or all of their own equipment and work materials.[8]

What Remedial Steps Are Necessary?

Based upon the extensive documentation of past exploitation of industrial homeworkers, the inability of government agencies at all levels to regulate homework, the evidence for continued problems, including the experiences of clerical workers and electronic homeworkers, the need for government intervention is clear. What form the intervention should take may not be as obvious.

The AFL-CIO has taken the position that the greater good is served by banning all forms of homework where exploitation is a serious problem. It opposed the lifting of the ban on home knitting and is resisting the current proposal to lift the bans in the other six industrial areas. In addition, the 15th Constitutional Convention of the AFL-CIO, held in October 1983, passed a resolution calling for a ban on computer homework.[9] Again, it should be noted that the Fair Labor Standards Act, under which the bans are instituted, contains exemptions for executive, administrative, and professional employees, so that a ban on white-collar homework would primarily affect only clerical workers.

As noted earlier, the U.S. Department of Labor is experimenting with a certification system in the banned industrial homework categories. Under existing human resources and budgetary constraints, this effort is doomed to failure, and certainly could not be expanded to other areas.

If a ban on electronic homework is not feasible at this time, then it would seem that a combination of approaches is necessary to protect the large number of clerical and other white-collar workers who work at home now, or will be homeworkers in the future. In the first place, it is essential to provide conditions under which the decision to work at home is truly one of free choice. An extensive system of daycare facilities must be established around the country. This will probably require, at the least, federal incentives and coordination, and should involve state governments and local agencies. Similarly, much study will have to be given to the needs of the handicapped and of people who care for infirm relatives, with a goal of providing as many outside support programs as possible so that, again, the decision to work at home is not made on the basis of a lack of viable alternatives.

Second, federal legislation is needed to ensure that homeworkers receive no less in pay and benefits than office workers doing comparable work. A determined effort must be made by the Department of Labor to eliminate as much as feasible the misuse of the independent contractor designation.

Third, detailed records of each individual employee's work at home are essential if abuses are to be minimized. This necessity might require greater sharing of data among relevant government agencies. In addition, penalties for employer infractions need to be strengthened substantially.

Assistance must be given to homeworkers, themselves, so that they may be better able to avoid difficulties. For example, annual income tax packages might include a special message for homeworkers, with a worksheet or form to determine if they are likely to be employees rather than self-employed, and another worksheet to calculate if the work time actually spent on all aspects of the job is compensated, at least at the minimum wage. These worksheets should be compared with employer reports, and remedial action then taken by the Labor Department.

Where a union contract exists, or in situations where office workers are attempting to organize, homeworkers must be included in units of office workers doing similar work. This inclusion will ensure that homeworkers receive the same treatment as their office counterparts and would probably make it easier for homeworkers to reenter the office environment if and when they choose to do so.

Recent developments require that these recommendations be expanded to include some protection from unfair competition from overseas workers. I noted earlier that advances in computers and telecommunications permit office work to be done at home. In fact, electronic work becomes completely independent of geography. Not only can work be shifted from office locations to homes, but it can, in fact, be performed anywhere in the world where computers and either telephone lines or communications satellites are available. Even the latter are not required if a slight delay can be tolerated because, at the worst, all one need do is mail a few disks or tapes to transfer the results of the work to an office in another country.

Many countries seek to protect domestic industries and their employees. For example, Canada's 1980 Banks and Bank Revision Act requires that processing both original documents and books of entry must be done in Canada. Brazil prevents foreign companies from providing technical services unless there are no Brazilian firms able to do so.[10]

At the present time, competition from other countries in data entry and other kinds of clerical work is based almost entirely on differences in wage rates. It is impossible for U.S. typists, for example, to compete with mainland Chinese keyers who are paid about US$5 a *day*. If knowledge of English is important, a company can use workers in Jamaica, for example, who are paid about US$50 a week, just over a third of the U.S. minimum wage for a 40-hour week, which itself is much less than most skilled typists earn.

As a society, we cannot afford to have our manufacturing employment shrink through an increase in imports and, at the same time, permit unrestrained entry of clerical and other white-collar work done overseas. We cannot have a society of only producers and no consumers. Maintaining employment must be considered just as important, from a national interest point of view, as reducing labor costs to be more "competitive."

Old arguments about relative competitive advantages between nations must be cast aside when faced with the ability to almost instantaneously shift the location of work. U.S. import restrictions may need to be placed on clerical and computer work done overseas for domestic employers.

Unrestrained competition is what brought on the sweatshop system so many decades ago. Regulation is needed today, both of domestic homework and unfair international competition, to ensure that large numbers of our citizens who need assistance are able to work with dignity.

Notes

1. Ruth Crawford, "Development and Control of Industrial Homework," *Monthly Labor Review* (June 1944):1153.
2. U.S. Department of Labor, Employment Standards Administration, Press release USDL-81-225, May 4, 1981.
3. Statement of the AFL-CIO before the Subcommittee on Labor Standards, House Committee on Education and Labor, September 23, 1986.
4. U.S. Congress, Office of Technology Assessment, *Automation of America's Offices* (Washington, D.C.: U.S. Government Printing Office, 1985).
5. *The Nation,* April 2, 1983, p. 390.
6. Hearing testimony of Mary Dworjan, Employment and Housing Subcommittee, House Committee on Government Operations, February 26, 1986.
7. Ibid.
8. Steven S. Kawakami, "Electronic Homework: Problems and Prospects from a Human Resources Perspective" (Report for a tutorial seminar LIR 494, Institute of Labor and Industrial Relations, University of Illinois at Urbana-Champaign, September 7, 1983).
9. The complete text of the AFL-CIO convention resolution has been printed in *Office Workstations in the Home* (Washington, D.C.: National Academy Press, 1985), pp. 152–153.
10. Office of the United States Trade Representative, *National Trade Estimate: 1986 Report on Foreign Trade Barriers* (Washington, D.C.: U.S. Government Printing Office, 1986).

13 Retirement and Health Coverage: Problems Affecting Homework

Charlotte Muller

Through direct government programs and group arrangements most members of the U.S. labor force have won rights to income in old age and in the event of disability as well as protection against the high costs of medical care. Such benefits are considered a necessity in meeting the risks of living in advanced industrial societies. However, the protection level is far from equal throughout the workforce. Homeworkers who have discontinuous careers, part-time schedules, ambiguous relationships to employers, and low earnings may lack the entitlements that are enjoyed by those regularly employed in workplace sites in uninterrupted careers. The decision to do homework may fulfill current preferences and needs but leave the individual vulnerable to future risks. Various program characteristics influence the degree of protection that may be achieved. This chapter considers these issues in relation to social security, pensions, and health insurance.

Social Security

Social security retirement income for homeworkers is affected by the level of their earnings, which reflects the labor market conditions faced by these workers. Retirement income may also be affected by characteristics of the social security program as they interrelate with worker and employer behavior. Research is needed in order to identify problems that may result in inadequate coverage, to measure their magnitude, and to devise legal, organizational, and educational solutions.

Entitlements for women in general under social security is analogous to and can serve as the context for examining entitlements for homeworkers. In December 1985, women made up 47 percent of retired-worker beneficiaries and 33 percent of disabled-worker beneficiaries.

Their benefit level was much less than that of men in these two categories: for retired workers, $412 per month versus $538 for men, and for disabled workers, $381 versus $534 for men. Women's benefits as widows of qualified workers—$434—were higher than benefits derived solely through their own earnings. The proportion of women among the disabled and retired beneficiaries is increasing, and the proportion entitled on the basis of both their own and husband's record is now almost one-fifth of women 62 and older (U.S. Social Security Administration (SSA), 1986).

Acquiring social security retired-worker benefits requires fulfilling a number of conditions. Since 1978 the Secretary of Health and Human Services annually applies a formula to determine the minimum amount of income that must be earned in the form of wages, self-employment income, or a combination in order to get credit for one quarter of coverage. In 1984 this amount was $390; in practice, $1,560 earned in a year is interpreted as four quarters' worth. For fully insured status, at least one quarter of coverage is needed for each calendar year after 1950 or, depending on year of birth, for each year between 21 and 62 years of age. Persons born in 1929 or later, who could have entered the labor force in the late 1940s, must have 40 quarters of coverage.

Additional time requirements are imposed for disability insurance; for those who are disabled after age 31, 20 quarters in the last 40 are required. Today 75 percent of women 20 or older are insured for retirement benefits but only 58 percent of those 25 to 64 are insured for disability benefits.

A woman homeworker may have an earnings record that is solely self-employment-based or solely wage-based, or that includes both in the same time period, or has different bases in different time periods over her work life. For those contributions that are derived from working for others, the worker's protection depends on whether her social security account has been credited by all her employers, which may be problematic. For example, an employer may accrue liability and accumulate the worker share of payment but may go out of business before the payments under FICA have been made for a given year. Presumably all federal tax liabilities would be presented for payment, but the protection of the employee's interest in having taxes paid in may be less than ideal. For a woman who works for marginal employers and in industries with a short firm-life, assurance of employers' continuous adherence to social security requirements may be more difficult than in more stable firms. Something depends, too, on the attitude of Social Security Administration leadership toward the administrative investment needed to tie up such loose ends. In a deregulated economy many surprises are possible.

A woman who has two or more employers is entitled to claim the excess tax that may be paid in against her personal income tax. Because the FICA contribution is large there is strong motivation to reclaim the excess. That no refund of interest accrued is payable to the covered person is a small but negative feature of U.S. law. In addition, educational level and familiarity with the English language may affect how well a worker monitors the status of her account.

A woman who is self-employed is required to make additional contributions to attain eligibility. The rate in 1988 is nearly twice that for the employer or employee share alone instead of 1.4 times, which was the ratio in 1983. Low-income workers may have conflicting motives about following through on these payments, even if their status as self-employed is unambiguous, because their immediate income is reduced.

The line between self-employment and working for others is a significant element of social security administration. The common law test is that workers are employees if the one for whom they work has the right to tell them what to do and how, when, and where to do it. The *Social Security Handbook 1984* presents specific criteria as to the distinction between the two statuses, but these are not free from ambiguity. Employer control is indicated if hours of work are set and if the worker must work full-time in the service of one employer; however, a person may be an employee of several firms at once. Working off premises shows some freedom from control but is admittedly not a clear guide because some businesses call for off-premises activity. Payment by the hour, week, or month is indicative of employee status; however, lump sum payments to independent contractors may be computed by hours required to do a job times a fixed hourly rate, or weekly or monthly payments if convenient. Employer control is shown by payment of business or travel expenses and by furnishing of tools and materials; however, in reality, contractor/consultants can be reimbursed for travel. A related criterion is that if the worker makes a significant investment in facilities, independence is indicated.

For any worker, interpretation of the foregoing could affect who is liable for social security taxes, and, specifically, whether the worker must pay at the higher, double rate for self-employment. For homeworkers, presumably all this is bypassed by specific clauses affecting homework. The handbook includes homeworkers as one of four occupational groups for which an employee relationship is affirmed even if the common law test is not met, so long as three conditions are met: (1) there is a contract of direct service, (2) there is no worker investment in facilities, and (3) a continuing relationship exists.

If a worker at her own or another's home or in a home workshop works in accordance with the employer's specifications and on supplied materials and returns the product to the employer or designee, she is an employee. A minimum amount of cash must be received per year in order for the total of cash plus in-kind payments to be credited and considered for benefit determination (and for the earnings test of retirement status).

The purchaser of labor services is motivated to avoid having the arrangements construed as employment in order to reduce social security tax liability and to escape regulation under other laws affecting employers. The employer may do this by claiming—or creating—a contractual rather than an employment relationship. Taking still another pathway, the employer may simplify the management burdens by contracting with another party who becomes the employer of record for all contingent workers whose services are used. This agent may be less accessible to the worker for surveillance and complaints than an established producing firm.

The continuing relationship standard is weakened by the possibility of termination of a bona fide employee relationship shortly after it starts. The standard based on investment in facilities is not clearcut if the worker adapts her home for the conduct of economic activity. A firm may be motivated to interpret the law one way and the worker another. What happens when an employer and worker view the nature of their relationship differently depends on SSA attitudes and the resourcefulness of workers in bringing cases to agency attention. Furthermore, an employer may "solve" the problem of liability not by expression of views but by noncompliance, and if that occurs, the outcome depends on the degree of countervailing power held by workers and the SSA.

Pensions

Pension plans are very popular in the United States as a source of retirement income but data from the Commerce Department's *Current Population Reports* for 1983 show that only three of every eight employed women have pension plan coverage through their employer or union. Among recent retirees, the New Beneficiary Survey of 1982 shows an increase in pension plan coverage for women from 21 percent in 1968 to 1970 to 39 percent a decade later (Snyder 1986).

For employed women with coverage in 1983, the median income is $14,565, 71 percent above the median income for all employed women ($8,510), which suggests that those lacking pensions are not likely to be able to provide individually for retirement needs. Both their social security and their saving potential will be limited.

The low rate of coverage for women is largely associated with part-time work: About one-third of women workers (32.5 percent) work part-time, and of these, 61.2 percent work less than 50 weeks per year. Of this group only 7.7 percent are covered, compared with 20.7 percent for those working 50 to 52 weeks part-time and with 58.2 percent for those working full-time, year-round. See Table 13.1 for further comparisons.

Thus, the descriptive data point to a probability of little coverage for women working at home part-time and for women homeworkers in general. The figures also show the lowest rates of coverage for women in the following demographic subgroups: in metropolitan areas but outside central cities; of Spanish origin; relative of household head, other than spouse; under 25 and over 65; and in service occupations and service industries (both business and repair services and personal services).

Relatively favored groups are professional occupations and, among industries, public administration, transportation and utilities, and nondurable manufacturing.

The demographic variables probably have an impact on coverage rates because the factors of residence, ethnicity, and so forth affect the type of jobs individuals are able to get. Age groups with higher percentages covered also have higher incomes. Similarly, income correlates with frequency of coverage for most of the other demographic factors indicated above. However, public administration employees have incomes not much higher than other industries with far lower percentages covered (U.S. Department of Commerce, *Current Population Report* 1983).

Coverage statistics are only part of an assessment of the robustness of pensions as a reliable retirement income source. Achievement of vesting of the employer portion of contributions is another necessary ingredient in establishing protection. Vesting is affected by the minimum age at which service is credited and the handling of breaks in service. Also, the amount of the benefit and the link between the amount and years of service help define the quality of benefits. If the age-earnings profile of the homeworker is different from that of the career employee in the centralized workplace—specifically, if there are fewer increases based on seniority and/or skill—one's ability to accumulate substantial entitlement is limited. Full-time employees in the central workplace often change jobs to better their terms, but homeworkers may have limited duration with one employer for a different reason, that is, because they are hired for the length of a particular project and for peak needs.

Private pensions can provide an important retirement income source for women who have individual or collective bargaining strength and employers who are interested in a long-term relationship. If one attraction of women homeworkers from the employer's point of view is a lean payroll and minimum fringe benefits, the pension route to security may

Table 13.1
Female Civilian Wage and Salary Workers 15 Years Old and Over with Employer- or Union-Provided Pension Plan Coverage: 1983

	Total workers	Number with coverage	Percent covered	Median income of covered workers
	(in thousands)			
Total	50,069	18,864	37.7	$14.6(000)
Type of residence				
Inside metropolitan areas	35,299	13,736	39.0	$15.5
Inside central cities	14,110	5,585	39.6	15.1
Outside central cities	21,189	6,150	29.0	15.7
Outside metropolitan areas	14,759	5,128	34.7	12.2
Region				
Northeast	10,762	4,227	39.3	14.8
Midwest	12,581	4,692	37.3	14.6
South	16,047	6,387	37.9	13.8
West	9,869	3,558	36.1	15.6
Race and Spanish Origin				
White	43,176	16,110	37.3	14.7
Black	5,635	2,309	41.0	13.8
Spanish origin	2,627	819	31.2	12.7
Relationship to Householder*				
In families	41,838	15,254	36.5	14.0
Household	7,338	3,186	43.4	14.9
Spouse of householder	25,039	10,480	41.9	14.0
Other relative of householder	9,461	1,582	16.7	12.4
Unrelated individuals	7,938	3,538	44.6	16.6
Age (years)				
15-24	12,251	1,776	14.5	10.7
25-34	14,117	5,872	41.6	15.1
35-44	10,325	4,828	46.8	15.9
45-54	6,985	3,545	50.8	14.9
55-64	5,063	2,540	50.2	14.3
65+	1,335	303	22.6	9.6

(continued)

Table 13.1 (continued)
Female Civilian Wage and Salary Workers 15 Years Old and Over with Employer- or Union-Provided Pension Plan Coverage: 1983

	Total workers	Number with coverage	Percent covered	Median income of covered workers
	(in thousands)			
Total	50,069	18,864	37.7	$14.6(000)
Weeks Worked in 1983				
Full-time	33,780	16,791	49.7	15.4
50-52 weeks	24,024	13,992	58.2	16.2
Other	9,756	2,799	28.7	na
Part-time	16,279	2,073	12.7	7.0
50-52 weeks	6,318	1,308	20.7	8.5
Other	9,961	765	7.7	na
Occupation				
Executive, administrative, etc.	3,881	2,048	52.8	19.6
Professional specialty	6,792	3,991	58.8	18.7
Technical, sales and administrative support	22,402	8,704	38.9	13.5
Service - private households	1,408	21	1.5	*
Service - except private households	8,735	1,635	18.7	9.7
Precision production, etc.	1,080	441	40.8	14.8
Operatives, fabricators, etc.	5,212	1,986	38.1	11.6
Industry*				
Manufacturing - durable goods	4,111	1,708	41.5	12.8
Manufacturing - non-durable goods	3,507	1,889	53.9	15.5
Transportation and utilities	2,072	1,259	60.8	18.8
Wholesale trade	1,329	459	34.5	14.7
Retail trade	10,335	11,721	16.7	10.9
Finance, insurance, etc.	3,902	1,828	46.8	14.0
Business and repair services	2,072	522	25.2	14.9
Personal services	3,130	232	7.4	10.8
Professional and related services	15,486	11,279	47.0	15.0
Public administration	2,204	1,549	70.3	15.4

*Categories with small numbers omitted.

Source: Bureau of the Census, Current Population Reports: Characteristics of Households and Persons Receiving Selected Noncash benefits: 1983, Tables 4, 14.

mean little. It can mean more if the contingencies that prevent crediting of both earned service and legally recognized leave periods, including disappearance of firms or their pension plans from the scene, are anticipated and planned for. Leonard Apcar noted in the *Wall Street Journal* both a growing number of terminations of pension plans and the inadequacy of regulations to protect beneficiaries in such cases (March 23, 1984). In another *Journal* article, Randall Smith also reported reductions in funding of corporate plans resulting in risk of inability to support pledged benefits (October 11, 1984).

Some recent improvements have been legislated. Passage of the Tax Equity and Fiscal Responsibility Act in 1982 provided some narrowing of a previous gap between pension rights of highly paid employees and other employees of the same firm by limiting the maximum benefits and contribution in qualified plans that would get favored tax treatment (Carter 1983). In 1984 the Retirement Equity Act amended ERISA (Employee Retirement Income Security Act of 1974) and the Internal Revenue Code to improve the share of women in the private-pension system. Key provisions include the following: (1) Employers are not permitted to require a minimum age of over 21 (with one year of service) for participation in pension plans (age 26 for educational institutions), but only future workers are affected. (2) All years of service after age 18 must now be counted for vesting of employer contributions (1 year = 1,000+ hours of service). (3) A worker can leave the job for up to five years, early in his or her career, and keep credit for initial service even if the break-in-service years exceed the credited years. (4) Service credit of up to 501 hours is given for maternity and paternity leave even if unpaid and even if not approved by management. Credit is based on the hours a person would normally have worked or, if this amount is unknown, on an assumed eight-hour day. The credit is used only to prevent a break in service and is not used to calculate benefits (Donovan 1985). These amendments would strengthen the capabilities of pension plans to bend to the life-cycle needs of women homeworkers—if, and only if, they are covered at all.

The public route, provision of a universal floor of benefits through social security, is probably more important. The program needs scrutiny and monitoring for the reasons suggested above.

Health Insurance

Several different aspects of health insurance coverage may be important to women homeworkers. First, the probability of being in a group health plan is less for women than for men. This results from working part-time instead of full-time, and from working in certain industries. Nondurable manufacturing, retail trade, and service industries—fields where many women work—have less coverage and a big sex gap in coverage rates (*Current Population Reports* 1983). Although many employed women have coverage through their husbands, in 1977 there were 1.2 million uninsured women workers, mostly wives, whose dependents were also uninsured (Monheit et al. 1985).

Second, the total premium outlay determines the benefit package and the share paid by the employer. These are influenced by whether a firm is unionized, but on further analysis this effect does not remain after allowing for characteristics of the firm such as size, whether it is staffed for the most part with full-time workers, location outside the South, and whether the firm is in manufacturing rather than service or trade (Rossiter and Taylor 1982). The average employer contribution for female-headed families was only three-fifths that for male-headed families, and the sex gap in total premiums was roughly similar (Cafferata 1984).

The ultimate outcome of all the relevant factors is that about half of employed women and two-thirds of employed men have another party paying some or all of their health plan premium costs (*Current Population Reports* 1983). More infrequently, the employer or union pays the whole cost. This is the case for 23 percent of the women and 30 percent of the men.

Third, cost-sharing limits the value of premiums as full or substantial protection. The last decade has seen a flowering of contract provisions to restrain plan expenditures, including incentives to use cheaper types of care. As dependence on family caregivers is integrated with or implicit in some of these provisions, women as family members may find a conflict between caregiving and their economic activity, and women as patients may find it difficult to arrange for caregiving support.

Fourth, coverage may be contingent on marriage relationships. Divorced women are less likely to be covered (Berk and Taylor 1984). Recent legislation has allowed continuation of group coverage after divorce or death of a spouse, but the cost to the individual is high because both employer and employee contributions must be paid for by the person continuing coverage.

Fifth, self-employed women acquire coverage, other than through a husband, via individual insurance, which is a second-class arrangement because it is more costly than group policies and may have a restricted benefit package. In addition, there is no provision for continuation during periods of no income.

Sixth, the ultimate step in cost containment is discontinuance of group plans. An employer's commitment is no longer to be taken for granted; at least one major firm has been reported to have discontinued coverage for both retirees and active workers.

Seventh, Medicare provides limited coverage. Because of deductibles, coinsurance, Medicare's method of calculating allowed charges, and excluded services, Medicare's shortfall in covering health care expenses is great, and consequently two-thirds of the elderly carry supplementary insurance. But today's low-income workers are at risk of becoming low-income elderly who cannot afford this.

Eighth, the Pregnancy Discrimination Act of 1978 is restricted to employers of 15 or more. Equal treatment of pregnancy in regard to disability and health care benefits does not apply to the self-employed and employees of small firms.

Ninth, insurance fails to cover preventive services needed by women, notably the Pap smear test and mammograms. The age distribution of homeworkers indicates that many of them are in age groups where services for prevention of disability and death from chronic disease are part of the recommended health care package. The poor coverage for ambulatory care, in general, and prevention, in particular, in private insurance implies that a financial barrier to these services still exists.

Finally, there is limited coverage for short-term disability. Just how many homeworkers have protection against income loss resulting from short-term disability is not known but it is likely that many do not. Nationally, only three-fifths of all workers had some kind of formal plan in 1981, and this proportion has been stable for many years. Another subgroup is protected by Temporary Disability Insurance (TDI) laws in several states. Still others have informal sick leave; just how many is unknown. Absence for pregnancy is now covered on the same basis as other disabilities in voluntary plans under the Pregnancy Discrimination Act, and state TDI laws have been amended in the same direction. Because of the subjectivity of reporting, short-term disability insurance has traditionally covered only part of the income loss; only 38 percent of the $41.3 billion lost in 1981 was recovered by workers. Administration of formal plans is likely to be more difficult for homeworkers because of the blending of family duties and gainful employment activities.

Findings from a study that examines the relation of employment, family factors, and gender to health and health care (Muller 1986a, 1986b) have several implications for homework. For example, although employed women have more restricted-activity days than employed men, most of the difference can be accounted for by women taking nonwork days (vacation days, weekends, and holidays) for illness; whereas work days lost to illness are almost identical for men and women. We do not know which activities women will reduce in order to cope effectively with illness when the boundary between home duties and paid work is not clear, or whether there is enough slack time in the daily schedule to provide for adequate rest in case of illness.

In addition, although women who work tend to have better health than women who are not in the labor force (which is probably related to the selection of healthier women into gainful work), health among employed women varies with the psychological and physical characteristics of their jobs. Jobs with more complexity and autonomy correlate with better health, an association that is also true for men (Muller 1986a). Job stress, associated with scant autonomy combined with frequent peak demands, seems to lead to poor physical health. Workers who are on a standby basis and take the brunt of a company's peak needs may be especially vulnerable.

Third, women's health is affected by having a sick child or sick spouse, with "sick" defined in terms of reported poor health status, chronic limitations, or heavy use of physician services. Men's health is more affected by having a sick spouse than a sick child (Muller 1986b). The findings suggest the importance of role burdens for the health of homeworkers.

Finally, having insurance increased the probability of receiving ambulatory physician care and having better health status. Thus, fringe benefits or their absence have both financial and health consequences for homeworkers.

Future Monitoring and Analysis

An appreciation of homework issues can result in, and in turn be aided by, an inclusion of questions regarding work location in national survey instruments used to collect data on acute illness and disability, long-term care needs and family caregivers, health care utilization and insurance, decisions as to partial and full retirement, and other subjects. Currently, these topics either are routinely researched in continuing data systems or have been addressed in large-scale national survey programs. The larger databases available, compared to limited special surveys of homework, make possible interesting and important disaggregations of an obviously heterogeneous group. The large databases permit tracing the implications of homework for health, welfare, and economic security while taking into account numerous influential and possibly interactive variables such as the number of earners in a family, race, and job history.

We also need to develop a comprehensive matrix of the set of federal and state laws and standards that impinge on the work choice framework and welfare outcomes of individuals who are either engaged in or deciding on homework, taking into account the diversity of situations that may exist. A person may gain from one set of criteria or interpretations of one law, but this may be offset by losses from another law. Tax law, labor standards, social security, welfare, and so forth should be considered comparatively and integratively. Theoretical or abstract models can be tested against empirical data collected from special surveys or special-purpose analysis of regular surveys and data flows.

References

Apcar, Leonard M. "Reagan Pension-Safeguard Plan Pleases Business, But Others Seek Stiffer Action." *Wall Street Journal*, March 23, 1984, 9:1.

Berk, Marc L., and Amy K. Taylor. "Women and Divorce: Health Insurance Coverage, Utilization, and Health Care Expenditures," *American Journal of Public Health* 74 (1984): 1276–1278.

Cafferata, Gail Lee. NCHSR National Health Care Expenditures Study. *Private Health Insurance Premium Expenditures and Source of Payment*. DHHS Pub. No. (PHS) 84-3364, 1984.

Carter, Gene. "Private Pensions: 1982 Legislation." *Social Security Bulletin* 46 (1983): 3–8.

Donovan, Edmund T. "The Retirement Equity Act of 1984: A Review." *Social Security Bulletin* 48 (1985): 38–44.

Monheit, Alan C., et al. "The Employed Uninsured and the Role of Public Policy." *Inquiry* 22 (1985): 348–364.

Muller, Charlotte. "Health and Health Care of Employed Adults: Occupation and Gender." *Women and Health* 11 (1986a): 27–46.

______. "Health and Health Care of Employed Women and Homemakers: Family Factors." *Women and Health* 11 (1986b): 7–26.

Price, Daniel H. "Cash Benefits for Short-Term Sickness, 1948–81." *Social Security Bulletin* 47 (1984): 23–38.

Rossiter, Louis H., and Amy K. Taylor. "Union Effects on the Provision of Health Insurance." *Industrial Relations* 21 (1982): 167–177.

Smith, Randall. "Business Reduces Pension Funding to Cut Costs, Fend Off Takeovers." *Wall Street Journal*, October 11, 1984, 35:4.

Snyder, Donald C. "Pension Status of Recently Retired Workers on Their Longest Job: Findings from the New Beneficiary Survey." *Social Security Bulletin* 49 (1986): 5–21.

U.S. Department of Commerce, Bureau of the Census. *Current Population Reports: Characteristics of Households and Persons Receiving Selected Noncash Benefits*. Washington, D.C.: U.S. Government Printing Office, 1983. Consumer Income Series P-60.

U.S. Social Security Administration, ORSIP. *Fast Facts and Figures About Social Security* (1986).

U.S. Social Security Administration. *Social Security Handbook 1984*, 8th ed. SSA Pub. No. 05-10135, 1984.

14
Local Zoning Ordinances Governing Home Occupations

JoAnn C. Butler

The opportunity to be one's own boss and to schedule one's job makes home-based work attractive to many people.* Although not everyone could or would wish to earn a living by working at home, for some this is the ideal work environment, and the number of home-based workers is growing.

For many families, having two breadwinners has become the norm. For those families with children and elderly relatives, home-based work offers family members an excellent opportunity to contribute income while remaining available to oversee the household. For families living in sparsely settled areas with no public transportation, and for the growing number of women who head single-parent families and are faced with inadequate child care, working at home may be the only way to achieve economic self-sufficiency. The advantages to working at home are apparent for the elderly and handicapped populations. Thus, the ability to work at home can benefit those who find it difficult to travel to work because of physical disabilities, age, location, or family responsibilities. Although the ability to work at home offers many advantages to workers, many home occupations often present problems for the local community. Home occupations are not limited to typically unobtrusive industries such as crafting quilts, word processing, and offering legal advice. Small-engine repair, auto bodywork, and furniture refinishing are home occupations that can be noisy, smelly, dangerous, and basically unattractive. Residential streets are often narrower and

*The original research for this chapter was funded by a grant from the U.S. Department of Health and Human Services and was conducted while the author was a Research Associate with the American Planning Association.

sewerage capacity less than commercial areas of a community. Home-based businesses can generate heavy traffic or demands for parking, and some businesses may use noisy machinery or bright lights at late hours.

Although planners and zoning administrators recognize the need to allow—sometimes even to promote—home occupations that meet the needs and demands of residents, local officials are also called upon to enhance the residential qualities of a neighborhood and preserve the neighborhood as a comfortable place for the people who live there. In view of the employment changes over the last several years—growth in the service industry, personal computing capabilities, and recent higher rates of unemployment—many local governments find that their present home occupation ordinances are inadequate to control the undesirable impacts upon neighborhoods that are associated with some home occupations.

Regulating Work in a Residential Setting

Local officials—and the regulations they enforce—must maintain a balance between the needs of the individual who works at home and the needs of the residents who do not. The problem for zoning officials is to know where to draw the line.

A difficulty with many home occupation ordinances is that they do not always balance the concerns of neighbors with those of workers in the neighborhood. Those who would like to work at home complain either that they are prevented from doing so for reasons that are not clear to them, or that if they stay within the bounds of the local zoning law they are put at an unfair disadvantage relative to existing illegal home occupations. On the other hand, neighbors complain that their retreat from the work-a-day-world is being invaded by traffic, noise, and hazards of the workplace; even guitar lessons and typesetting can be seen by some as the thin edge of the wedge of other businesses moving into the neighborhood.

With funding from the U.S. Department of Health and Human Services, the American Planning Association surveyed over 1,100 local planning agencies to find out how and why those agencies regulate home occupations. The high response rate—60 percent—along with the content of the surveys themselves, indicated that the impact of home occupations on neighborhoods had raised substantial concerns in communities around the country.

Many local officials among the survey respondents were dissatisfied with their home occupation ordinances, which were considered too vague to enforce. Vague ordinances also hindered home-based workers trying to establish legal workplaces.

Organizations that promote homework reported dissatisfaction with home occupation ordinances that they considered obsolete. However, given the number of neighbor complaints that many home occupations prompt, regulations would seem not to be obsolete at all, but, rather, not well drafted.

Drafting techniques can be exceedingly important. For example, Berkeley, California, recently found that its insurance carrier cancelled the city's liability insurance because of the way in which the city's home occupation ordinance was drafted. Although the ordinance stipulates that a permit would be granted only for nonhazardous home occupations, nowhere in the ordinance is nonhazardous defined. As far as the insurance company is concerned, the ordinance as drafted exposes apartment building dwellers to too high a risk from potentially hazardous home occupations.

Except in those places that use permits or licenses to regulate home occupations (a procedure that allows the number of home occupations to be monitored), the change in the number of home occupations over the past several years remains an educated guess. For the majority of the communities that responded to the survey, the number of home occupations is only recorded through the number of neighborhood complaints, local media advertisements, and the overt display of merchandise or signs on a residential lot. Nevertheless, most of the survey respondents indicated that they believed that home occupations had increased in their communities.

According to most survey respondents, the increase in the number of home-based businesses had little to do with inflation or a downturn in the economy. Whether this belief is justified, most respondents believed that it was the advances in the high-technology industries and the ready availability of personal computers that made it easier for people to engage in service industries at home.

But even computer-based occupations are not wholly benign in their effects on the residential neighborhood. Although home occupations involving quiet, unobtrusive equipment such as telephones and/or computers may appear to have limited land-use impacts, these occupations might still generate an inordinate amount of traffic through client contact or merchandise deliveries.

Ninety percent of the survey respondents had an ordinance regulating home occupations, and most respondents had revised their ordinance at least once so that it more clearly reflected the concerns of both home-based business persons and nearby neighbors. Bridging the gap between these two opposing groups often falls to planners and zoning officials such as the survey respondents. The lessons learned by these respondents in trying to serve both groups provide useful information on how to and how not to draft an ordinance regulating home occupations.

Elements of a Home Occupation Ordinance

Home occupation ordinances typically contain the following elements:

1. A definition of home occupations
2. The background or history preceding the ordinance enactment or amendment
3. An intent and purpose or policy statement describing why home occupations were being regulated in the community
4. A listing of permitted and prohibited home occupations
5. A series of conditions or set of performance standards that home occupations must meet
6. A statement of review procedures applied to home occupations
7. Enforcement procedures.

Very few home occupation ordinances contain all of these elements. However, those ordinances that provided the clearest guidance to both zoning regulators and potential home-based workers contain most of the elements.

The first, and most important, element of the ordinance is a concise definition of a home occupation. The definition must be simple and must avoid ambiguous words. For example, a home occupation can be defined as "any activity carried out for financial gain by a resident conducted as an accessory use in that resident's dwelling." More elaborate examples include:

- A home occupation is defined as any business or commercial activity that is conducted or petitioned to be conducted from property that is zoned for residential use (Blaine, Minn.).
- Home occupation is an occupation or business activity which results in a product or service and is conducted in whole or in part in the dwelling unit, and is clearly subordinate to the residential use of the dwelling unit (Port Angeles, Wash.).

Three ambiguous words to be avoided in a definition of a home occupation are "customary," "professional," and "family." For example, many ordinances define a home occupation as "a customary activity carried on in a dwelling unit by a professional or family member."

Home occupations traditionally have been required to be customarily found in a neighborhood. But one has to question (and inevitably someone who wants to work at home will question) the logic behind a zoning official determining that practicing medicine and dressmaking are customary while real estate sales and typesetting are not. Another problem that arises is how do new uses become acceptable as customary uses without operating illegally to begin with? A good example here may be personal computers: Even in the early 1980s they were certainly not customarily found in a person's home.

There is also little value in trying to make a distinction between professionals and nonprofessionals in a home occupation definition. How can one say that a doctor is any more professional than a dentist, or an accountant any less professional than a realtor? Also, such a limitation can be read as discriminatory against clerical or blue-collar workers.

Professional status and the customary criteria have been retained in a number of ordinances as the easiest way to control the effects of a home occupation on the surrounding neighborhood. But the favored status given to professionals and customary uses cannot be justified on the basis that these uses produce less harmful consequences to a neighborhood than other home occupations. The terms are an inappropriate surrogate for the regulation of general nuisances (for example, noise and odors), high volumes of traffic, parking, and aesthetics.

Some home occupation ordinances also limit employment to "family" members. But, as it becomes more usual for unrelated individuals to share a household and its expenses, the use of the word "family" has become challengeable. To prevent problems, many communities in 1988 require home occupations to be carried on by the "occupant" or "resident" of the dwelling. Ordinances are much less likely to be challenged when they concentrate on uses and not the users.

Better ordinances contain a concise history of home occupation regulation in the community. This administrative, and sometimes social, background, which describes the setting within which the ordinance was enacted, is much easier to amend when local officials have a good idea as to why the ordinance was adopted in the first place. A clear documentation of the history surrounding adoption is found in the St. Petersburg Beach, Florida, ordinance:

> WHEREAS, currently all requests for occupational licenses for home occupations must be granted by the Board of Adjustment, a costly and time-consuming process; and
> WHEREAS, more citizens, particularly mothers and the handicapped, are being forced into the employment market to help offset rising costs; and

> WHEREAS, a business in the home is the best way for many persons to work, due to obligations to family or for health reasons; NOW, THEREFORE, THE CITY OF ST. PETERSBURG BEACH, PINELLAS COUNTY, FLORIDA, DOES ORDAIN: (ORD. NO. 200)

Some communities, like St. Petersburg Beach, make their short history almost a social policy statement. For example, clauses in an ordinance may indicate that the council recognizes that at the present time a large portion of the community's population has been forced into the job market to offset rising costs, and that home occupations may be the best way for many people to work, given family obligations or health concerns. These policy statements can also recognize the rights of those living in the neighborhood but *not* working at home to be free of those nuisances sometimes caused by homework.

For example, the following purpose and intent statement is found in the Yakima, Washington, ordinance:

> 1. Purpose. The conduct of business in residential units may be permitted under the provisions of this section. It is the intent of this section to: (a) Ensure the compatibility of home occupations with other uses permitted in the residential districts; (b) Maintain and preserve the character of residential neighborhoods; and (c) Promote the efficient use of public services and facilities by assuring these services are provided to the residential population for which they were planned and constructed, rather than commercial uses.

And from Blaine, Minnesota, the intent of the city's home occupation ordinance is described as follows:

> a. Intent. In order to provide peace, quiet, and domestic tranquillity within all residential neighborhoods within the city, and in order to guarantee to all residents freedom from excessive noise, excessive traffic, nuisance, fire hazard, and other possible effects of commercial uses being conducted in residential areas.

A very common, although usually not helpful, technique used in home occupation ordinances is a listing of those occupations permitted or prohibited in one, some, or all residential areas. For example, for those occupations not listed, the question becomes, is the exclusion deliberate or simply an oversight? And for those drafting amendments to the ordinance, such a list is difficult to keep up-to-date. An outdated list does little to guide a zoning administrator in handling new, unprecedented home occupations that might even be desirable in a neighborhood.

An unusual and useful example of an ordinance that incorporates a listing of occupations is from Long Beach, California. The ordinance begins by specifying the standards that any home occupation in the city must comply with and then lists those home occupations that actually have been, and those that have not been, approved by zoning officials. In structuring its ordinance this way, it would seem that the Long Beach zoning administration has a flexible set of guidelines for assessing individual home occupations, and the person trying to establish a home-based business has a good idea of what the city is likely to accept as appropriate home-based work.

The main element of a home occupation ordinance contains reasonable restrictions on home occupations to ensure that they start and stay secondary to the main use of a residence. Home-based work is often used to incubate small businesses. However, the concern of both zoning administrators (and neighbors) is that the home occupation tail does not begin to wag the residential dog. Reasonable restrictions or conditions are the appropriate way to prevent neighborhood problems, rather than, as mentioned earlier, limiting home occupations to customary uses carried out by professionals.

Restrictions usually include limiting the floor area that can be used as a workspace (usually something like 10 percent or 500 square feet); structural alterations are not usually allowed. Also, most ordinances limit work from being done in accessory buildings or even attached garages. Zoning officials report that doctors are the single worst abusers of these provisions; medical offices often expand to fill an entire home until the doctor eventually moves out while maintaining the office in the neighborhood.

Zoning officials often limit the allowed number of employees as a way to prevent home occupations from taking over the primary use of the home. Employees are usually limited to the actual residents plus one additional employee. More employees than this is usually a good indication that the home occupation has outgrown its incidental character and has become a full-fledged commercial business. Requirements that the worker actually reside on the premises ensures that an absentee landlord situation does not develop.

Limiting the amount of goods stored within the home and restrictions on sales from the home are other means to control the size of the occupation. Restrictions on sales also help ensure that traffic volume in the neighborhood does not increase. Potential traffic problems are one of the negative impacts of home occupations that neighbors fear most.

Reducing the negative impacts on the surrounding neighborhood is the rationale behind home occupation ordinances. A major concern of neighbors is that general nuisances such as traffic, fire, noise, odors, fumes, electrical interference, and glaring visual impacts will invade the neighborhoods along with home occupations. To combat these potential nuisances, ordinances may preclude equipment from being used that is not ordinarily found in a home. However, just what is ordinary home equipment again presents a problem of ambiguity.

Examples of standards set for the prevention of nuisances are as follows:

- Conditional use permits shall not be granted when it appears to the City Council that the proposed home occupations will constitute a fire hazard to neighboring residences, will adversely affect neighboring property values, or will constitute a nuisance or otherwise be detrimental to the neighbors because of excessive traffic, excessive noise, odors, or other circumstances (Blaine, Minn.).
- No traffic shall be generated by such home occupation in greater volumes than would normally be expected in a residential neighborhood, and any need for parking generated by the conduct of such home occupation shall be met off the street and other than in a required front yard (Southern Pines, N.C.).
- There shall be no storage of equipment, vehicles, or supplies associated with the home occupation outside the dwelling (Visala, Calif.).
- There shall be no exterior indication of the home occupation; no exterior signs shall be used; no other on-site advertising visible from the exterior shall be used that informs the public of the address of the home occupation (Forest Grove, Ore.).
- A home occupation shall limit any external evidence of an occupation to one (1) identification sign not to exceed two (2) square feet in area (Washington County, Ore.).

Neighbor complaints are not the only concern of zoning officials. A common complaint from the potential home-based worker is that home occupations are treated arbitrarily. These complaints are probably justified when the zoning ordinance gives the worker and the zoning official little guidance on what review procedures are used to determine if a home occupation should be allowed.

Some communities go to one extreme and allow home occupations by right in all residential districts; some go to the other extreme and do not allow home occupations at all. But most communities regulate home occupations with special use permits, sometimes in combination with a business license. Most communities place a time limit on a home occupation permit: usually a year or two. The permit usually is not transferable to subsequent occupants of the home and the permit holder cannot take the permit along to a new residence.

A permit is usually issued as long as the conditions spelled out in the zoning ordinance are met. But unless the conditions are explicit, it is very difficult to determine if an applicant has complied. More than once courts have overturned the denial of a home occupation permit if the zoning ordinance only vaguely defines what a home occupation is and only vaguely stipulates the conditions attached to home occupations.

Communities and their zoning officials are split as to whether to hold public hearings before granting permits. Those communities that do require public hearings believe strongly that, because home occupations have the potential to interfere with the residential character of a neighborhood, there should always be a public hearing where neighbors could, at the very least, voice their opinions. Those communities that do not require public hearings often do away with the requirement in an attempt to streamline their procedures. This streamlining tactic often has the effect of preventing clandestine home-based business. Evidently, the more cumbersome the review procedures the more likely home occupations are to go underground.

Enforcing regulations controlling home occupations is a major problem for most zoning administrators. In part, this stems from the fact that many home-based business operators are unaware that there are local regulations to be met. Even if the homeworker is aware of the regulations, unclear zoning ordinances lead many homeworkers to believe that the ordinance just does not apply to them.

In addition, an ill-drafted home occupation ordinance hinders officials in enforcing their own regulations. Although home occupations very often go undetected, this is not a problem to many local agencies simply because they do not have enough staff members to worry about enforcing ordinances. The unwritten rule in enforcement of home occupations for most communities is that if no one complains, there is no problem.

Generally, any violation of the conditions set forth in the zoning ordinance, such as a change in the extent of use areas of the dwelling unit being used, outdoor storage, hours of operation, and so forth, is grounds for the revocation of a home occupation permit. Some ordinances provide for very strict fines and penalties for the violation of the conditions stipulated in the ordinance. The Marquette, Michigan, ordinance, for example, provides that any violation of the ordinance is declared to be a public nuisance per se, and the violator is guilty of a misdemeanor. If convicted, that person will be fined by not more than $100 or spend up to 30 days in the county jail. Of course, any ordinance that is to be enforced through criminal law must be very clear and provide fixed standards as to what is permitted and prohibited in any particular instance. The typical civil penalty incurred for the violation of a home occupation ordinance is the revocation of a home occupation permit.

Conclusion

Few communities have experienced legal challenges to their home occupation ordinances to date. Many local planners and zoning officials, however, have indicated that they see legal challenges looming on the horizon. Most legal challenges that have been encountered have been based on neighborhood impact caused by high-intensity home occupations, including automobile body shops, bakeries, and beauty shops.

In general, courts have upheld zoning ordinances dealing with home occupations as long as the homeowner/business operator has not been subject to unreasonable restrictions on the use of the residence. However, for a zoning regulation to be considered unreasonable, application of the regulation would have to render a person's property almost worthless; an ordinance is not invalid or contradictory in nature because it does not allow a person to put his or her property to its most profitable use. An ordinance regulating home occupations will not be considered invalid unless, because of the regulation, the property cannot yield a reasonable return if used only for the purposes allowed in the district. Any home, used as a home in a residential district, is presumed to yield a reasonable return upon resale.

Proponents have argued that to deny the use of a home for home-based businesses will reduce the value of the property, and that, if the ability to develop a home occupation was part and parcel of owning the house, an owner could get a greater return on his or her investment. With regard to zoning law, the limitations of profits as a consequence of the zoning restriction and the highest and best use of the property involved are factors that a court would usually consider in its determination of the validity of a home occupation ordinance. Other factors, however, would also be considered—for example, the depreciation of value to adjoining properties that may be caused by allowing home occupations.

Some innovative approaches to dealing with the issue of home-based work and investment returns on housing are taking place. In fact, whole subdivisions are springing up in which people live and work. Market Place in Oak Creek, Wisconsin, for example, consists of 20 homes built especially to accommodate home occupations ranging from dentists' offices to craft studios. And each home in the Eaglecrest subdivision in Foresthill, California, was designed to include a teleport containing a personal computer and modem so that the occupant could link up to computers (and employment). This phenomenon reflects the view that the opportunity to work from one's home is an asset that can increase the market value of a house. Furthermore, some believe that the importance of homework may grow to the point that zoning away the ability to work in one's home may impair the value of the property.

One community is even experimenting with a zoning technique that accommodates both residential and commercial uses in what would traditionally have been strictly a residential area. In the village of Lynwood, Illinois, a development has been started with one-acre lots in which the front of the lot is zoned for a single-family residence and the rear of the "dual-zoned" lot is for commercial use. Village officials were skeptical at first about the concept but allowed the zoning to proceed with proper architectural controls in place. Residents of the subdivision, who have drafted restrictive covenants governing the neighborhood businesses, find that because the dual zoning requires large lots, the commercial aspect of the development does not detract from its residential character.

In determining the validity of any zoning ordinance, including one that regulates home occupations, the community interest must be balanced against the property rights of individual owners. A zoning ordinance is not going to be held invalid if individual rights are restricted for the greater good of the public. The welfare of the community is not going to be subordinated to the profit motive of a single individual. On the other hand, there is no basis for the exercise of a local government's zoning power if the public gain is small compared with an individual's loss and hardship.

A local government, through the use of its zoning power, can easily permit or provide for incidental, accessory uses such as home occupations in a residential district. A local government can just as easily exclude all or some home occupations from residential districts. Again, restricting all or some home occupations from a residential district will not be valid when the restriction would seem to be capricious or without relation to the public welfare.

The exclusion of places of business from residential districts is not a declaration by the local government that such businesses are nuisances or that they are to be suppressed as such. But occupations that are liable to become nuisances per se, or which may become nuisances by reason of the inappropriateness of the places in which they are conducted, may be legally excluded from particular localities. Whether a zoning ordinance is arbitrary in prohibiting the use of the property for such an occupation in certain districts is a question for the courts to answer.

There have not been many legal challenges to home occupation ordinances in the past. Yet, as home occupations have become more prevalent throughout the country, zoning ordinances that regulate them are often viewed as regulations that unduly restrict personal liberty. Several home-based work groups have been building challenges to local zoning ordinances that they believe to be vague, inconsistent, or discriminatory. The International Association for Home Business has been soliciting support from its members for a class action suit on "the right to choose the workplace."

In order to prevent legal challenges to an ordinance, drafters must indicate clearly how their ordinance provides for the general welfare. It is only within the text of the zoning ordinance that the intent can be made clear and the ordinance made legally defensible.

Residential and commercial uses are not necessarily incompatible, and allowing home-based work in a residential setting can be a positive, even a necessary, policy for a community. However, in order to encourage the pursuit of a broad range of home occupations, as well as retain the advantages of a residential environment, home occupations need to be regulated at the local government level. Local zoning ordinances that successfully balance the rights of home-based workers with the concerns of neighborhood residents must be clearly drafted to provide guidance to both zoning regulators and home-based business persons.

Conclusion: Directions for the Future

Kathleen E. Christensen

As the chapters in this book attest, home-based work defies simple conclusions. For some, it is an arrangement that works out extremely well; for others it provides the best of not very good alternatives. Yet, there are several questions to which I would like to respond in light of the insights and data provided in these chapters.

What Does the Future Look Like?

In the early 1980s there was a belief on the part of some futurists that rapid advances in telecommunication technology would lead to the eventual demise of the office as we now know it. Predictions by futurists Alvin Toffler in his book *The Third Wave* and Jack Nilles of the University of Southern California led us to believe that up to 10 percent of U.S. employees would work out of their homes by the turn of the century. Yet several authors in this book have challenged the notion of such rapid decentralization of the workforce on the grounds that the U.S. corporate culture is not yet ready for a radical decentralization of employees. Even though computers and communications technology have made the decentralization of millions of jobs a concrete possibility, the prevailing norms of U.S. management will likely counteract that. U.S. managers value visibility, and by and large, measure productivity on their ability to see employees at work. In addition, few have been trained to manage flexible work arrangements, including home-based work. In effect, therefore, the strength of corporate culture will likely override the power of advanced technology in the near future.

Although there does not appear to be evidence of any immediate large-scale growth in the numbers of employees working in their homes, there is, nonetheless, likely to be an increase in the overall figure of

1.9 million who work exclusively in their homes. The main factor contributing to this growth of home-based work will be due to the rise in self-employment, including sole proprietorships, limited partnerships, and incorporations. Already, according to the May 1985 Bureau of Labor Statistics, the majority of exclusively home-based workers are self-employed.

Several factors are converging to promote self-employment in the home. The first is highly voluntary and involves the genuine desire to go into business for oneself. But four other factors have elements of involuntarism. First, working parents increasingly find that one of them, typically the woman, needs more flexibility than the current job market offers. Second, older women seeking to reenter the workforce after raising their children often cannot find the jobs they want or for which they feel qualified. Third, retirees frequently find that starting a small business at home provides the income they need to supplement their social security or pension checks. And, finally, there are large numbers of men and women who are the victims of recent layoffs. The people in these four groups typically turn to self-employment not out of a desire to be entrepreneurs, but rather because of their financial and family needs.

For these people, self-employment offers more opportunities than does company employment. In these cases, the decisions to be self-employed and to locate the business in the home go hand-in-hand, for the home offers definite cost savings in terms of overhead and capital investment. Furthermore, within the ranks of the self-employed are an unknown number of people hired as self-employed independent contractors who, in fact, may be fraudulently hired as such and should instead, given their relationships to their firms, have been hired as employees. The extent to which they are genuinely small businesses is truly in question.

What Should Be the Response of the Government?

If it is correct that the real growth in home-based work will be due to self-employment of all types, then the federal government may have to address issues broader than those related solely to home-based work. First, as many of the authors called for, there must be explicit enforcement of the U.S. Department of Labor and the Internal Revenue Service's definitions of employee status versus self-employment status to ensure that there are not flagrant abuses of "contracting out" as a way to save both direct wage costs and indirect benefit costs.

Second, the issue of worker protection must be addressed if the rise in self-employment is signaling, as it appears to be, a rise in the number of workers unprotected for health coverage. In the United States, health coverage is tied to one's employment status. This is in stark contrast to most other industrialized nations where health coverage is tied to citizenship. As a result, benefit coverage now costs U.S. businesses, on average, 39 percent of their payroll. Increasing numbers of U.S. businesses are seeking alternative ways to cut these costs, including transferring workers from the status of employees with benefits to self-employed contractors or part-time employees without benefits. The move to this type of contingent workforce may save the corporation, but force the federal government to query whether in effect what is going on is a quiet de facto shift of health care from a private sector responsibility to a public sector one.

Federal and state governments might consider several possible alternatives to meet this problem: mandatory benefits for part-time workers; creating state or federally sponsored health care plans; or providing incentives for the formation of guilds of self-employed workers that would be eligible for lower group rate plans. Regardless of the policy direction, the federal government must recognize that U.S. home-based business owners need more cost-efficient ways to protect their own health needs and those of their families than are currently available.

In addition to issues of protection, home-based work also raises the need for the federal, state, and private sector to work together to enable home-based working parents to choose to, rather than be forced into, working at home. A primary effort should be directed to providing adequate child care and elder care facilities so that if a family member, typically a woman, decides to work at home, the decision is made relatively freely and not forced because there are no other alternatives for caring for dependent family members. Federal and state efforts could take a variety of forms: implementing better tax write-offs for families for their dependent care expenses; promoting tax incentives to corporations, which would provide on-site or subsidized child care services; and providing demonstration models, within governmental agencies or in cooperation with private sector industries, that would highlight the importance of employer involvement in both child care and elder care facilities. Although the private sector, by and large, has shied away from the provision of on-site facilities, they might consider more family-support services if the federal and state governments set the lead.

The government could also take the lead in ensuring that home-based business owners have adequate information on starting and running a business. The Small Business Administration would be well served to step up their efforts to provide locally and regionally accessible information regarding financing a new business, writing a business plan, marketing services and products, setting up health care and retirement programs, and working with clients. Although the SBA has been involved with efforts directed to small businesses, they might direct particular attention to the *home-based* business owner who may be more vulnerable to the already high rate of failure of small businesses in the United States due to their relatively small scales of operation and the isolation bred by being at home.

The government should also provide funding for a more grass-roots, self-help approach to helping home-based small businesses. This could take the form of establishing a national clearinghouse of home-based workers that would serve several purposes. It could provide a way that home-based workers could meet others in similar industries or occupations to exchange information on a variety of important business matters, including price-setting. A national clearinghouse could also constitute the seedbed for establishing a national network of local guilds of home-based workers.

In summary, any federal approach to home-based work would be well-served to situate homework within broader health, family, and business issues rather than focusing on it as an isolated, unique work phenomenon.

How Should U.S. Employers Respond?

U.S. businesses are caught between two strong crosscurrents. One is their goal to cut costs and maintain a "mean-and-lean" staffing; the second is their need to attract and retain valuable employees. The pursuit of the first goal has had an immediate effect on the numbers of home-based workers insofar as firms have found that contracting out work, which often is done by people working in their homes, results in a flexible workforce and substantial savings. But the second objective may have more long-term effects over the next 15 to 20 years as public and private firms recognize that they have to provide work arrangements that suit the needs of those employees they want to recruit or retain. In this context, U.S. businesses would benefit by following the lead of such companies as Pacific Bell, Mountain Bell, and J.C. Penney. Each company has institutionalized model programs that remunerate employees equally, regardless of where they work, and that ensure that all employees are afforded equal opportunities for advancement. In addition, the newly instituted telecommuting program by the state of California provides important insights into ways that public organizations and institutions can deal with home-based work programs. All of these programs guarantee that people who work at home retain the rights and privileges of office-based employees. Any large-scale move in the directions taken by these particular employers, however, will require serious rethinking of the spoken and unspoken rules of corporate cultures that place high premium on employee visibility in rewarding employees.

What Should Organized Labor Do?

U.S. trade unions have a long history of opposing industrial homework, largely on the grounds of the potential violations of such work arrangements to minimum wage, overtime compensation, and child labor laws. In their efforts to avoid further exploitation resulting from such arrangements, the AFL-CIO and the Service Employees International Union (SEIU) have both passed resolutions calling for a ban on all computer homework. Rather than focusing exclusively on the computer and technology issues, the unions would be well served to examine, as Dennis Chamot does, the employee status and occupational structure of white-collar home-based workers and to mount their oppositions on those grounds. In addition, the unions may find that they would have a relatively responsive audience of self-employed contractors or small business owners who would value affiliate membership with a union in order to obtain better health care or pension coverage at premium prices.

Summary

The roles played by government, employers, and trade unions will have a good deal to do with defining what white-collar home-based work will look like in the years ahead. Individually and collectively, they can do a lot to make the arrangements better and more rewarding. Although the potential for exploitation from working at home obviously is real, there is an equal potential that work-at-home, when well understood, supported, and executed, can meet serious needs among U.S. workers and businesses.

As important as what government, employers, and trade unions do will be the efforts and concerns of people who entertain the notion of working at home. Homeworkers are not a generic group. They vary by age, income, gender, and family circumstances. Yet the majority of those who work in their homes want to retain the right to work there. In addition, they may want other opportunities—better jobs outside the home; better child care opportunities; adequate compensation and health care coverage and pension. But, by and large, they do not want to be forbidden nor penalized for working in their homes.

The desire to work at home is there. Only government, employers, and trade unions can create the conditions so that it is not a forced option that can lead to exploitation, but rather a choice that legitimately meets the needs of U.S. workers and businesses.

Acronyms

ACYF	Administration for Children, Youth and Family
ADEA	Age Discrimination in Employment Act
ADP	Automated data processing
AFL-CIO	American Federation of Labor and Congress of Industrial Organizations
AT&T	American Telephone and Telegraph
BLS	U.S. Bureau of Labor Statistics
BNA	Bureau of National Affairs
CPI	Consumer Price Index
CPI-X	Experimental Consumer Price Index
CPS	Current Population Survey
DOL	U.S. Department of Labor
DPE	Department of Professional Employees, AFL-CIO
EEOC	Equal Employment Opportunity Commission
EPA	Equal Pay Act
ERISA	Employment Retirement Income Security Act
ESA	Employment Standards Administration
FICA	Federal Insurance Contributions Act
FLSA	Fair Labor Standards Act
GDP	Gross Domestic Product
GNP	Gross National Product
HHS	U.S. Department of Health and Human Services
IBM	International Business Machines
ILAB	Bureau of International Labor Affairs
ILGWU	International Ladies Garment Workers Union
IRS	Internal Revenue Service
ISDN	Integrated Services Digital Network
NLRA	National Labor Relations Act
NRA	National Recovery Administration
OECD	Organization for Economic Cooperation and Development
OPEC	Organization of Petroleum Exporting Countries
OSHA	Occupational Safety and Health Act
OTA	Office of Technology Assessment
PC	Personal Computer
PCE	Personal Consumption Expenditures
SECA	Self-Employment Contributions Act

SEIU	Service Employees International Union
SMSA	Standard metropolitan statistical area
SSA	Social Security Administration
TDI	Temporary Disability Insurance
WPS	Wisconsin Physicians Services Insurance Corporation

About the Contributors

Eileen Boris is assistant professor of history at Howard University and will be on leave as a fellow at the Woodrow Wilson Center for International Scholars, Washington, D.C., during 1988–89. She is the coeditor, with Cynthia Daniels, of *Homework: Historical and Contemporary Perspectives on Paid Labor at Home* (forthcoming) and the author of *Art and Labor: Ruskin, Morris, and the Craftsman Ideal in America* (1986). She is writing a history of industrial homework and its regulation in the United States.

JoAnn C. Butler is an attorney specializing in land use and environmental law at the firm of Sachnoff, Weaver & Rubenstein, Ltd., in Chicago. She is the author and coauthor of a number of studies and articles on land use.

Dennis Chamot is associate director of the Department for Professional Employees of the AFL-CIO. A chemist by formal training, he has written and spoken extensively on a variety of issues, and in particular on the effects of workplace technological changes. He has served on numerous panels at the National Science Foundation, the National Research Council, the Congressional Office of Technology Assessment, and the U.S. Department of Labor, among others.

Kathleen E. Christensen is director of the National Project on Home-Based Work and associate professor of environmental psychology at the Graduate School and University Center, City University of New York. She is the author of *Women and Home-Based Work: The Unspoken Contract* (1988) and of numerous articles on contingent work and the changing structure of the workforce.

Vary T. Coates, a political scientist, is a senior analyst and project director at the Office of Technology Assessment of the U.S. Congress. She directed a major study, *Automation of America's Offices* (1984–1985), and is currently directing a study of the effects of automation on the securities and futures markets.

Cynthia B. Costello is coordinator of the Employment and Voluntarism Program at the Villers Foundation in Washington, D.C. She is the author of *"We're Worth It!" Women, Work, and Organizing* (forthcoming) as well as of numerous articles on women workers.

Judith M. Gerson teaches sociology and women's studies at Rutgers University. She is the author of numerous articles on gender relations as well as of *At Home and in the Office* (forthcoming).

Gil E. Gordon is president of Gil Gordon Associates in Monmouth Junction, N.J., a consulting firm specializing in the implementation of telecommuting programs. He edits the newsletter *Telecommuting Review* and coauthored *Telecommuting: How to Make It Work for You and Your Company.*

Kristine Iverson is employment policy director for the Minority Staff of the Committee on Labor and Human Resources in the U.S. Senate. She has made numerous conference presentations on labor and employment policy issues.

Robert E. Kraut is manager of the Behavioral Science Research Group at Bell Communications Research. He previously taught sociology and psychology at the University of Pennsylvania and Cornell University and is coeditor of the National Academy of Sciences report on technology and women's employment, *Computer Chips and Paper Clips* (1986), and editor of *Technology and the Transformation of White-Collar Work* (1987).

Roberta V. McKay is a labor economist in the Office of Policy Analysis and Information, Women's Bureau, U.S. Department of Labor. Her writing and research issues concern working women, including current labor force status, work force 2000, new technology, competitiveness, and women in science and technology careers.

Charlotte Muller is director of the Division of Health Economics at the Department of Community Medicine, Mt. Sinai School of Medicine. She has written extensively on her research on Medicare, fertility services, health care of employed women, and other subjects.

Margrethe H. Olson is associate professor and director of the Center for Research on Information Systems at New York University. She is the editor of *Technological Support for Work Group Collaboration* (forthcoming) and of numerous articles on telecommuting as an organizational work option.

Joy R. Simonson is a professional staff member of the Employment and Housing Subcommittee, Government Operations Committee, U.S. House of Representatives. She has prepared committee hearings and reports on home-based clerical work, federal Equal Employment Opportunity procedures, and the contingent workforce.

Conference Participants

Chair

Kathleen Christensen, director, National Project on Home-Based Work, Graduate School and University Center, City University of New York

Moderator

Alan Gartner, professor and director of sponsored research, Graduate School and University Center, City University of New York

W. J. (Buck) Benham, staff manager—special assignments, U.S. West Learning Systems, Lakewood, CO

Eileen Boris, assistant professor, Department of History, Howard University

JoAnn Butler, attorney, Sachnoff, Weaver & Rubenstein, Ltd., Chicago, IL

Lanny Catz, senior vice president—administration, The NPD Group, Port Washington, NY

Dennis Chamot, associate director, Department for Professional Employees, AFL-CIO, Washington, DC

Patrick Cleary, deputy assistant secretary for policy, U.S. Department of Labor, Washington, DC

Vary Coates, project director, Communications and Information Technologies Program, Congress of the United States Office of Technology Assessment, Washington, DC

Cynthia Costello, coordinator of employment and volunteerism programs, Villers Foundation, Washington, DC

Susan Cowell, executive assistant to the president, International Ladies Garment Workers Union, New York, NY

Faye Duchin, director, Institute for Economic Analysis, New York University

Joyce Durgerian, senior labor standards investigator, Division of Labor Standards, New York State Department of Labor, Albany, New York

David Fleming, telecommuting program manager, Telecommuting Division, California Department of General Services, Sacramento, CA

Marcia Freedman, Urban Research Institute, New York University

Joan Gaffney, Family and Youth Services Bureau, Administration for Children, Youth and Family, U.S. Department of Health and Human Services, Washington, DC

Audrey Gartner, editor, *Social Policy,* CASE, City University of New York
Judith Gerson, assistant professor, Sociology Department, Rutgers University
Gil Gordon, president, Gil Gordon Associates, Monmouth Junction, NJ
Rick Higgins, project manager for telecommuting, Pacific Bell, San Ramon, CA
Paget Wilson Hinch, associate commissioner, Family and Youth Services Bureau, Administration for Children, Youth and Family, U.S. Department of Health and Human Services, Washington, DC
Francis Horvath, Office of Employment and Unemployment Statistics, Bureau of Labor Statistics, Washington, DC
Kristine Iverson, employment policy director—minority staff, U.S. Senate, Commitee on Labor and Human Resources, Washington, DC
Alex Kotlowitz, staff reporter, *Wall Street Journal,* Chicago, IL
Robert Kraut, Bell Communications Lab Research, Morristown, NJ
Marie MacBride, National Alliance on Home-Based Businesswomen, Midland Park, NJ
S. M. Miller, professor, Sociology Department, Boston University
Thomas E. Miller, director of research ESU—Division of Link Resources, New York, NY
Charlotte Muller, professor of economics and sociology, Graduate School and University Center, City University of New York
Margrethe H. Olson, associate professor and director, Center for Research on Information Systems, New York University
Joanne H. Pratt, president, Joanne H. Pratt Associates, Dallas, TX
William Price, legislative associate for the minority staff, Education and Labor Committee, U.S. House of Representatives, Washington, DC
Jackie Ruff, clerical division director, Service Employees International Union, AFL-CIO, Washington, DC
Stephen M. Settle, senior legislative officer, U.S. Department of Labor, Office of the Secretary, Washington, DC
Joy R. Simonson, Government Operations Subcommittee on Employment and Housing, U.S. House of Representatives, Washington, DC
Paula Smith, administrator, Wage and Hour Division, U.S. Department of Labor, Washington, DC
Donna R. Wiesner, special assistant to the assistant secretary for postsecondary education, Department of Education, Washington, DC

Index

For Product Safety Concerns and Information please contact our EU
representative GPSR@taylorandfrancis.com
Taylor & Francis Verlag GmbH, Kaufingerstraße 24, 80331 München, Germany

www.ingramcontent.com/pod-product-compliance
Ingram Content Group UK Ltd.
Pitfield, Milton Keynes, MK11 3LW, UK
UKHW011006180926
475701UK00004B/594

9780367309817